D0911086

DISCOVERING JESUS IN THE NEW TESTAMENT

DISCOVERING JESUS IN THE NEW TESTAMENT

KEITH WARRINGTON

Discovering Jesus in the New Testament
© 2009 by Hendrickson Publishers Marketing, LLC
P. O. Box 3473
Peabody, Massachusetts 01961-3473

ISBN 978-1-59856-011-4

All rights reserved. No part of this book may be reproduced or transmitted in any form or by any means, electronic or mechanical, including photocopying, recording, or by any information storage and retrieval system, without permission in writing from the publisher.

Except where otherwise noted, Scripture quotations are from the New Revised Standard Version of the Bible (NRSV), copyright © 1989 by the Division of Christian Education of the National Council of the Churches of Christ in the United States of America. Used by permission. All rights reserved.

Biblical quotations marked ESV are from the The Holy Bible, English Standard Version®, copyright © 2001 by Crossway Bibles, a publishing ministry of Good News Publishers. Used by permission. All rights reserved.

Printed in the United States of America

First Printing — September 2009

Photo Credit: Mark Sadlier, Trevillion Images. Used with permission.

Cover Design: Stefan Killen Design

Hendrickson Publishers is strongly committed to environmentally responsible printing practices. The pages of this book were printed on 30% post consumer waste recycled stock using only soy or vegetable content inks.

Library of Congress Cataloging-in-Publication Data

Warrington, Keith.
Discovering Jesus in the New Testament / Keith Warrington.
p. cm.
Includes bibliographical references and indexes.
ISBN 978-1-59856-011-4 (alk. paper)
1. Jesus Christ—Person and offices—Biblical teaching. 2. Bible. N.T.—Criticism, interpretation, etc. I. Title.
BT203.W38 2009
232—dc22

2009019493

Contents

Acknowledgements

I am grateful to my undergraduate and postgraduate students at Regents Theological College, Malvern, England, with whom I have had the opportunity to walk this path towards a greater appreciation of Jesus, and from whom I have learned much. For improving the style throughout, I am very grateful to my research assistant, Dr. Timothy Walsh.

I dedicate this literary exploration of the person and mission of Jesus to my wife Judy, who has followed him for as long as I have. Her readiness to walk in his footsteps is a constant encouragement to me. I also dedicate this to my children, Luke and Anna-Marie, and to their spouses Laura and Chris, who have stimulated me to more intentionally relate to and rely on Jesus throughout our lives together.

Abbreviations

1QH	Dead Sea Scrolls *Hoyadot (Thanksgiving Hymns)*
1QS	Dead Sea Scrolls *Serek Hayahad (Rule of the Community or Manual of Discipline)*
4Q521	Dead Sea Scrolls *Messianic Apocalypse*
As. Mos.	*Assumption of Moses*
b. 'Arak.	Babylonian Talmud Tractate *'Arakin*
b. Ned.	Babylonian Talmud Tractate *Nedarim*
b. Sanh.	Babylonian Talmud Tractate *Sanhedrin*
2 Bar.	*2 Baruch*
B.C.E.	before the common era
BECNT	Baker Exegetical Commentary on the New Testament
c.	century
C.E.	common era
cf.	compare
ch(s).	chapter(s)
1–2 Chr	1–2 Chronicles
Col	Colossians
1–2 Cor	1–2 Corinthians
Dan	Daniel
Deut	Deuteronomy
e.g.	*exempli gratia,* for example
1 En.	*1 Enoch*
Eph	Ephesians
esp.	especially
ESV	English Standard Version
Exod	Exodus
Ezek	Ezekiel
Gal	Galatians
Gen	Genesis

Gk.	Greek
Heb	Hebrews, New Testament Book of
Heb.	Hebrew
Hos	Hosea
i.e.	*id est,* that is
Isa	Isaiah
Jas	James
Jer	Jeremiah
Jub.	*Jubilees*
Judg	Judges
1–2 Kgs	1–2 Kings
Lev	Leviticus
lit.	literally
LXX	Septuagint (Greek translation of the OT)
m. Šabb.	Mishnah Tractate *Šabbat*
Mal	Malachi
Matt	Matthew
Mic	Micah
Neh	Nehemiah
NIGTC	New International Greek Testament Commentary
NRSV	New Revised Standard Version
NT	New Testament
Num	Numbers
OT	Old Testament
p(p).	page(s)
1–2 Pet	1–2 Peter
Phil	Philippians
PNTC	Pillar New Testament Commentary
Prov	Proverbs
Ps(s)	Psalm(s)
Pss. Sol.	*Psalms of Solomon*
Rev	Revelation
Rom	Romans
1–2 Sam	1–2 Samuel
Sib. Or.	*Sib Oracles*
Sir	Sirach
T. Benj.	*Testament of Benjamin*
T. Jos.	*Testament of Joseph*

T. Jud.	*Testament of Jud.*
T. Sol.	*Testament of Solomon*
T. Zeb.	*Testament of Zeb*
1–2 Thess	1–2 Thessalonians
1–2 Tim	1–2 Timothy
v(v).	verse(s)
WBC	Word Biblical Commentary
Wis	Wisdom of Solomon
Zech	Zechariah
Zeph	Zephaniah

Introduction

In my previous book, *Discovering the Holy Spirit in the New Testament,*[1] I sought to examine both the common and unique ways in which the various writers of the NT present information about the Holy Spirit. This volume follows a similar journey by exploring the NT portrait of Jesus. While on occasion the NT writers offered similar messages concerning Jesus to their disparate audiences, at other times the various writers revealed information that was of particular value to their readers in their individual life settings. By examining both the commonality and the rich diversity in the NT writers' teaching about Jesus, contemporary readers are better able to appreciate how Jesus' person and mission speak to their own world.

The numerous books that have been written about Jesus can generally be placed in one of three groups. The first comprises academic, theological volumes on the person of Jesus (sometimes these have concentrated on technical debate and overlooked Jesus' dynamic nature). In the second group are more popular books that focus on equipping unbelievers or believers to understand the historicity and authenticity of Jesus' life. This category also includes surveys of Jesus' life and mission. The final group consists of books that concentrate on particular aspects of Jesus' life or ministry (e.g., his prayer life, evangelism, leadership, or miracles) or his teaching (e.g., on the kingdom of God, discipleship, faith, or the Holy Spirit).

This book, in contrast, intentionally explores each NT author's presentation of Jesus' person and mission with reference to its commonality with that of the other NT writers and its unique contribution to the larger portrait of Jesus depicted in the NT. Because there is some overlap between the NT books in their portraits of Jesus, there will unavoidably

[1] Keith Warrington, *Discovering the Holy Spirit in the New Testament* (Peabody, Mass.: Hendrickson, 2005).

be some repetition of information. The assumption is that a number of readers will want to peruse the chapters of this book that relate to the NT books that specifically interest them rather than reading the book from cover to cover.

Despite the diversity of the various authors' presentations of Jesus, there are common theological threads that run through each of their writings. This book assumes that the NT writers were convinced of the full deity, sovereignty, and sinless humanity of Jesus as well as the historical nature of his incarnation, death, bodily resurrection, and ascension. These are all integral markers of Jesus' mission, and the NT writers confirm that they have significant implications for an accurate understanding of Jesus.

Over the past hundred years, there has been much discussion concerning the reliability of the Gospel sources, especially as they speak of Jesus. Many scholars have explored these issues, and the debate is beyond the scope of this book. The assumption made here is that the NT texts are the work of Spirit-inspired writers who sought to offer clear and authentic portraits of Jesus for the benefit of their readers.[2] The NT text in its current canonical form will constitute the basis for the exploration of Jesus in this book.

There is no reason to think that each NT author has mentioned every aspect of his christology in a given NT book. It is possible that some writers did not mention or stress particular issues simply because they assumed that their readers shared their views. The NT as a whole, however, presents Jesus' person and ministry as a mosaic that explores and reflects his multi-faceted mission in various complementary ways.[3] Each chapter of this volume will explore a NT book or collection of books in search of christological or soteriological characteristics that

---

[2]For discussion concerning these issues, see I. Howard Marshall, *The Origins of New Testament Christology* (Downers Grove, Ill.: InterVarsity, 1977); N. T. Wright, *Jesus and the Victory of God* (London: SPCK, 1996), 3–124; James D. G. Dunn, *Christianity in the Making, Volume 1: Jesus Remembered* (Grand Rapids: Eerdmans, 2003), 11–308.

[3]See David Wenham, *Paul: Follower of Jesus or Founder of Christianity?* (Grand Rapids: Eerdmans, 1995); Darrell L. Bock, *Jesus according to Scripture: Restoring the Portrait from the Gospels* (Grand Rapids: Baker, 2002); Larry Hurtado, *Lord Jesus Christ: Devotion to Jesus in Earliest Christianity* (Grand Rapids: Eerdmans, 2003); Oscar Cullmann, *The Christology of the New Testament* (Louisville: Westminster John Knox, 1959, 1980); Gordon D. Fee, *Pauline Christology: An Exegetical-Theological Study* (Peabody, Mass.: Hendrickson, 2007).

best reflect the author's presentation of Jesus in order to highlight some of their distinctive emphases to their respective audiences.

It is not always an easy task to compile a comprehensive christology[4] of the NT, for it is sometimes unclear where the writers are intentionally making explicit theological statements about Jesus as opposed to mentioning aspects of his character in passing. Sometimes, NT writers seamlessly merge christology and soteriology,[5] not always carefully delineating the material dedicated to each. Instead, as they portray Jesus they sometimes combine aspects of his person and mission, his deity and his ministry, his divine role and his resources, in generalized descriptions. Our task will be to glean christological material both from the explicit and implicit references made to Jesus by the various authors, as well as to sift general statements to distinguish descriptions of Jesus' person from those that relate to his work.

The NT writers did not intend to provide all of the answers to the complex Trinitarian issues that have surfaced from time to time in the history of the church. The NT does not elucidate the interrelationship between Jesus, the Father, and the Spirit; Jesus' dual natures; the virgin birth; the resurrection; how Jesus could live sinlessly as a human being; or many other topics that have excited the curiosity of many. No single NT writer set out to provide a systematic and comprehensive christology. It was not their intention to present data that could easily be downloaded into encyclopedic volumes. Their christology was practical and relevant, and its goal was to meet their readers' needs for spiritual development. These writers did not want to simply teach about the nature of Jesus. They wanted to transform lifestyles. Their aim was to provide not so much a comprehensive portrait of Jesus as a personal model to follow. They sought to inspire transformation and worship as they provided information to provoke wonder and provide truth to combat error.

The NT writers had two main ambitions. First, they wanted to reveal who Jesus truly was and to explore his mission (past, present, and future). Second, they wanted to relate these facts to their audiences. While we may discover lessons that are similar to those that the earliest readers learned, often our reading of these texts will inspire us to learn about Jesus in ways that are fresh and particularly relevant for our own

---

[4] The term "christology" will refer throughout to the person *and* mission of Jesus.

[5] "Soteriology" is understood as relating to the mission of salvation achieved by Jesus.

circumstances. Such is the privilege of those who read a book that is dynamic by its very nature, since it is Spirit-inspired. The adventure ahead (for that is what I hope it will be) beckons us to enjoy the experience of encountering Jesus.

We will concentrate on what the texts reveal about Jesus' identity rather than on his ministry—on who he is rather than what he did. Thus, for example, we will not have the space to explore Jesus' many teachings and miracles.[6] This volume is not a commentary on individual NT books. It includes minimal discussion concerning dating, the identity and geographical location of the original readers, and authorship. The emphasis throughout is on an accessible and balanced approach. Where the text is unclear, this will be frankly acknowledged, and the most significant interpretive options will be considered.

In many ways, this book follows the pattern I recommend to my students when they prepare research papers based on the NT. We will discover Jesus in the NT largely through exploring the textual evidence. The text itself is the focus and sets the agenda, and the result is a text-driven awareness of its message to the first-century reader. The hope is that, as a result of such close readings of NT texts, believers will better appreciate Jesus' character, his comprehensive commitment to them, and his significance for their lives.

---

[6]See Keith Warrington, *Jesus the Healer: Paradigm or Unique Phenomenon* (Carlisle: Paternoster, 2000).

chapter 1

The Synoptic Gospels

Jesus, God Incarnate

The Gospels present the life and teachings of Jesus from the perspective of four of his early followers. The first three Gospels are referred to as "synoptics" (from Gk. "viewed together") because of the parallel and sometimes overlapping nature of their presentations. Because the synoptic Gospels repeat so many of the references to Jesus' words and deeds, the major themes in Matthew, Mark, and Luke will be treated together. However, although much of the information in the synoptics displays a general agreement, each of the writers refers to Jesus in unique ways and with a multiplicity of terms and titles. Also, certain themes are more prominent in one synoptic Gospel than another. Therefore, after the unified presentation of Jesus as seen throughout the synoptic narratives, we will explore each synoptic Gospel's unique contribution to our understanding of Jesus. The portrayal of Jesus from the fourth Gospel will be taken up separately in the following chapter.

The Unified Synoptic Portrayal of Jesus

The Gospels provide a narrative christology, a story in which the main character is Jesus. He is central to the story, and everyone else has been invited to play a part, as it were, in order to reveal more of him. The Gospels offer readers a front-row exposure to Jesus, who at first glance looks like a man but, when explored further, begins to take the form of the eternal God who has a personal concern for all in the audience. Jesus lives in the text but also in the shadows and between the lines, permeating the narrative with his ubiquitous presence. The challenge is, and has always been, whether readers can see him as he truly is and take the step of faith needed to accommodate the remarkable possibility that he is God.

Unique Savior

The central message of the Gospels is that Jesus, the eternal Son of God, became a man in order to save people from the punishment that awaited them because of sin. Throughout his life, he demonstrated the character of God, initiated the means whereby people can enjoy a relationship with God, and gave the Spirit to those who followed him.

Fundamentally, Jesus was a Savior, but uniquely so. Despite, and perhaps because of, the supermarket choice of religions available in the first century, despair was beginning to spread to all parts of society. Political, social, economic, and moral pressures that pervaded the first-century world only exacerbated this growing sense of hopelessness. Hope for a life after death was practically nonexistent in non-Jewish communities and uncertain in Judaism. People sought comfort where they could, often in degenerate, impersonal, superstitious, and syncretistic religious practices which only increased their fear for the future and uncertainty in the present.

Of all the many bitter disappointments of the Jews, the greatest was the apparent absence of God. The representatives of God in Jewish religion, particularly the Pharisees and the Sadducees, offered little hope for the future or sensitive guidance for the present. Into this near-suicidal situation of despair and desperation, conscious need and unconscious longing, came John the Baptist bringing news of a savior. The synoptics record the fulfillment of this promise in the life and mission of Jesus.

The people's greatest need, of course, was not economic, political, or social improvement but spiritual rescue. Unless their personal sin could be dealt with they had no hope of establishing a relationship with God or of receiving eternal life. But because they did not recognize their need, the Jews who were expecting a messiah who would provide political and economic benefits had trouble recognizing the Messiah when he came. Many Jews assumed that the Law's sacrificial system provided a route to forgiveness and that, as Jews, they were already God's children. So they were looking for a messiah who would subjugate their enemies,[1] not save them from hell. They did not need, or want, a suffering savior

[1] *Pss. Sol.* 17:6, 26–27; 4 Ezra 12:32–34.

but a superstar; not a friend of sinners but a dynamic king; not another rabbi to teach them how to live but a wonder worker to take them out of this life and lead them to a promised land where Messiah would reign. Although Jesus offered what they really needed, he did not fulfill their dream.

Writing years after the events, the synoptists tell the story of Jesus' mission and his rejection by most of those he came to save. Their Gospels also demonstrate who he truly was and what he came to do for those who placed their trust in him.

The Birth and Youth of Jesus

Although Mark's Gospel does not cover the years before Jesus' baptism in the Jordan, Matthew and Luke offer extended narratives concentrating on the events leading up to, and immediately following, Jesus' birth.

Matthew (1:18, 20) and Luke (1:35) both record the role of the Holy Spirit in Jesus' birth. Matthew describes the Spirit initiating the conception, and Luke shows the Spirit's oversight of the entire birth process. The Spirit's involvement in Jesus' incarnation is reminiscent of his role in creation (Gen 1:2). The Spirit was not providing a medical safeguard to ensure that the birth of Jesus was successful. Rather, his presence demonstrated the significance of the birth. Nothing like this had happened before and, because the child was God in the flesh, it was essential to clearly and supernaturally signal the event. Thus, the verb Luke uses (1:35) to describe the overshadowing presence of the Spirit (Gk. *episkiazō*) was used in the LXX to describe the divine cloud that rested on the tabernacle (Exod 40:34, 35) and God's protective presence as he led his people to the promised land in the OT (Ps 91:4). Although the filling of the Spirit predicted for John the Baptist (Luke 1:15) was unusual, the overshadowing of the Spirit prior to Jesus' birth was unique and astounding.

The Holy Spirit inspires Simeon to go to the temple in order to see Jesus (who, he is told, is the Messiah) and to prophesy of his mission to come (Luke 2:25–35). The Spirit also encourages Elizabeth to prophesy concerning Jesus (Luke 1:42–45). Both refer to the beneficent ministry of Jesus for the Jews, though there are also hints of suffering and pain in the prophecies. Although the Spirit was with some OT characters, especially the prophets, this presence reaches a superlative expression in the life of Jesus, who was divinely overshadowed by none other than "the Holy Spirit . . . and the power of the Most High," even before he was born (Luke 1:35).

This supernatural support indicates that Jesus is worthy of the highest acclamation. The message of Matthew and Luke, even before Jesus begins his ministry, is that Jesus is worthy of consideration. He is not just a man with a divinely inspired mission but he is united with none other than the Holy Spirit.

The Authoritative Jesus

Although Jesus' physical birth demonstrates his humanity, Matthew and Luke significantly exalt his birth by relating how angels announced it to Joseph (Matt 1:20), to shepherds (Luke 2:8–12), and to Mary (Luke 1:26–33). His name is Jesus (Matt. 1:21); he will save his people from their sins (Matt 1:21); he has received from his Father an everlasting kingdom over the "house of Jacob" (Luke 1:33); and he is set apart (Luke 1:35). Furthermore, his birth fulfills OT prophecy (Matt 1:23) even down to the detail of its location in Bethlehem (Matt 2:6).

These narratives also ascribe a number of important names to Jesus. He is called Emmanuel ("God with us," Matt 1:23), the king of the Jews (Matt 2:2) who is worthy of worship (Matt 2:11), the Christ (Messiah[2]), the ruler of the Jews (Matt 2:6), Savior (Luke 2:11), and the Son of the Most High (Luke 1:32). He is also "called holy, the Son of God."[3] In particular, he is referred to as the Lord (Luke 2:11).[4] The early chapters of Luke, in particular, also present the theme of redemption (Luke 1:68; 2:38). It is as a twelve year old, while speaking to the religious leaders in Jerusalem, that Jesus identifies the temple as "my Father's house" (Luke 2:49). Although his intelligence is worthy of consideration, as his learned conversational partners were astonished by his wisdom, it is his self-identification that is the sensational aspect of the narrative.

---

[2] Matt 2:4; Mark 1:1; Luke 2:11. In the Gospels, "Messiah" is mainly used as a title, whereas in the Pauline literature it is generally always a proper name, often being used as the name to replace "Jesus" or to precede it (Rom 3:24; 6:3).

[3] Mark 1:1; Luke 1:35.

[4] This will be one of Luke's key titles for Jesus (Acts 2:36); Luke 2:11; 3:4 (see also John 20:2, 13, 18, 20, 25, 28; 21:7; Rom 10:13; Heb 1:10; 1 Pet 3:14–15; Jude 14–15; Rev 17:14; 19:16). See also Marshall, *Origins of NT Christology,* 97–108.

For it is not only that Jesus has divine characteristics or that he has been appointed to his commission by God the Father and thus fulfills it in supernatural power; Jesus is none other than God in the flesh. Thus the unique "prophet of the Most High," John the Baptist (Luke 1:76), prefigures him. The genealogies exalt him. He receives a catalogue of illustrious names and titles. He fulfills OT prophecies. Angels acclaim him. The Holy Spirit partners with him and affirms him. Although kings try to kill him, Jewish shepherds and Gentile wise men (both marginalized in their own way) choose to worship him. Jesus the Savior is for all people, Gentiles and Jews (Luke 2:10, 32). He came to bring good news (the gospel) to everyone (Mark 1:1).

Baptism

John, the Unique Forerunner

Each of the synoptics records Jesus' baptism by John the Baptist as well as John's testimony about him. Luke, in particular, describes John in exalted prophetic terminology (1:5–25, 57–80). Not only are his parents "righteous before God, living blamelessly according to all the commandments and regulations of the Lord" (1:6), but the birth of their son (which is itself a miracle, given their age and the inability of Elizabeth to have children [1:7]) is preceded by the appearance of an angel who prophesies it (1:11–13).

Luke describes John himself as being "great in the sight of the Lord" and "filled with the Holy Spirit," "even before his birth" (1:15). His role is to function in the power of Elijah "to make ready a people prepared for the Lord" (1:16, 17, 76). Mark (1:2–6) affirms John's status by commencing his Gospel with a description of him fulfilling OT prophecy,[5] wearing the clothes of a prophet (2 Kgs 1:8; Zech 13:4), and living in the wilderness. The wilderness was a place associated with OT prophets and was also a place where, in the past, God's people had received revelation.[6]

For all his worth and pedigree, however, John was only Jesus' forerunner. He came to prepare the people by encouraging them to repent and to prove their penitence by being baptized in water—so that they

---

[5] Isa 40:3; 43:7; Mal 3:1.

[6] Exod 3:1; 1 Kgs 19:4.

could be ready to benefit from the superior mission of Jesus.[7] John's coming may have fulfilled OT prophecies, but Jesus fulfilled prophecies that had reference to God (Isa 40:3–5; Mal 3:1).[8]

Jesus Who Baptizes with the Holy Spirit and Fire

Although it might appear that it is Jesus' baptism in the Jordan that is most important to the synoptists on that occasion, it is more appropriate to recognize that the baptism is the context for a number of other more important elements, each of which portrays Jesus as an exalted figure. Even before Jesus is baptized, each author identifies him as the one who will baptize with the Holy Spirit (Mark 1:8; Matt 3:11; Luke 3:16) "and fire," which in the OT connotes judgment, cleansing, and transformation. The Jews believed that the Messiah would be endowed with the Spirit (Isa 11:2), though there is no indication in the OT that he would bestow the Spirit. The readers of the Gospels, therefore, would not have expected the Messiah to do this. But the synoptists present Jesus not only as partnered with the Spirit, but also as having the authority to bestow the Spirit upon others. Jesus was not just an anointed man with supernatural powers. Each of the authors reminds his readers of the incomprehensible nature of Jesus, who was able to give the Spirit to people—an exclusively divine prerogative.[9]

Jesus Endorsed by the Spirit

The fact that the Holy Spirit descended on Jesus (John twice reveals that the Spirit also remained with him [1:32–33]) indicates his importance as one who the Spirit affirms. The Spirit's association with Jesus reveals not Jesus' helplessness or need for such supernatural aid; rather, it emphasizes his unique status. Jesus' traveling companion is none other than the Holy Spirit. More important still is the fact that the description is a fulfillment of the prophecy of Isaiah (11:2; 42:1) that God would place his Spirit upon his Servant. This does not mean that his baptism in the Jordan was the first occasion that Jesus was closely identified with the Spirit, but it does designate that he was God's unique Servant with a message from God. Jesus was about to embark on his mission to preach

---

[7] Matt 3:11–12//Mark 1:7–8//Luke 3:16.
[8] Matt 3:2–3; Mark 1:2–3; Luke 3:4–6.
[9] Num 11:29; Isa 42:1.

the good news of the kingdom of God, and this anointing declared that the Spirit would be his partner for the duration of the journey.

Empowerment is an important element of the Holy Spirit's activity in the OT, and it is possible that Jesus was being empowered by the Spirit. However, the Gospels do not explicitly record that the Spirit enabled Jesus to perform miracles. Indeed, they often present Jesus as functioning in his own power and authority without any explicit mention of the Spirit.[10] The synoptists do not describe Jesus as a mere man who needed the Spirit, without whom he had little authority or power. It is therefore more likely that Jesus is being revealed to the world as the legitimate initiator of the kingdom, whose inherent worth warrants his walking with the Spirit and the Spirit walking with him. The message is clear. If the Spirit is with Jesus, he must be authentic.[11] The Spirit legitimizes Jesus, validating him as the promised Messiah. While the Spirit may be empowering him, the primary purpose is to confirm the Spirit's endorsement of Jesus. As Bock writes, "The Spirit leads and confirms more than he empowers Jesus."[12] The one with whom the Spirit chooses to remain is the one with whom readers should also choose to remain.

Jesus the Son Who Is Affirmed by His Father

The words of the Father indicating divine pleasure in Jesus, "my Son, the Beloved"[13] recall two OT texts. Psalm 2:7 links sonship to the king and Isaiah 42:1 proclaims God's endorsement of, and delight in, the Servant. Before Jesus commences his mission, he receives the affirmation of the Father. It is not necessary to assume that Jesus is being adopted as the Son of God or that he is, for the first time, made aware of his unique sonship. Rather, the words reflect the close, eternal communion between the Father and Son. Although this was apparently a private revelation for Jesus and John the Baptist, the Gospel authors use the account to inform their readers of the superiority of Jesus. He has received the highest accolade possible—the heavens are metaphorically ripped apart in order to bestow the affirming touch of the Spirit and words of the Father upon Jesus. The readers are thereby let in on the

---

[10] Luke 4:36; 5:12–13, 17; 6:19; 8:46; 9:1; 10:19; 21:27.

[11] In the OT, the Spirit functioned as a "marker," identifying leaders (Exod 33:15, 16; Judg 6:34; 1 Sam 16:13).

[12] Darrell L. Bock, *Luke 1:1–9:50* (BECNT; Grand Rapids: Baker, 2003), 345.

[13] Matt 3:17//Mark 1:11//Luke 3:22.

secret. While Jesus may look like a mere man, his association with the Spirit and the Father tells a different story. He truly is heaven's ambassador and, in this narrative, the Father and the Spirit reveal their pleasure in accompanying him on the journey to save the world.

The identification of Jesus as the son of a father does not imply inferiority or suggest in any way that the Son is not an eternal being. Rather, this description of the relationship between the incarnate Jesus and his Father is intended to elevate his status in the minds of readers. He enjoys a unique, familial relationship with the Father and, as the Father's Son, he is the best ambassador because he reflects his Father better than anyone else could.

Temptations

After the divine endorsement of Jesus at his baptism, one would expect the result of his confrontation with the devil to be a foregone conclusion. Although the devil may hope for a knockout, he is in for a shock as his opponent stands before him, having received the affirmation of the Spirit and the applause of his Father. The battle commences but the odds are unfair, for Jesus has already been identified as supreme.

Matthew (4:1–11) and Luke (4:1–13) record three temptations of Jesus. Although there are differences in the accounts, the main thrust is clear—the devil is no match for Jesus. The devil attempts to divert Jesus from his mission by suggesting that he could prove that he is the Son of God, demonstrate it publicly, and own the nations by following an agenda other than the divine one. The devil challenges Jesus to achieve his ambitions without the pain of life and the rejection of those he came to save, without the denials, betrayals, and the flight of his followers, without suffering crucifixion and separation from the Father. The Gospel writers are not merely introducing Jesus as one who is above the attraction of food (even after forty days of fasting), selfish ambition, or gain. Rather, Jesus is the one who sees through the malevolence, the trickery, and the empty claims of the devil.

The fact that Jesus was led by the Holy Spirit (Matt 4:1//Luke 4:1) indicates his willing submission to the Father, but more importantly, it signifies his status. The Spirit is not leading Jesus in order for him to function as Messiah; it is because Jesus is the Messiah that the Spirit is leading him. The authors provide this information not to demonstrate the association between leading and following, but to illustrate that the destiny of the one is inextricably entwined with the destiny of the other. It is as if they are asking their readers the question, "What kind of man receives the attention of the Spirit in this way?"

Furthermore, the presence of the Holy Spirit indicates that Jesus' journey into the wilderness is part of the divine agenda. It was not his fault that he was tempted by the devil, nor did he foolishly wander into his territory.[14] The Spirit's presence affirms that Jesus is walking in the center of the Father's will for him. Although the devil clearly hoped to surprise Jesus and deflect him from his mission, it was God the Father who had sprung the trap and the devil was the prey as Jesus defeated him.

There is no indication that Jesus was anxious about this confrontation or weakened by his abstinence from food. This was not a battle between two equals and the result was never in doubt. Jesus responds to each temptation immediately with words from the OT. When the devil offers an OT verse, Jesus silences him with yet another OT verse: "Do not put the Lord your God to the test."[15] This reminds the devil of the one he addresses and puts him firmly in his place. His intrusion into Jesus' journey concludes with a reprimand by Jesus and a reminder of his true status. Jesus' use of this title "Lord" is significant. Earlier, Matthew and Luke used the title to refer to God the Father,[16] but here it refers to God the Son.

Following this narrative, Matthew and Mark refer to the angels who "waited on" Jesus (Matt 4:11; Mark 1:13). However, the Greek verb *diēkonoun* is best translated "served." The angels did not arrive to soothe the worn out Savior but to serve the one who is Lord. It is in this light that Mark's shorter account may best be understood. Although it is possible that his reference to Jesus being with the wild beasts (1:12) may indicate a hostile environment, it is more likely that he intends to demonstrate that Jesus was in control, even over the wild beasts—after all, he created them (Heb 1:2). This is less a story about the determination of Jesus to overcome temptation (though it is that) and more an

[14]Many Jews viewed the wilderness as the home of demons (Luke 11:24); similarly, water was viewed as being a fearful place for demons (Luke 8:33). In *T. Sol.* 5:11, the demon Asmodeus begs not to be sent into water (cf. 11:6). Thus, entering the wilderness may have seemed presumptuous or foolish to readers. The fact that Luke emphasizes the presence of the Spirit with Jesus militates against such an assumption.

[15]Matt 4:7//Luke 4:12.

[16]Matt 1:24; 2:13, 19; Luke 1:6–46; 2:9–39.

insight into the remarkable nature of Jesus, who demonstrates his ability to win the cosmic war before the battle has properly commenced. The rest of the story is the path to victory.

Ministry Years

A number of events dominate the years between Jesus' baptism and temptation and the final few weeks of his life. Each of these reveals crucial truths about Jesus and his mission. He preaches and teaches, calls and develops disciples, performs miracles, and responds to the needs of people. He exhibits his divine authority and exquisite character throughout. One of the fundamental aims of Jesus' mission and of those who recorded it was to provide people with the opportunity to place their trust in him. Although he was also a prophet, healer, exorcist, and stimulating teacher, the Gospel writers want readers to come to the most important conclusion: that Jesus came to save—to offer a relationship with God and the forgiveness of their sins.

The concept of faith, therefore, is a common ingredient in each of the synoptics. To those who are unwilling to place their faith in him and accept him, Jesus is forceful. He denounces religious authorities,[17] warns about the Pharisees,[18] and dismisses the attempt of Herod Antipas to kill him (Luke 13:31–33). In responding to those who place their trust in him, however tentatively, Jesus offers warm acceptance, encouragement, affirmation, and hope.[19] Jesus' authority is foundational, and the synoptists demonstrate this in a number of ways.

Jesus' Authority Demonstrated by Events

The transfiguration, one of the most remarkable events in Jesus' life, demonstrates his authority. Here the past, present, and future come into focus, the divine and human interlock, and glory and suffering merge.[20] Each synoptist describes the event differently, though the overall effect is similar—Jesus is supernaturally changed, and the brightness of his appearance is the common denominator in each description. While the

---

[17] Matt 23:1–36//Mark 12:38–40//Luke 20:45–47; Luke 11:42–52; 16:14–15.

[18] Matt 16:5–12; Mark 8:14–21; Luke 12:1.

[19] Mark 6:25–34//Luke 12:22–32; Matt 10:29–31//Luke 12:6–7; Matt 26:6–13//Mark 14:3–9//Luke 7:36–50.

[20] Matt 17:1–9//Mark 9:2–20//Luke 9:28–36.

authors do not state the significance of this metamorphosis, the effect is to surprise the reader with the sensational nature of such a transformation. The event indicates the true character and status of Jesus, best reflected in intense light that banishes all vestiges of darkness. Such brightness elsewhere in the Bible relates to the manifestation of the glory, authority, or presence of God.[21] Here, this light intimates the divinity of Jesus. This episode in Jesus' life is probably also intended to remind readers of the occasion when Moses' face shone after he had talked with God (Exod 34:29). It is significant, however, that Jesus shines before God the Father speaks.

The fact that Moses and Elijah are present is significant for a number of reasons. Not only do they represent the history of God's revelation in the Law and the Prophets, but they also signal the past and the future, since Elijah was expected to precede the end times (Mal 4:5). Their importance as messengers of God emphasizes the prominence of Jesus as the one they are to meet. Moses and Elijah also experienced suffering as well as success in their ministries and so are best placed to speak to Jesus about the journey that will end with his "departure" in Jerusalem (Luke 9:31). In the context of the three disciples who were frightened and offered inappropriate suggestions (Mark 9:6), the presence of two heroes from the past lends an air of kingliness to Jesus and dignity and gravity to the occasion.

The conversation between Moses, Elijah, and Jesus appears to relate solely to the events of the passion that are soon to come. The words of the Father, however, identify Jesus as his Son and instruct all to listen to him. Soon, however, the one to whom all should listen is ignored, ridiculed, and rejected. This narrative and those that follow present a combination of glory and suffering, sorrow and success, painful rejection and royal precedence.

Jesus' Authority Associated with His Teaching

Jesus was often referred to as a rabbi or teacher, but his style of teaching and its content distinguish him as being different from other teachers. Although Jesus' teaching style is worthy of consideration, it is the content of his instruction that is most important—in particular because what he says reveals his authority. He offers timeless lessons

[21] Dan 7:9; Rev 1:14, 16; 4:5.

through his miracles, deeds, and lifestyle as well as through his words. Matthew concentrates the teaching of Jesus in a number of sermons and also in his miracles; Mark largely transmits Jesus' teaching through the miracles he performs; while Luke uses miracles, teaching, and stories to reveal characteristics about Jesus (John uses incidents and miracles as well as extended discourses to act as signposts to Jesus).

To provide a comprehensive presentation of all the issues Jesus taught about would be impossible for a book this size.[22] Much of Jesus' teaching focused on the kingdom of God. The term "kingdom of God" is absent from the OT, but the concept of the rule of God where God is king[23] and ruler over creation[24] permeates the Bible. The concept of the kingdom of God was developed in the intertestamental literature and resulted in some extreme expectations: that the Romans would be destroyed, that Satan would be removed, and that the Jews would be vindicated and provided with supernatural prosperity (*Pss. Sol.* 17, 18). Jesus takes the theme of the kingdom of God and puts his stamp on it. He identifies it as the reign of God, most dramatically characterized by the presence of God, that can be experienced in the present as a foretaste of all that is to come. He establishes his personal authority by announcing the presence[25] and priority of the kingdom[26] while he declares that he has the authority to provide and determine entrance to it,[27] which is free to all[28]—a prerogative that belongs to God.[29] Although people's responses to the kingdom vary,[30] Jesus promises its growth.[31]

---

[22] These subjects include information concerning the devil and demons (Matt 12:25–30//Mark 3:22–27//Luke 11:16–23; Matt 12:43–45//Luke 11:24–26), the Spirit (Matt 12:31–32//Mark 3:28–30//Luke 12:10–15), eternal life (Matt 19:16–22//Mark 10:17–22//Luke 18:18–23), faith (Matt 17:19–21//Mark 9:28–29//Luke 17:5–6), and the second coming (Matt 24:1–51//Mark 13:1–23, 35//Luke 17:22–37).

[23] 1 Sam 12:12; Ps 24:10.

[24] Ps 29:10; Isa 6:5.

[25] Matt 4:17, 23; 9:35; Mark 1:14//Luke 8:1; Luke 17:20–21.

[26] Matt 6:19–21//Luke 12:33–34; 13:44–52; Matt 25:1–13.

[27] Matt 7:21–23; Luke 12:32–34; Matt 18:1–5//Mark 9:33–37//Luke 9:46–48; Matt 22:29–30.

[28] Matt 22:1–14//Luke 14:15–24.

[29] Matt 19:23–30//Mark 10:23–27//Luke 18:24–27.

[30] Matt 13:1–23//Mark 4:1–20//Luke 8:4–15; Matt 13:24–30//Mark 4:26–29.

[31] Mark 4:26–32; Matt 13:31–32//Mark 4:30–32//Luke 13:18–19; Matt 13:33//Luke 13:20–21.

Jesus' sermons identify key elements of his mission and assert his personal authority to achieve them. Thus, at the commencement of his ministry, Luke informs his readers that Jesus came to "bring good news to the poor . . . release to the captives . . . sight to the blind . . . to let the oppressed go free . . . to proclaim the year of the Lord's favor" (4:18–19). These are high aims, especially given their OT pedigree,[32] but the Spirit's presence with Jesus (Luke 4:18) is evidence of his authority not only to proclaim them but also to accomplish them. He is not simply functioning as did the OT prophet who prophesied future events. Jesus is taking it upon himself to deliver the divine agenda and, even in the face of malevolent opposition, he will succeed.

Jesus' Authority Associated with His Prophecies

The Gospel writers portray Jesus as one who has knowledge of the future.[33] He predicts the destruction of the temple;[34] the persecution of his followers;[35] global devastation;[36] the arrival of false prophets and pseudo-messiahs;[37] and the coming of the Son of Man.[38] He also prophesies concerning his own suffering, betrayal, and denial.[39] Although some thought he was "the Prophet" who was to come before the end times (probably based on Deut 18: 15–19),[40] the synoptists reveal Jesus as one more exalted still.

Jesus' Authority Associated with Actions

Jesus' actions also verify his supreme authority. He regularly confirms his readiness to set his own agenda, or that which he perceives to be the Father's agenda for him, even when it contradicts the expectations and established behaviors in Jewish society. Jesus chooses where and to whom to preach. Even when crowds are waiting for him, on

---

[32] Isa 58:6; 61:1–2.

[33] Matt 11:20–24//Luke 10:13–15; Matt 16:27–28//Mark 9:1//Luke 9:27.

[34] Matt 24:1–2//Mark 13:1–2//Luke 21:5–6.

[35] Matt 24:9–14//Mark 13:9–13//Luke 21:12–19.

[36] Matt 24:15–22//Mark 13:14–20//Luke 21:20–24.

[37] Matt 24:23–28//Mark 13:21–23.

[38] Matt 24:29–31//Mark 13:24–27//Luke 21:25–28.

[39] See the following passages on his sufferings (Matt 16:21//Mark 8:31//Luke 9:22; Matt 17:22–23//Mark 9:30–32//Luke 9:43–45; Matt 20:17–19//Mark 10:32–34//Luke 18:31–34), betrayal (Matt 26:21–25//Mark 14:18–21//Luke 22:21–23), and denial (Matt 26:30–35//Mark 14:26–31//Luke 22:31–34).

[40] Matt. 21:11.

occasion he moves to different towns. It is not that he is indifferent to people's needs, but rather that he is sensitive to a divine agenda.[41]

He chooses to eat with those with whom he wishes to eat.[42] Even though standard rules of behavior dictated that certain people were undesirable and even inappropriate guests at a meal, Jesus chooses to eat with those who are most marginalized, including tax collectors. His rationale is that in order to save people he will cross barriers to meet them where they are.

Similarly, he chooses the appropriate times for fasting.[43] When religious leaders question him concerning fasting, Jesus responds by declaring that he is to be the judge of when fasting should be undertaken. He does not defend his attitude to fasting; he simply offers three metaphors which support the view that there is a right time and a wrong time to fast. As it is inappropriate for people to fast with a bridegroom prior to his wedding, or to place a new piece of cloth on an old garment, or to pour new wine into old wineskins, so also Jesus concludes that it is inappropriate for his disciples to fast. Although he may be suggesting obliquely that he is the divine bridegroom,[44] it is more likely that he is stating bluntly that it is up to him to decide when it is appropriate to fast. He leaves his audience with the dilemma of whether or not to accept his authority.

Jesus also asserts his authority to determine legitimate activity on the Sabbath.[45] Religious leaders accuse him of allowing his disciples to work on the Sabbath by taking grain and eating it.[46] He responds to the accusation with a conundrum, asking his questioners if they would similarly criticize David for having broken the Law by eating bread that was dedicated to the priests. Again, rather than defending his position, he presents his audience with a challenge. Will they trust Jesus to determine that which is acceptable (as they did David)? Or will they demand an explanation that will satisfy their logic and accommodate their presuppositions? Each of the synoptic Gospels

---

[41] Mark 1:35–38//Luke 4:42–43.

[42] Matt 9:10–13//Mark 2:13–17//Luke 5:27–32.

[43] Matt 9:14–17//Mark 2:18–22//Luke 5:33–39.

[44] Judaism does not link this title to the Messiah, though it is an OT image of God (Isa 61:10; 62:5).

[45] Matt 12:1–8//Mark 2:23–28//Luke 6:1–5.

[46] This violated the laws prohibiting the harvesting and threshing of grain on the Sabbath (*m. Šabb.* 7.2), though see Deut 23:25.

concludes these narratives with the words of Jesus, "the Son of Man is lord of the Sabbath." He is the supreme arbiter of the validity of Sabbath activities.

When Jesus finds himself being questioned by religious leaders concerning purity laws and washing one's hands before eating,[47] he does not answer immediately but instead requests that they explain some of their behavior in the light of Jewish laws. He does not seek to embarrass them; he is, rather, asserting once again his authority to determine which aspects of the Law have the highest moral priority. He declares his superiority to the Law by pronouncing all foods to be clean and thus edible. He also sets standards even higher than the Law as he speaks against infidelity and not simply divorce, against lust and not just adultery, against anger and not only murder. He calls people not just to refuse to retaliate, but to be ready to go beyond the call of duty. His followers are not simply to abstain from oaths, but also to develop integrity. They are not just to reject hatred, but to support love (Matt 5:17–20). In this respect, Jesus fulfills the Law by embodying its heart and essence and not simply its rules and external regulations.

Jesus' declaration of his authority to call for repentance and, more radically, to forgive sins, is of fundamental importance.[48] Although he heals a paralytic, it is Jesus' forgiveness of the man's sins that is central to the narrative.[49] The scribes assume that Jesus' claim to be able to forgive sins is blasphemy. The physical healing, then, is the proof that he offers of his authority—that his verbal forgiveness of sins is not a forlorn claim. The healing, though it is important to the paralytic and those who brought him, carries a more profound lesson—Jesus has the authority to forgive sins.

When the Gospel writers described Jesus as having the authority to forgive sins, they did so knowing that in Jewish tradition this was a prerogative belonging exclusively to God. Rabbinic tradition assumed that sin would not be forgiven, nor would sickness be healed, until the sin that caused it had been confessed.[50] Jesus, however, pronounces forgiveness when no confession had been offered. The Gospel writers declare

---

[47] Matt 15:1–20//Mark 7:1–23//Luke 11:37–41.

[48] Luke 5:27–32; 7:47–49; 19:9–10.

[49] Matt 9:1–7//Mark 2:1–12//Luke 5:17–26.

[50] See *b. Ned.* 41a.

that Jesus is not only a healer or a prophet who speaks on behalf of God, but one who himself uniquely functions as God.[51]

When Jesus cleanses the temple he demonstrates his authority there as well.[52] For the religious leaders, the important issue is not the action itself but the authority Jesus assumed in undertaking it. While John indicates that Jesus' concern is with trade in the temple, the synoptists include Jesus' references to Isaiah 56:7 and Jeremiah 7:11, which identify the temple as a house of prayer now transformed into "a den of robbers." Jesus reevaluates the significance of the temple, which is coming to the end of its earthly use. It will be replaced by a new temple, the church, and the sacrificial system will be superseded once and for all by the supreme sacrifice—his death on the cross. Jesus further demonstrates his authority to decide appropriate activity in the temple when he allows blind and lame people to come to him there (Matt 21:14)—those who some religious Jews would have forbidden. He is the Lord of the temple who will reinstitute authentic worship. Jesus is the judge of people, activities, and words.[53]

Titles of Authority

Son of Man

Jesus referred to himself as the "Son of Man" over fifty times in the Gospels (excluding parallel references).[54] Matthew is the author who uses the title most regularly, though Mark and Luke use it on occasions when Matthew does not.[55] It is possible that the title refers to Jesus as a (mere) member of humanity,[56] but it is much more likely that it refers to a supernatural being who receives authority directly from God and

---

[51] Luke alone in the NT uses the Greek word *paradoxa,* "strange things" (5:26). There was an incongruity about Jesus offering someone spiritual healing before a physical healing.

[52] Matt 21:10–17, 23–27//Mark 11:11–17, 27–33//Luke 19:45–46; Luke 20:1–16.

[53] Matt 3:12//Luke 3:17; Matt 10:34–36//Luke 12:49–53; Matt 11:20–24//Luke 12:12–15.

[54] Matt 8:20//Luke 9:58; Matt 10:23; 11:19; 12:40; 13:37; 16:13; Luke 12:8; Matt 17:9, 12//Mark 9:9, 12; Matt 17:22//Mark 9:30//Luke 9:43; Matt 20:18//Mark 10:33//Luke 18:31; Matt 20:28//Mark 10:45; Matt 25:37, 39//Luke 17:26, 28; Matt 26:24//Mark 14:21//Luke 22:22; Matt 26:45//Mark 14:41.

[55] Mark 8:31//Luke 9:22; Luke 17:25; 18:31–33; 22:22; 24:7.

[56] Num 23:19; Ps 146:3; Isa 51:12; Ezek 2:1.

comes on the clouds of heaven[57]—an action elsewhere associated with God.[58] The Gospels often use the term in eschatological contexts,[59] but it occurs mainly in settings where it refers to the authority of Jesus. Jesus, as the Son of Man, has authority to forgive sins,[60] to determine Sabbath practice,[61] to eat and drink with anyone he wishes (Luke 7:34–35), to be a sign to "this generation" (Luke 11:30), and "to seek out and to save the lost" (Luke 19:10). Jesus radically adds suffering to the role of the Son of Man.[62]

Messiah

The synoptists clearly present Jesus as the Messiah.[63] He is the Son of David,[64] a title first used in Psalm 110:1 to refer to someone who is more important than King David. The term, though generally identifying the bearer as someone who was born in the lineage of David, also had a more specific and significant sense that the Jews understood as referring to the coming Messiah. However, Jesus is portrayed as having a prestige that is far beyond that of even the predicted Messiah. Jesus owns authority that belongs exclusively to God and thus is worthy of worship.

Although the OT provides information concerning the messianic age,[65] it gives very few specific details about the Messiah. The Jews were expecting a messiah, and many hoped that Jesus might be that person. But the Gospel writers demonstrate that Jesus does not fulfill the popular expectations for the Messiah. The Jews were expecting a dynamic conqueror who would smash through the pagan opposition to God

---

[57] Dan 7:13; 4 Ezra; 1 Enoch 46:16; 48:2–10; 62:5–16; 63:11; 69:26–29.

[58] Exod 34:5; Num 10:34; Ps 104:3.

[59] Matt 16:27//Mark 8:38//Luke 9:26; Matt 24:30//Mark 13:26//Luke 21:27; Matt 26:64//Mark 14:62//Luke 22:60; Matt 24:44//Luke 12:40; Matt 24:27//Luke 17:24; Matt 24:37//Luke 17:26; Matt 13:41; 19:28; 24:30; 25:31; Luke 12:8; 17:22, 30; 18:8; 21:36.

[60] Matt 9:6//Mark 2:10//Luke 5:24.

[61] Matt 12:8//Mark 2:28//Luke 6:5.

[62] Matt 8:18//Luke 9:58; Mark 8:31//Luke 9:22; Matt 17:12//Mark 9:12; Matt 17:22//Mark 9:31//Luke 9:44; Matt 20:18//Mark 10:33//Luke 18:31; Matt 20:28// Mark 10:45; Matt 26:45//Mark 14:41; Matt 12:40//Luke 11:30; Luke 6:22.

[63] Matt 1:16–17; Matt 16:13–20//Mark 8:27–30//Luke 9:18–21 (John 20:31); Mark 14:61–62; Luke 2:11, 26; see pp. 6, 34–35.

[64] Matt 22:41–46//Mark 12:35–37//Luke 20:41–44; see pp. 34–35.

[65] Isa 26–29; Joel 2:28–3:21.

and forcefully establish his kingdom. The Gospels, on the other hand, speak of the Messiah's suffering, pain, and sadness on his journey to procure redemption.

At the same time, the writers establish that Jesus is not just Messiah but someone who functions with divine power and authority at a higher level of authority than Messiah. There is limited direct evidence in the OT that the Messiah was expected to effect miracles, though later Judaism[66] and Qumran[67] anticipated that power. Jesus exceeded their most optimistic expectations of a restorative and caring messiah.[68] Although as Messiah he was expected to be anointed by the Spirit and reign as a king,[69] Jesus bestows the Spirit on others and functions as the king of a superior kingdom.[70] There are other contrasts as well. Messiah was expected to bless materially, but Jesus promises to bless spiritually; Messiah was expected to destroy sinners, but Jesus came to save them; Messiah was to come specifically for the Jews, but Jesus came for the world; Messiah was expected to be a man, appointed by God, but Jesus was God become man and radiated God perfectly. Similarly, Jesus offered a fresh interpretation of the coming messianic kingdom. Jesus expanded upon the OT vision of a life of prosperity and blessing where the rule of God is constant and Eden is recreated[71] with the promise of a kingdom where God reigns but the blessings are specifically related to a personal relationship with him.

Son of God

The Gospels often refer to Jesus as the Son of the Father,[72] the Son of God,[73] and the Son of the Most High.[74] Demons referred to him as the Son of God (Mark 3:11; 5:7) as did the devil (Mark 4:3, 6) but,

---

[66] *Pss. Sol.* 3:16; 13:9–11; 14:13–15; 18:7–10; *As. Mos.* 10:1–10; *Jub.* 23:29–31; 4 Esd 7:12, 27–31; 8:53; *1 En.* 96:3; *2 Bar.* 29:5–8; 73:2–74:4; *Sib. Or.* 3.373–380, 619–623, 744–759; *b. Sanh.* 91b; *T. Zeb.* 9.8; *T. Jud.* 18.12.

[67] 1QH 11:22; 1QS 4:6; 4Q 521.8, 12. The Dead Sea scrolls refer to two messiah-figures—one, like David, who would rule, and the other who would function as a priest.

[68] Isa 11:1–4; 35:5; Jer 23:5–6; Ezek 34:23–24.

[69] Isa 9:2–7; 32:1–5; Jer 23:5; 30:9; 33:15, 17; Ezek 37:24; Hos 3:5; Mic 5:2–5.

[70] Matt 3:11//Mark 1:7–8//Luke 3:16.

[71] Isa 11:6–9; 32:13; 35:1, 10; 65:20–22; Amos 9:13.

[72] Matt 11:25–27//Luke 10:21–34.

[73] Luke 1:32; 2:49; see also Marshall, *Origins of NT Christology,* 111–23.

[74] Matt 11:25–27//Luke 10:21–22.

more importantly, God the Father refers to him as his Son.[75] Although Jesus never uses the term of himself, when asked, "Are you the Messiah, the Son of the Blessed One?," he responds, "I am."[76] This term referred to people who, by virtue of their being created by God, may be defined as sons of God (including Adam, Luke 3:38). The Israelites were also sons of God,[77] as were the nations (Hos 11:1). The term also refers to the king in the singular form,[78] to angels,[79] and to believers.[80]

When the Gospel writers use the term Son of God to refer to Jesus, however, it is clear that they are describing a different quality of sonship. The synoptic authors build a number of features into the term so that readers cannot misunderstand it to indicate an inferior status in relationship to the Father. Rather, the clear implication is that Jesus enjoys the most exalted status possible. Thus, Jesus knows the Father as much as the Father knows the Son (Matt 12:27). As the Son of God, Jesus partakes of God's very nature. Furthermore, this knowledge is exclusive and immediate. Others may only enter into this relationship with the express permission of the Father of the Son. As a son best reflects his father, so also Jesus in the flesh offers the most accurate and authentic portrayal of God possible on earth. He is the unique revelation of God, the most perfect mediator. He is a Son, the Son of the Father, the Son who came to save.

Unique Mentor

One of Jesus' earliest acts is to call his disciples.[81] Each of the synoptics records this act, which is significant for a number of reasons. First, it indicates that Jesus did not anticipate that his ministry would end with him—others would continue his work. The disciples' readiness to follow him immediately reflects his authority. Normally the disciples of rabbis asked to be taught by a particular rabbi, but Jesus chooses those he will mentor. Second, Jesus gave his disciples commissions and

---

[75] Matt 3:17//Mark 1:11//Luke 3:22.

[76] Matt 26:63–64//Mark 14:61–62//Luke 22:69.

[77] Deut 14:1; 32:8; Isa 1:2; Jer 3:19.

[78] 2 Sam 7:14; Pss 2:7; 89:27.

[79] Gen 6:2, 4; Job 1:6; 2:1; 38:7; Heb 1:5.

[80] Matt 5:9; Luke 20:36; Rom 8:14, 19; Gal 3:26.

[81] Matt 4:18–22//Mark 1:16–20//Luke 5:10–11; Matt 9:9//Mark 2:14//Luke 5:27.

granted them his supernatural authority to fulfill them.[82] He instructed them to preach the good news of the kingdom, to make disciples and baptize them in water, to cast out demons, and to heal the sick. In effect, he authorizes and equips the disciples to emulate him.

Jesus does not offer abstract aspirations but rather gives clear lifestyle guidelines for any who seek to follow him. He encourages his followers to recognize that following him is a priority, for he demands total commitment.[83] Jesus' followers also need to remember that they have been granted authority and should exercise it when appropriate.[84] Their role is to preach concerning the principles of the kingdom,[85] recognizing that such a commission will involve suffering and self-denial.[86] In all of this, though, Jesus himself will support them.[87]

Jesus identifies a number of important lifestyle characteristics of the kingdom, including forgiveness;[88] obedience;[89] faithfulness;[90] trust;[91] service;[92] mercy;[93] sacrifice;[94] forgiveness;[95] authentic relationships;[96] giving;[97] love;[98] and humility,[99] amongst others. As the initiator of the kingdom, he instituted the code of conduct and also determined the

---

[82] Matt 10:1–25; 28:18–20; Mark 3:13–19; 6:7–12; 16:15–18; Luke 6:12–16; 9:1–6; 10:1–12; 22:36–38.

[83] Matt 6:19–21//Luke 12:33–34; Matt 6:24//Luke 16:13; Matt 7:13–14//Luke 13:23–24; Matt 8:18–22//Luke 9:57–62; Matt 10:37–39//Mark 8:34–35//Luke 4:25–27.

[84] Matt 10:40–41//Luke 10:16; Luke 9:1.

[85] Matt 10:7; Luke 9:2–5.

[86] Matt 10:16–39//Mark 13:9–13; Matt 16:24–28//Mark 8:34–9:1//Luke 9:23–27; Matt 20:20–28//Mark 10:35–45//Luke 22:24–27.

[87] Matt 10:28//Luke 12:4.

[88] Matt 18:23–35//Luke 11:27–28.

[89] Matt 5:17–20; Matt 7:24–27//Luke 6:47–49; Matt 12:46–50//Mark 3:31–35//Luke 18:19–21.

[90] Matt 24:42–51; Matt 25:14–30//Luke 19:11–27; Luke 16:10–12.

[91] Matt 19:13–15//Mark 10:13–16//Luke 18:15–17.

[92] Matt 20:24–28//Mark 10:41–45//Luke 22:24–30; Matt 24:45–51//Luke 12:41–46; Matt 25:14–30//Luke 19:11–28.

[93] Matt 9:9–13; 12:1–8.

[94] Matt 8:18–22//Luke 9:57–62; Matt 10:34–39//Luke 14:25–33; 12:49–53.

[95] Matt 6:14–15; 18:15–22//Luke 17:3–4; Matt 26:6–13//Mark 14:3–9//Luke 7:36–50.

[96] Matt 18:15–20//Luke 17:3.

[97] Matt 6:1–4; Mark 12:41–44//Luke 21:1–4.

[98] Matt 5:43–48//Luke 6:27–28, 32–36; Matt 7:12; 22:34–40//Mark 12:28–34//Luke 10:25–28.

[99] Matt 23:12//Luke 18:9–14; 14:7–14.

rewards.[100] Jesus offers guidance concerning numerous issues including temptation;[101] prayer;[102] possessions;[103] stewardship;[104] spirituality;[105] anger;[106] adultery;[107] divorce;[108] oaths;[109] and retaliation.[110]

Miracle Worker

The miracles Jesus performed tell us far more about Jesus than that he was a remarkable wonder worker. They illustrate his authority.[111] The miracle narratives raise the question: *Who is this man?* Because Jesus often performed deeds that only God was authorized to do, people who observed him often wondered about his identity. The Gospel writers clearly present Jesus as one who has no peer. His authority is superior to that of anyone from his own time or who preceded him. Indeed, the Gospel writers affirm that Jesus was not just a miracle worker but God incarnate, and his miracles authenticated him as such.

Thus, the healings and exorcisms that Jesus performed provided opportunities for people to consider his identity. Those who witnessed these powerful acts could choose either to accept Jesus, to trust him and recognize that he was far more than a healer, or they could reject him. The miracles of Jesus did not always lead to discipleship. However, they always functioned as evidence that a new kingdom was present, and that demanded a response.[112]

---

[100] Matt 10:40–42//Mark 9:38–41//Luke 9:49; Matt 19:27–30//Mark 10:28–31//Luke 22:28–30.

[101] Matt 18:6–9//Mark 9:42–50//Luke 17:1–2.

[102] Matt 6:5–8, 9–13//Luke 11:1–4; Matt 7:7–11//Luke 11:9–13; Matt 21:21–22//Mark 11:20–24; Luke 11:5–13.

[103] Matt 13:22//Mark 4:19//Luke 8:14.

[104] Luke 16:1–13.

[105] Matt 5:14–16//Mark 4:21–25//Luke 8:16–18; Matt 7:15–23//Luke 6:43–44; Matt 12:33–35; 21:18–20//Mark 11:12–14//Luke 13:6–9.

[106] Matt 5:21–26//Luke 12:57–59.

[107] Matt 5:27–31.

[108] Matt 5:31–32//Mark 10:11–12//Luke 16:18; Matt 19:9.

[109] Matt 5:33–37; 23:16–22.

[110] Matt 5:38–42//Luke 6:29–30.

[111] Wright, *Jesus*, pp. 191–97. See Matt 8:23–27//Mark 4:35–41//Luke 8:22–25; Matt 14:13–21//Mark 6:32–44//Luke 9:10–17; Matt 14:22–23//Mark 6:45–52; Matt 15:32–30//Mark 8:1–10.

[112] Matt 9:1–8//Mark 2:1–12//Luke 5:17–26; Matt 9:32–34; Matt 12:22–29//Mark 3:22–27//Luke 11:14–23; Matt 20:29–34//Mark 10:46–52//Luke 18:35–43.

Although there are references to compassion in a few cases, it is not the prime motivation in the healings of Jesus.[113] Although Jesus is merciful, he is also, and more particularly, fulfilling the prophecies concerning a new age as well as demonstrating his supreme authority and unique mission.

The Miracles Demonstrated Jesus' Authority

Jesus demonstrates his authority over nature by calming storms;[114] walking on water;[115] and feeding thousands supernaturally.[116] He has authority to heal sickness;[117] he can also heal on the Sabbath;[118] he casts out demons;[119] and he raises people from the dead.[120] Jesus has supreme power over all the forces of darkness, and he illustrates this as he confronts them and breaks their dominion over people's lives with ease.[121] The Gospels do not simply describe his power but also his authority. Jesus healed whenever, whoever, and wherever he wished, and he also chose not to perform miracles where appropriate.[122] There is no record of him praying for the healing of the sick. Instead, he removed the sickness instantaneously, often with a word or command.[123] Jesus regularly used his hands in healing people,[124] which is further evidence of his authority. Although touch is often viewed as a symbol for compassion, in a Jewish context it indicated authority and power. He who could not be contaminated by sickness, ceremonially or otherwise, touched the sick while at the same time transmitting wholeness to them. The authoritative touch of Jesus reflects the authority associated with the hand of God spoken of in the OT.[125]

---

[113] Matt 14:14; 20:34; Mark 1:41 (though see the variants); Luke 7:13.

[114] Matt 8:23–27//Mark 4:35–41//Luke 8:22–25.

[115] Matt 14:22–33//Mark 6:45–52.

[116] Matt 15:32–39//Mark 8:1–10.

[117] Matt 8:14–16; Luke 13:32.

[118] Matt 12:9–14//Mark 3:1–6//Luke 6:6–11; Luke 14:1–6.

[119] Mark 1:23–28.

[120] Luke 7:11–17.

[121] Matt 8:28–34//Mark 5:1–20//Luke 8:26–39; Matt 12:22–29//Luke 11:14–26; Matt 17:14–21//Mark 9:14–29//Luke 9:37–43.

[122] Matt 12:38–42; 16:1–4//Mark 8:11–12//Luke 11:16, 29–32; Matt 13:53–58//Mark 6:1–6//Luke 4:16–30.

[123] Matt 8:3; Mark 5:41; Luke 13:12.

[124] Matt 8:3, 15; Mark 5:41; Luke 13:13.

[125] Num 11:23; Deut 33:3; 1 Chr 29:12.

The OT taught that God was the one who inflicted people with sickness and the one who healed them.[126] Now, Jesus undertakes the latter role. Where no one else could help, Jesus authoritatively provided restoration. The Gospel writers present the healings of Jesus in such a way as to make the inquisitive reader consider whether he could be divine. The healings functioned as springboards for a step of faith that had the potential of developing into a relationship with him. It was because of this authority that Jesus was able to achieve his mission to initiate the kingdom, to reinstate the outcast, and to forgive people's sin. However, while many welcomed Jesus' authority over sickness and demons, few had the understanding to move beyond this to recognize his authority to take away sin.

Jesus' Authority to Include the Marginalized

In addition to providing startling object lessons, demonstrating Jesus' supreme authority over sickness and its taboos, the healings also proved his authority over people and societal codes of conduct. People who were ill in the time of Jesus often led lonely lives. This was due, in part, to their inability to function as normal members of the community in contrast to their able-bodied colleagues. But their loneliness was also due to a widely-held belief that personal sin had caused the illness, which God had sent as a form of chastisement. Social ostracism, or at least a form of marginalization in the community, often resulted. If God had punished a person, it was difficult for the community to be seen to be undermining that action by accepting the afflicted person back into society as if nothing had happened to them. In healing them, Jesus dissolved the social barriers that separated people from each other and introduced them to a God who was not so far from them as perhaps they feared.[127]

The significance of this is not so much that Jesus had compassion on those rejected by society but rather that he demonstrated his authority to incorporate them back into their communities as fully contributing members. This reintegration was coupled with the new revelation that God had not rejected them—the evidence for this being that their illness had been removed. Since God was reckoned to be the only one capable of this transformation, the authors of the Gospels assumed that God

---

[126] Gen 12:17; Exod 15:26; Num 11:33.

[127] Matt 8:2–4//Mark 1:40–45//Luke 5:12–16; Matt 9:18–26//Mark 5:21–43//Luke 8:40–56; Matt 15:21–28//Mark 7:24–30; Luke 7:11–17; 13:10–17; 17:11–19.

must have caused it. In this regard, the Gospels present Jesus fulfilling the prophecies concerning a new age in which God's mercy would be fully revealed.[128] God, in the person of Jesus, had come to touch hurting humanity and infuse wholeness into lives that had been broken and scarred.

The healing of lepers provides an example of this authority to reintegrate those who had been excluded by society (Matt 8:1–4//Mark 1:40–45//Luke 5:12–16). Although Moses (Num 12:10–15) and Elisha (2 Kgs 5:1–14) were involved in the healing of lepers, they did not touch them in the process. The Gospels record, however, that Jesus stretched out his hand and touched the leper. This is not an incidental detail. By touching the untouchable, Jesus broke the Jewish Law and also risked ceremonial uncleanness (Lev 5:3). Rather than view this as a deliberate act of presumption or provocation designed to undermine the sanctity or importance of the Law, it is preferable to understand this as the commencement of a process of reintegration for the victim—a journey back into society that will be formally completed by his visit to the priests as prescribed by the Law. It is possible that, by touching those who are ill, Jesus simply shows his compassion for outcasts. However, it is more probable that Jesus touched the leper to establish his authority.

Leprosy ceremonially contaminated those who came into contact with it. Jesus proved himself to be above the legalism that marginalized people and to be immune to ceremonial contamination. He lived among the powerless and the poor, touching and transforming them without ever becoming tainted. He facilitates this transfer from a living death to a fulfilled life. By reaching out to touch and heal the marginalized, Jesus made their reintegration into society possible. Jesus transformed the lives of outcasts by restoring them and sent a clear message to religious leaders: "I am the one who determines the entrance and the boundaries of the kingdom, not you." The Gospels record these healings to show Jesus meeting the marginalized and dispossessed and providing hope for the hopeless and help for the helpless.

Jesus' Authority to Initiate the Kingdom

The healings and exorcisms of Jesus also demonstrated that a new kingdom had been established.[129] Moltmann said that, after the procla-

---

[128] Isa 49:13; Ezek 39:25.

[129] Matt 4:23–24; 9:35; 12:22–29//Mark 3:22–27//Luke 11:14–22; 7:19–23; 9:1, 2.

mation of the gospel, "The healing of the sick is Jesus' most important testimony to the dawning of the Kingdom of God."[130] In healing people, Jesus revealed something of life as God intended it, unburdened by physical weakness. In this respect, every one of Jesus' healings anticipated his final victory over death and authenticated his message of the arrival of a new kingdom. The healings functioned as parables, demonstrating that Jesus had initiated a new kingdom.

Risen and Ascended Lord

Jesus the Savior

Throughout his life, Jesus enabled people to enjoy a relationship with God and to begin to experience eternal life as members of the kingdom that he had come to initiate. The very first verses of the Gospel narratives, therefore, announce that he is the Savior.[131] He had come to rescue people from grave danger—not from a life of bondage to a pagan emperor but from ownership by the devil. His deliverance is not merely from sorrow and isolation because of physical circumstances, but from sin and separation from God. Repentance and faith in Jesus are important keys to access this freedom.[132] A fundamental motivation for this unilateral desire to save helpless people from their sins is love, and it is no surprise to read of this attribute throughout the Gospels.[133]

One of the most traumatic events that demonstrated Jesus' willingness to fulfill his salvific agenda, despite personal cost, occurred when he was welcomed into Jerusalem, an event that each of the Gospels records.[134] This occasion, more than most, illustrates the expectation of the Jews with regard to Messiah. Jesus was praised for being the Messiah they wanted him to be and was simultaneously rejected for being the Messiah he was. The words that the people used to acclaim Jesus were from Psalm 118:26 (Luke 19:38//John 12:13). This was a conqueror's psalm. Some years earlier, Simon Maccabee

---

[130] Jürgen Moltmann, *The Source of Life* (trans. M. Kohl; London: SCM, 1997), 64.

[131] Matt 1:21; Mark 1:1; Luke 2:11.

[132] Matt 4:17; Mark 1:15; Luke 5:32.

[133] Matt 9:36–38//Mark 6:34; Matt 14:14; 15:32//Mark 8:2; Luke 7:13; 10:33; 15:20.

[134] Matt 21:1–9//Mark 11:1–10//Luke 19:28–40.

had returned to Jerusalem after a victorious battle against the Syrians and the crowds had sung these verses to him, the military conqueror (1 Macc 13:51). They waved palm branches before him, as they did before Jesus, as a celebration of his military prowess. This was a common practice before kings (2 Kgs 9:13). Most of the people who welcomed Jesus would have been expecting a dynamic warrior who would be installed as king, as a nation builder, as a wonder worker. Jesus, however, had come as the Suffering Servant and Savior. Surely Jesus was conscious of their misunderstanding concerning him, resulting in his tears (Luke 19:41).

Jesus the Redeemer

A feature of the salvation that Jesus achieved relates to his being a ransom (Mark 10:45). In order for people to receive forgiveness for their sins, Jesus willingly took their punishment upon himself and suffered separation from God on the cross in their place. The result of this was that he was forsaken by his Father (Matt 27:46).

The rejection and sufferings Jesus endured reach their climax towards the end of his life and include the plot to kill Jesus;[135] his betrayal;[136] the pain of Passover;[137] the Last Supper;[138] Gethsemane;[139] and Peter's denial.[140] Thereafter, he was arrested[141] and presented to the Sanhedrin,[142] to Pilate,[143] and to Herod (Luke 23:6–16) after being scourged and beaten.[144] Then, instead of Barabbas,[145] Jesus is crucified and buried.[146] Matthew records the cataclysmic events that took place at the moment of his death (27:51–53). However, although it was at the end of his life that Jesus was forsaken by his disciples and separated from his Father, the theme of rejection is present from the

---

[135] Matt 26:1–5//Mark 14:1–2//Luke 22:1–2.

[136] Matt 26:14–16//Mark 14:10–11//Luke 22:3–6.

[137] Matt 26:17–20; Mark 14:12–17//Luke 22:7–14.

[138] Matt 26:26–29//Mark 14:22–25//Luke 22:15–20.

[139] Matt 26:36–46//Mark 14:32–42//Luke 22:39–46.

[140] Matt 26:69–75//Mark 14:66–72//Luke 22:56–62.

[141] Matt 26:47–56//Mark 14:43–52//Luke 22:47–53.

[142] Matt 26:57–58//Mark 14:53–65//Luke 22:54–71.

[143] Matt 27:1–2//Mark 15:1//Luke 23:1; Matt 27:11–14//Mark 15:2–5//Luke 23:2–5; Matt 27:24–26//Mark 15:15//Luke 23:24–25.

[144] Matt 27:28–31//Mark 15:17–20.

[145] Matt 27:15–23//Mark 15:6–14//Luke 23:17–23.

[146] Matt 27:31–61//Mark 15:20–47//Luke 23:26–56.

earliest chapters of the Gospels.[147] Each of the synoptists records the fact that one of the most significant elements of Jesus' death was the inauguration of the new covenant with God.[148] As a result of these events, salvation was achieved at a severe physical, emotional, mental, psychological, and spiritual cost to Jesus. Jesus achieved redemption—but at an appalling price.

Jesus the Resurrected Lord

The conclusions of the Gospel accounts describe Jesus' literal resurrection, its aftermath, and his ascension.[149] The resurrection of Jesus is significant for a number of reasons. First, it demonstrated that Jesus had been victorious over death. He conquered death and overcame its power as he died and uttered his triumphant cry, "It is finished." He may have died in physical weakness, but morally and spiritually he was the master of death before he entered its gates. Although supernatural forces of evil may have anticipated that they would meet a weak, disfigured, defenseless foe, they would soon realize that he was a victorious, and not a vulnerable, intruder into their domain. His authority swept all before him. The resurrection simply let readers into the secret. The Gospels publicly declared the truth of his triumph—Jesus is alive and has achieved his salvific sacrifice. The resurrection of Jesus was also important because of all that occurred afterwards, including the authoritative commissioning of the disciples (Matt 28:18–20), the bestowal of the Spirit, the establishment of the church (Acts 2:1), and Jesus' ascension to a new role in heaven (Luke 24:51).

Individual Synoptic Portrayals of Jesus

On many occasions, the Gospel writers tailor their individual stories and teachings concerning Jesus to their respective audiences. When their presentations of Jesus are compared, we can identify not only the

[147] Matt 9:34; 12:24//Mark 3:22–23//Luke 11:14–15; Matt 11:18–19//Luke 19:47–48; Matt 13:10–17//Mark 4:10–12//Luke 8:9–10; Matt 10:34–36//Luke 12:51–53; Matt 10:39; 12:14//Mark 3:6//Luke 6:11; Matt 13:57–58//Mark 6:3–6//Luke 4:23–30.

[148] Matt 26:28//Mark 14:4//Luke 22:20.

[149] Matt 27:62–28:20//Mark 16:1–20//Luke 24:1–53.

common themes that are of substantial importance to them, but the important features that are specific to each of the individual authors.[150] The synoptic Gospels function as a prism, with each writer reflecting different christological perspectives on Jesus' incarnate life. Taken together, these individual portrayals lead to a composite portrait of Jesus that is more comprehensive than that of any of the Gospels considered independently. This clear and wide-ranging presentation of Jesus' remarkable nature and mission enables readers to more fully assess his potential impact on their lives.

Matthew: The Initiator of God's Kingdom

As in the other Gospels, the author's name does not appear in the text of Matthew, but authorship was attributed to him from before the end of the second century. Matthew's aim appears to have been to present Jesus in such a way that he would appeal to Jews.[151] For his Jewish readers, Matthew presents Jesus as a true Jew with a superlative ancestry that includes Josiah, Solomon, David, Ruth, Jacob, Isaac, and Abraham (1:1–16). By tracing the genealogy through Joseph, his father by adoption, Matthew defines Jesus' legal right to the throne of David. Matthew also presents his genealogy carefully, identifying three sets of fourteen generations each,[152] a literary form using a number that was significant to his Jewish readers.[153]

Yet while Matthew presents Jesus with clear reference to a Jewish audience, he also underscores the universal application of his Gospel. One way he does this is by demonstrating Gentiles coming to great

---

[150] See also Richard A. Burridge, *Four Gospels: One Jesus?* (London: SPCK, 1994) and Mark L. Strauss, *Four Portraits, One Jesus: An Introduction to Jesus and the Gospels* (Grand Rapids: Zondervan, 2007).

[151] He includes information of relevance to Jews (cf. Mark 13:18 with Matt 24:20, where Matthew adds the Sabbath; also cf. Mark 7:24–30 with Matt 15:24, where Matthew refers to the house of Israel).

[152] Not only does Matthew split the genealogy into 3 sections of 14 generations each, but David is also of central importance. The Heb. word for David is made up of consonants that are represented by numbers (d = 4, v = 6, d = 4). The sum of these numbers is 14 (4 + 6 + 4). Thus, the word *David* forms an example of *gematria*, a literary device used by Jewish scribes in which numeric significance was attached to important words.

[153] Numerology was of considerable interest to Jewish scribes and rabbis and is of particular value in exploring some biblical texts, esp. apocalyptic literature. The number 7 represents perfection or completion.

faith in Jesus. Thus, the eastern Magi[154] offer worship to Jesus (2:1–12), a Canaanite woman expresses great faith (15:21–28), and Roman centurions recognize that he is the Son of God (8:10; 27:54). In addition, the "Great Commission" includes Gentiles as being recipients of the disciples' message (28:18–20).

Jesus Is Authoritative

The Gospels often describe Jesus as functioning with authority. Thus, Matthew describes him as the inaugurator of the kingdom, the Lord,[155] and the supreme teacher who calls and commissions disciples. All the Gospel writers refer to Jesus as the "Son of God," but Matthew contains some unique references (14:33; 16:16) that emphasize this title. Matthew also refers to God as the Father of Jesus, and fifteen of these references are unique to his Gospel.[156] Jesus is described as the one whose authority is unrivalled and equal to that possessed by God.

Matthew defines Jesus as the one who is willing and able to provide restoration where needed.[157] The healing of Peter's mother-in-law (8:14–15) provides the opportunity for Matthew to demonstrate Jesus' authority and the importance of service to him. In contrast to the narratives in Mark and Luke, there is no reference to anyone else other than Jesus and the woman. Matthew records Jesus as taking the initiative in the healing and dealing with it effortlessly and instantly. Matthew restricts the woman's service to Jesus (8:15), whereas Mark and Luke refer to the restored woman serving others gathered, including Jesus. Similarly, in 8:5–13, Matthew records the healing of a centurion's servant and provides an opportunity for his readers to learn of Jesus' ability to heal instantaneously without being present with the one who was ill.

In Matthew, the authoritative Jesus carries the pedigree of the OT backed by supernatural authority. Matthew's hope is that readers will emulate the centurion and Peter's mother-in-law and actively place their

---

[154]The Magi (traditionally referred to as the "wise men") were probably Persian priests (not kings) who specialized in interpreting dreams and astrology, a belief that was prevalent in the ancient world. As such, they understood the significance of a new star that indicated to them that a new king was to be born. Given their knowledge of Judaism, they may have also been influenced by ancient Jewish prophecies concerning the Messiah. These refer to him as a star (Num 24:17) and a bright light (Isa 60:3).

[155]7:21–22; 8:21; 12:8; 15:22.

[156]4:6; 8:29; 14:33; 16:16; 26:63.

[157]9:22, 28–29; 15:28.

trust in Jesus and serve him thereafter. Central to Matthew's presentation is a desire to lead his readers to a more accurate perception of Jesus, as the one who alone can forgive their sins and provide them with a relationship with God. Consequently, the concept of faith is central to his narrative. Faith involves trust in both the person and mission of Jesus.[158] Throughout his Gospel, Matthew presents Jesus functioning authoritatively and offering the opportunity for those who observe his actions to trust him on a higher level.

Jesus Is the Messiah

In order to celebrate him as Messiah and the one who initiates the kingdom of God, Matthew quotes the OT regularly with reference to Jesus and, in particular, relating to his messianic mission.[159] Jesus is so central that the OT speaks of his coming, his mission, and his exalted relationship with God. In particular, Matthew presents him as the fulfillment of OT prophecies concerning the Messiah. This is especially true of his healing ministry (12:15–21). In 8:16, 17, Matthew records Jesus healing a large number of people, and he interprets this as the fulfillment of Isaiah 53:4, a passage which explicitly relates to the Messiah. Similarly, in 11:4–6, Jesus responds to a question from John the Baptist concerning his identity by pointing to his healing and preaching ministry as evidence of his status and mission which fulfilled the popular expectations of the Messiah.

True to his focus on Jesus as the Messiah, Matthew uses the title *Son of David,* a common messianic designation, more often than Mark, Luke, and John combined. It is an important marker for his Jewish audience to understand the significance of Jesus. First-century Jews, inspired by OT prophecy, envisioned that an heir of David would sit on a reconstituted throne.[160] Increasingly, in the years prior to Jesus' birth, the expectation had developed overtones of military conquest and political freedom. In contrast to this popular nationalistic expectation, when the title *Son of David* is used in Matthew, it most often appears

---

[158] 18:6; 21:25; 27:42.

[159] 2:15, 23; 4:14–16; 8:17; 11:5; 12:17–21; 13:35; 21:4. He quotes the OT 41 times, 37 of which carry the introductory formula "that it might be fulfilled." While half of these are common to Mark and Luke, the remaining quotations are unique to Matthew.

[160] Isa 11:1; Ezek 34:23–24; 37:24.

in the context of healing the blind and the marginalized,[161] emphasizing the nonpolitical and integrative aspects of Jesus' mission. The Davidic Messiah offers himself to all.

The ability to recognize the Son of David acts as a Matthean marker for an accurate perception of the Messiah. While the crowds misunderstand him, and the rulers repudiate him (21:15), the blind "see" him (9:27–28; 20:31), the Canaanite accepts him (15:22), and children applaud him (21:15–16). Those who succeed in making such a correct identification prove themselves to be candidates for the kingdom. Matthew chooses a title which, despite its political overtones, is familiar to the Jews in order to capture the Davidic heritage and hope for the readers. At the same time, he radically subverts the traditional expectations of such a figure and presents Jesus as the Son of David but with different characteristics. Jesus is not just descended from David; he is also from heaven (21:23–27).

Jesus Is a Teacher

One of the most important characteristics of Jesus as presented by Matthew is that he is a teacher. Both the style and the content of his teaching grab the reader's attention. Matthew provides five of Jesus' sermons relating to the kingdom of God, much of the contents of which are unique to his Gospel.[162] The kingdom is a major feature of Matthew's teaching, and Jesus is presented as the one who inaugurates it. He demonstrates this in his preaching (5:17) and in his miracles (5:23–24). Matthew introduces this emphasis on the kingdom early in the Gospel. Thus, after establishing Jesus' identity (Savior, 1:21; Son of God, 4:1–11) and identifying his mission (4:12–22), Matthew offers a summary of Jesus' ministry (4:23–24). The summary links Jesus' healing activity with his teaching and preaching concerning the kingdom. Although the people may have followed Jesus to receive healings, he went beyond healing and taught them concerning the kingdom. Only after an extended portion of Jesus' teaching in the Sermon on the Mount (5:1–7:29) does Matthew refer to a specific healing (8:2–4). The healing ministry that Jesus begins to undertake functions as a sign of the kingdom. The full significance of Jesus' healings and exorcisms

---

[161] Matt 9:27–31; 12:22–23; 15:21–28; 20:29–34; 21:15.
[162] Chs. 5–7; 10; 13; 18; 23–25.

is to be found in the context of the kingdom, and Matthew is eager to establish this relationship.

One aspect of Jesus' teaching in Matthew focuses on specific information for the young church. Matthew is the only Gospel that uses the term "church" (Gk. *ekklēsia*). Jesus grants Peter authority as representative of his followers (16:18, 19), provides guidance with regard to church discipline and authority (18:15–18), promises to be present in the midst of the gathered church (18:19, 20), and commissions his followers to baptize and teach using his authority (28:19, 20).

Matthew's presentation of Jesus' teaching also includes an extended eschatological discourse (chs. 24; 25), longer than both Mark's and Luke's, and a set of unique parables containing an eschatological element.[163]

Mark: The Suffering Redeemer

Early Christian tradition strongly affirms Mark's authorship of the Gospel that is associated with his name, as well as the fact that the Gospel was written in connection with the Apostle Peter. Although he was not one of the Twelve, Mark had a strong relationship with early Christians (Acts 12:12).[164] It is generally believed that Mark's was the earliest Gospel and that Matthew and Luke used it in writing their Gospels. It is also assumed that Mark addressed his Gospel to a mainly Gentile audience. The author presents Jesus as an activist by linking together series of interconnected stories. One of Mark's favorite words is "immediately" (Gk. *euthys*)—Jesus is busy. The first chapter provides a good example of the pace of Mark's presentation of Jesus, with *euthys* occurring eleven times.

Jesus Is a Teacher

The fact that Jesus taught is important to Mark. Even though the Gospel presents only two discourses[165] and four parables, Mark often refers to Jesus as a teacher or as teaching.[166] Much of the teaching is contained in the miracle narratives. Yet readers will do well to recognize

[163] 13:24–30, 36–43, 47–50; 25:1–13, 14–30, 31–46.

[164] Mark joined Paul and Barnabas (his cousin; Col 4:10) on a mission, but he later left them (Acts 12:25; 15:37–40). Peter (who had worked with him in Rome, 1 Pet 5:13) speaks of him affectionately, as does Paul (2 Tim 4:11).

[165] 4:1–33; 13:1–37.

[166] 1:21–22, 27, 39; 2:2, 13; 4:1, 38; 5:35; 6:1, 2; 10:1; 11:18; 12:35, 38.

that such miracle stories are not intended simply to present Jesus as a healer or even as the best healer, but to teach other lessons as well.

Mark's unique account of the healing of a deaf man who also has a speech defect (7:31–37) serves as an example of the author's desire to reveal that Jesus was more than a healer. Mark's attention to detail in relating Jesus' various actions conveys Jesus' readiness to give ample time to accommodate the deaf man's worldviews and recognize his unique situation. This is not just a story about healing but about Jesus' willingness to sensitively and carefully achieve healing in a way that perfectly relates to the individual circumstances of the man concerned.

Another unique miracle provides an additional example of this emphasis on Jesus' personal care of the individual (8:22–26). The healing of a blind man is not immediate but partial—Jesus lays hands on him twice. Although some have assumed that this may have been a difficult healing for Jesus or an acute form of blindness, this is unlikely, given his ability to heal all other sicknesses and even to raise people from the dead. Also, any delay in healing would have been counterproductive to Mark's presentation of Jesus as the all-powerful Redeemer.

It is more appropriate to consider the context that Mark presents. Prior to this narrative, Mark records a misunderstanding among the disciples relating to one of Jesus' statements. Jesus responds by asking them, "Do you have eyes, and fail to see? . . . Do you not yet understand?" (8:14–21). After the healing, Mark records another conversation between Jesus and his disciples concerning their understanding of his identity. In response to his question, "Who do people say that I am?," they provide answers. When he asks them for a personal opinion, Peter replies, "You are the Messiah." However, although Peter provides an accurate response, it is soon clear that he, as well as the other disciples, do not understand the implications of Jesus' messiahship (9:32; 10:32–45). Although Peter's identification is correct, the following verses reveal Jesus rebuking him for acting as an instrument of Satan (8:33). Peter's understanding of Jesus is at best partial. Like the blind man, he and the other disciples are still partially sighted (9:10, 32).

Mark's record of the gradual healing of the blind man parallels the developing perception of the disciples concerning Jesus: they will come to a fuller realization of his status only after receiving further ministry from him. As with the blind man, full restoration will occur, but not immediately and not at Caesarea Philippi. All would-be disciples can take comfort from the fact that even the Twelve failed to understand immediately and fully. The promise to them and to future believers is that their immature perception will be made complete. Such a message would have been a particular encouragement to suffering Christians in Rome, to whom Mark most probably addressed this Gospel. If Peter, the apostle, understood only partially, there is hope for others with misty perceptions of Jesus.

Jesus Is Authoritative

Mark presents Jesus as the authoritative Christ and Son of God.[167] Although Jesus heals physical illnesses, his victory over the demonic displays this authority most clearly.[168] Indeed, it is the subject of the first narrated miracle. Jesus is victor over the forces of evil. Even when they confront him malevolently, he defeats them easily. It is significant that the miracles in Mark are not described as signs to lead people to Jesus, as in John. Rather, they cause the onlookers to be amazed and to wonder.[169] However, Jesus intends wonder to lead to faith in him. Tragically, the religious leaders drew the conclusion that he was an imposter, and they sought to kill him (3:5). On another occasion, a leper disobeyed Jesus and told of his supernatural cleansing even after Jesus sternly charged him not to do so. As a result, Jesus' agenda to preach in the towns was temporarily restricted. Mark presents this account as a warning to the reader not to follow the leper's example (1:40–45). Jesus' authority demands the appropriate response of obedience.

Jesus Is the Suffering Savior

Mark emphasizes that Jesus is the one who suffers to redeem people. He devotes nearly the last quarter of the Gospel to Jesus' final sufferings, leading to his crucifixion, but this motif of conflict starts early in the Gospel. A demon disturbs him the first time Jesus preaches in the synagogue (1:23), and he has to silence demons who would otherwise have hijacked his plans by whipping up inappropriate attention in him (1:34). Jesus has to deal with people who see him as little more than a healer and almost immediately disobey him (1:43–45). Others are so determined to get what they need from him that they are even prepared to crush him in the attempt (3:7–10).

---

[167] 1:1; 2:1–3:5; 8:29; 15:39.
[168] 1:21–28; 3:20–27; 5:1–20; 7:24–30; 9:14–29.
[169] 1:27; 2:12; 4:41; 5:20, 42; 6:51; 7:37.

Both the religious leaders (3:5) and the people demonstrate their unwillingness to accept Jesus as the Savior he claimed to be. In 3:20–30, his home community concludes that he is mad, and even his family seem to take a step back from him (3:31–35). As a result, it is his followers who Jesus trains to do the will of God. Incongruously and sadly, the demons are the ones who recognize his true status (3:11). As Mark builds this theme of suffering, the shadow of the cross begins to creep towards Jesus even in the first three chapters of the narrative.

In 8:31–38, Jesus begins to plainly teach about his sufferings,[170] and he speaks of giving his life himself as a ransom in 10:45. Mark's narrative makes it clear that one of Jesus' priorities is to mentor those who will carry on after him (3:13–19). Jesus is someone who knows his destiny and its aftermath; he is a savior who was born to die. Mark portrays Jesus' journey to the cross with an emphasis on the importance of the destination. He allows nothing to slow him down—not those he came to save (1:37–39); not demons, who he commands to be silent and dismisses quickly (1:25); not the devil (1:13).[171]

Luke: The Inclusive Savior

Luke was not an eyewitness to the events he records in his Gospel, but he was a thorough investigator who used previous records to provide a full, literary, orderly account (1:1–4). From the late second century, the Gospel and Acts are attributed to Luke. Theophilus, the addressee, was probably a Christian, though a wider, mainly Gentile, audience for the Gospel is also assumed.

Jesus Who Became a Man

Luke's stress on Jesus' humanity is evident. He traces the birth and childhood of Jesus (1:31–33, 69) and reveals him engaging with others[172] and weeping (19:41). This feature is clearest, however, in Luke's account of Jesus' passion and resurrection. Luke adds significant details to much of the material shared in common with Matthew and Mark. These additional incidents include the reference to Jesus healing the

[170] 9:30–32; 10:32–34; 12:1–11; 14:6–9; 22–25.

[171] Note the absence in Mark's gospel of the devil's three temptations of Jesus referred to by Matthew and Luke.

[172] 5:29–32; 11:38; 14:1, 15; 19:7.

high priest's slave (22:51), the fuller description of Jesus before Pilate and Herod, the proclamation of his innocence (23:6–16), the forgiveness of the thief on the cross (23:39–43), and Jesus' discussion with Cleopas and his friend (24:13–35). Luke presents Jesus as a savior who, because of his own traumatic times of loneliness, understands the tensions and challenges that people experience. It is no surprise, then, that Luke records unique events in the life of Jesus that relate to suffering. These include the discussion concerning his death that took place during his transfiguration (9:31), the reference to an angel being sent to strengthen him, and the fact that he sweat drops of blood (22:43–44).

Jesus the Inclusive Savior

The genealogy that Luke offers (3:23–38) goes back to Adam. For his Gentile readers in particular, Luke identifies Jesus as a man of the nations who has a message of inclusion for all—regardless of their culture, gender, or occupation. Through Luke's careful presentation, readers know that Jesus cares for the marginalized, including Gentiles and Samaritans, as he seeks to give them a place in society as well as to bring them into personal relationship with God. Readers see this, for example, in the description of Jesus as a light for the Gentiles (2:32), and in the OT quote in his sermon at Nazareth that speaks of *all* flesh seeing God's salvation (3:6). Luke further emphasizes Jesus' inclusiveness in his positive treatment of Samaritans,[173] in welcoming people from all points of the compass into the kingdom (13:29–30; see also the parable of the Great Banquet, 14:15–24), in mentioning non-Israelites in the OT (4:25–27), and in giving his commission to the world (24:47).

Luke also shows Jesus taking time for individuals including Zechariah (1:5–23, 59–79), Simeon (2:25–35), Zacchaeus (19:1–10), the rich ruler (18:18–24), and Cleopas (24:13–35). Most of the parables unique to Luke concentrate on marginalized individuals: the two debtors (7:41–43), the good Samaritan (10:33), the friend in need (11:5–13), the lost coin (15:8–10), the prodigal son (15:11–32), the rich man and Lazarus (16:19–31), and the Pharisee and the tax collector (18:9–14). Often, individuals who are associated with Jesus are social outcasts (including the shepherds[174] and the repentant, crucified

[173] See 9:51–56; 10:33–37; 17:15–18; the animosity between the Jews and the Samaritans was centuries old by Jesus' time.

[174] 2:8–20; 7:36–50; 23:39–43.

robber [23:42–43]). Women were often marginalized in both wider society and in religious Judaism (4:25–26; 7:12). Luke mentions eleven women[175] associating with Jesus, as well as two women in parables (15:8–10). To such outsiders, Jesus offers a message of hope. The unique record of Jesus' proclamation in 4:17–21 most clearly exemplifies this hope, which is located in him.

Luke also focuses on the poor (6:20; 14:11–14), including beggars (6:30), as particular objects of Jesus' mercy. Jesus has special compassion for children as well. On three occasions, Jesus restores the only child of a parent (7:12; 8:42; 9:38). In their account of Jesus and the children, Matthew and Mark refer to Jesus welcoming children (Gk. *paidia*; Matt 19:13; Mark 10:13). Luke, however, identifies them as babies (Gk. *brephē*; 18:15). Jesus, Luke emphasizes, is prepared to receive those who are so young they have no perception of who is holding them—he is more desirous to give than to receive.

All who were sick in Jesus' day were outcasts to some degree because the majority of Jews assumed that sin caused illness. Since they believed that illness was a mark of God's displeasure, they found it difficult to accommodate those whom God had punished. Luke refers to some in particular whom society marginalized and who received Jesus' care and restoration. These include lepers (5:12–14; 17:11–19), Gentiles (7:1–10), tax collectors,[176] a widow (7:11–16), a woman in the city (7:36–50), a blind beggar (18:35–43), and the high priest's servant (22:51). Luke presents Jesus as a touchable savior who feels for a hurting humanity, a "friend of . . . sinners" (7:34).

Luke is the only Gospel writer who records the healing of the ten lepers, one of whom is a Samaritan (17:11–19). It is a valuable story because it affirms some of the emphases of Luke's presentation of Jesus' authority to restore the outcast, to heal those whose physical conditions are beyond human therapy, and to provide spiritual salvation. What is of particular significance here is the seriousness of the disease. In addition to being physically disfiguring, leprosy was also linked with ceremonial uncleanness[177] and divine judgment,[178] which resulted in

[175] 1:26–38, 46–56; 39–56; 2:36–38; 8:2; 10:38–42; 18:1–8; 23:49.

[176] 5:27–30; 15:1–2; 19:1–10.

[177] Lev 13:9, 45–46.

[178] Num 12:10–15; 2 Kgs 5:27. The Talmud (*b. 'Arak.* 15b, 16a, 16b) describes seven sins (including idolatry, blasphemy, incest, murder, theft, and false testimony) likely to be punished with leprosy.

the sufferer being excluded from the community and the temple.[179] Yet while the disease is a token of God's judgment, it is God alone who has the authority to heal (2 Kgs 5:1–14). But while the healing of the lepers is amazing, it is not Jesus' healing power that is the focus of the narrative, but rather the way that those who have been healed respond to Jesus.

As a result of the Samaritan's expression of faith, Luke records Jesus' declaration that "your faith has made you well" (17:19). While all are cleansed (Gk. *katharizō*, 17:17), only the one who recognizes that he has been physically healed (Gk. *iaomai,* 17:15) is made whole (Gk. *sōzō,* 17:19). This variation in words is unlikely to be accidental. The healing by Jesus has been a catalyst for a spiritual transformation. The leper was physically cleansed, but by the end of the narrative he has received a deeper restoration. Luke again demonstrates Jesus' desire and ability to restore the outcast. Though he was an outcast, Luke notes that this Samaritan was the first of many people on the fringes of society to respond gratefully to Jesus. Others followed suit, including a widow (18:1–8), a tax collector (18:9–14; 19:1–9), children (18:15–17), and a blind man (18:35–43). Luke's message is clear to those who had little and were pushed around by others, who were treated as nonentities, maligned and humiliated, used and abused—Jesus is on their side. Jesus, the Savior of the Jews, is also the Savior of the Gentiles. Indeed, he is the Savior of everyone who is lost (15:1–32).

Jesus Who Prayed

Luke records nine occasions when Jesus prayed, seven of which are unique: at his baptism (3:21), in the middle of his ministry (5:15–16), prior to choosing the Twelve (6:12), prior to Peter's confession (9:18–22), at his transfiguration (9:9), after the return of the seventy (10:21), prior to teaching his disciples about prayer (11:1), in Gethsemane (22:39–46), and on the cross (23:34, 46). Luke also includes unique details in connection with Jesus' prayers, including his prayer for Peter (22:31–32) and for his enemies (23:34), as well as his love of quiet places.[180] Each of these provides insight into the person of Jesus.[181]

---

[179] See *b. Ned* 64a. This element of excommunication, in addition to the illness itself, was devastating—especially given the nature of the first-century Jewish society, rooted as it was in interrelationships.

[180] 4:42; 9:10; 21:37.

[181] Two unique parables deal with prayer: the friend at midnight (11:5–13) and the unjust judge (18:1–8).

Jesus Who Fulfilled a Divine Agenda

The motif of fulfillment is prominent in this Gospel. One of Luke's key terms is the Greek word *dei,* meaning "it is necessary,"[182] by which he identifies Jesus as following the predetermined plan of God. The fact that Luke includes unique prophecies forecasting the ministries of Jesus and John the Baptist even before their births[183] supports this idea. It is clear that Jesus is in charge of his destiny (13:31–33; 24:44). He is the foremost prophet (24:19) who does not just prophesy but who also speaks decisively and authoritatively as the representative of God.[184] In Jesus' final words in the Gospel (24:49), he promises the Holy Spirit to his followers, who are destined to complete the work he has initiated, according to his promise (Acts 2:1). In a world that assumed that fate or the gods controlled one's destiny, it was important that Luke's readers appreciate the supremacy of Jesus, in whom they had placed their trust.

Conclusion

One of the aims of the Gospel writers was to demonstrate that Jesus was the Messiah. Yet they also wished to emphasize that he was of greater status than people initially realized. The Gospels introduced Jewish monotheists and Gentile polytheists to the One who is God in the flesh. This was incongruous to Jews, who for centuries had been used to the fact that there was only one God. It was folly to Gentiles, who struggled with the belief that a divine being should become a man, participate in human life, and die as a criminal. To the Jew, such a notion was blasphemous; to the Gentile, it was ridiculous. Would-be followers of Jesus needed the Spirit to affirm this revelation, but the Gospel writers did their part in preparing the way to affirm such supernatural truth.

The Gospels present Jesus as an astonishing person who is preceded by OT prophecies and the exceptional prophet, John the Baptist. Both the Father and the Spirit affirm him. Jesus demonstrated an unparalleled authority over the devil, sickness, death, demons, the Sabbath, the

---

[182] See, e.g., 2:49; 13:6. Luke uses the word forty times in Luke-Acts, nearly half of the total references in the NT; seven of these occurrences refer to the sufferings of Jesus.

[183] 1:14–17, 31–35, 46–55, 68–79; 2:8–14, 30–35.

[184] See 11:46–52; 13:34–35. See Wright (*Jesus,* 162–97) for a discussion of Jesus' estimate of himself as a prophet.

temple, and the Law. He established himself as one who followed a divine agenda that had, at its heart, a plan to redeem the world, to initiate the kingdom of God, and to enable people to enjoy a personal relationship with God. The challenge to readers of the Gospels is whether they will acknowledge not only that Jesus is remarkable, but also that he is the Savior; not just the Messiah, but as close to God as can be imagined—indeed, that he is God, however inexplicable that may be in the light of their preconceptions, logic or world views.

Not surprisingly, our examination of the Gospels leads to the deduction that they are fundamentally christological—they concentrate on making Jesus known. Not only do his titles define him, but also his teaching, miracles, lifestyle, and personality. Similarly, the perceptions of the Father and the human, angelic, and demonic responses to him dictate the lesson that he is unique—he is the eternal God who has taken on the likeness of humans. Thus, although the synoptists portray him as authentically human (he was a member of a human family who loved and cried, lived and died), they also identify him as comprehensively divine. Indeed, although the Gospels assert his humanity, they generally simply accept it, while they graphically state and regularly imply his deity.

chapter 2

The Gospel of John

Jesus, Eternal Son of God

This Gospel is traditionally believed to have been written by John the son of Zebedee, one of the Twelve. While his Gospel also focuses on Jesus, John writes from a different perspective than the synoptists and repeats only about ten percent of the material included in their Gospels.

Jesus Is Supreme

John clearly portrays Jesus' humanity—he was tired and thirsty (4:6–7; 19:28), he cried (11:35), and he was troubled (12:27). The emphasis for John, however, is not that the Word became *flesh* (highlighting his humanity), but that the *Word* became flesh (highlighting his divinity). John focuses on the divinity of Jesus even more explicitly than do the synoptics. John does not include any birth or childhood narratives. Instead, Jesus appears on the scene in John's Gospel straight from heaven. Here it is not the shepherds or the magi who are Jesus' companions; it is God the Father who is, and always has been, Jesus' constant companion. Jesus was not born in time; he was alive before time was created. Jesus was not a man who prayed to God; he was in direct and constant communication with God as his Father. He is not simply a servant of God with an important commission, nor is he only "with God"—Jesus is God (1:1–2). Jesus was not created; he is the one through whom everything was created (1:3). Jesus was not just a preacher who showed the way and pointed to the light; he is the way and the light (1:4–5).

The miracle is not so much that he was "the true light" (1:9) or "full of grace and truth" (1:14), for such descriptions are perfectly appropriate for such a regal being. The miracle is that he "became flesh" (1:14), came "into the world" (1:9), and dwelled "among us" (1:14). The world would not recognize him (1:10) and his own people would not receive him (1:11), but Jesus had the authority to make everyone who believed "the children of God" (1:12).

Thereafter, John's Gospel unfolds the miracle of the incarnation—God becomes a man to save his creation and offer grace to all (1:17). Although it is incongruous that he should live on earth, the term "lived" (Gk. *eskēnōsen*, 1:14) is reminiscent of the term from the LXX that describes the presence of God in the tabernacle (Gk. *skēnē*, Exod 25:8–9). Jesus "lives in a tabernacle," which is his human body. The presence (Heb. *shekinah*)[1] or glory of God (Exod 25:15–18) lives in him and he is "full of grace and truth" (1:14). To support his emphasis on Jesus' divine status, John quotes Jesus on a number of occasions when he refers to himself with the phrase "I Am," a saying reminiscent of the presentation of God in the OT (Exod 3:14).[2] This phrase in John generally refers to Jesus in his role as Savior.

This determination to elevate Jesus is clear from the beginning of John's Gospel, where he obliquely yet powerfully presents Jesus as the one who owns the highest credentials of divinity. John does not mention Jesus' baptism, and in his Gospel the role of John the Baptist is specifically to witness to Jesus, not baptize him.[3] In place of the elevated description of John the Baptist found in the synoptics, John's Gospel introduces him simply as "a man sent from God, whose name was John" (1:6). Indeed, even his disciples are described as leaving him and following Jesus (1:36–37), and Jesus is recorded as "making and baptizing more disciples than John" (4:1). Whereas Luke (1:15) describes John as being "filled with the Holy Spirit," "even before his birth," John de-

---

[1] Although the word *shekinah* does not occur in the OT, it was used by Rabbis to refer to the presence of God (without having to mention his name, which was highly revered). The notion of God dwelling among his people was a common one in the OT (Gen. 9:27; Exod. 25:8; 29:45, 46). It is possible that John intends his readers to make the connection with Jesus also dwelling among people.

[2] See also 4:26; 6:20; 8:24, 28, 58; 13:19; 6:35 ("I am the bread of life"); 9:5 ("I am the light of the world"); 10:9 ("I am the gate"); 10:11 ("I am the good shepherd"); 11:25 ("I am the resurrection and the life"); 14:6 ("I am the way, and the truth, and the life"); 15:1 ("I am the true vine").

[3] 1:19–27, 32, 36; 3:26, 28; 5:33; 10:41. Even the association between John and Elijah noted in the synoptics (Matt 17:12; Mark 9:13; Luke 1:17) is played down in John (1:21, 25).

scribes Jesus as being given the Spirit in an immeasurable way (3:34). Jesus is supreme (1:26).

Unlike the synoptists, John does not record Jesus' wilderness confrontation with the devil or his exorcisms. In John's Gospel, there is no uncertainty concerning the outcome of the battle with evil, no early diabolic intrusion into the divine agenda. John records no interruption of the journey of the majestic one who is marked with the stamp of heaven as God incarnate—who became man but remained as much God as ever he was. Instead of discourse on the establishment of the kingdom with its practical outworking in lifestyle, John's emphasis is on the bestowal of eternal life[4] and relationship with the Father.[5] There is not even an account of the transfiguration; it is as if John prefers the reader to envisage Jesus as glorious and glorified from the opening chapter rather than giving a glimpse of this in a window of revelation partway through the narrative. John declares that his aim is to prove that "Jesus is the Messiah, the Son of God" (20:31). He identifies Jesus as fully divine (1:1; 10:30; 20:28), and the titles he gives Jesus substantiate this characteristic.[6]

The Logos

A unique title that John uses in his writings to refer to Jesus is the Greek word *logos* ("Word," 1:1, 14; Rev 19:13). John probably uses the title to intrigue his readers. Both Jew and Gentile readers would have been aware of the term and recognized the *logos* as being central to their religious or philosophical worldviews and synonymous with, or closely associated with, the ultimate deity. The use of *logos* in a philosophical sense had a long history before John adopted it. The earliest Greek writer to use it was Heraclitus (6th c. B.C.E.), who proposed that behind the universe, which was continuously changing, there existed an abiding, eternal principle, a creative force, which he referred to as *logos*. It acted as an inanimate power which controlled the universe.

[4]See 20:30–31. John closely aligns eternal life with the life experienced by God. It is life of "the age to come" or "of heaven above," the very life of God, the experience of enjoying God and experiencing God's capacity to live—but in the present, as well as the future.

[5]1:14–18.

[6]Jesus is associated with light (1:5), life (1:4), witness (1:15), truth (1:14), grace (1:14), glory (1:14), and knowledge (1:10).

Stoicism, a popular ancient philosophy, also used the term *logos* to describe the primordial source of all things that represented the wisdom needed to create the universe. Philo, an Alexandrian Jew who lived in Jesus' time, sought to describe Judaism to an intellectual audience as attractively as possible. He used the term *logos* 1,300 times in his writings and spoke of it as the second being after God who owns creative power and directs and sustains the universe. Since the *logos* bore many supernatural characteristics in the non-Jewish worldview, these readers would have been impressed by the writings of this elderly Jew who used their language to speak of such mysteries.

The Jews also used the term *logos,* but in their writings it referred to the verbal and written word of God (the Torah) with reference to its capacity to save,[7] create,[8] heal (Ps 107:20), sustain,[9] perform God's will,[10] provide light,[11] and reveal knowledge.[12]

In order to intrigue and then retain his audience, John used a term with which his diverse audience was familiar (although for different reasons and with different content). Once they are "hooked," he gently leads them to the startling conclusion that the *logos*, that they both accept in their different worldviews, is none other than Jesus (1:14). This enables him to elevate the status of Jesus to a position of prominence in their minds. John's revelation that he has met the *logos* and become a child of God as a result is astounding (1:12). Thereafter, and throughout the Gospel, John presents witnesses to Jesus who will declare the truth of this assessment and portray Jesus as the unique, authentic, and authoritative one who perfectly reflects God because he is fully divine.

The Son of God

John uses the title "son of God" more than the other Gospels do to refer to Jesus.[13] In view of the fact that the term was used to describe Israel, the king, or angels,[14] it is not surprising that John uses it distinc-

[7] Ps 107:20; Isa 4:8; Ezek 32:4–5.

[8] Gen 1:3, 6, 9; Pss 33:6–9; 42:15.

[9] Pss 147:15–18; 48:8.

[10] Isa 55:11; Jer 23:29.

[11] Ps 119:105, 130.

[12] Jer 1:4; 20:9; Ezek 33:7.

[13] 1:34, 49; 3:18; 5:25; 10:36; 11:4, 27; 19:7; 20:31 (18 times in the Johannine Epistles).

[14] See p. 23.

tively when referring to Jesus, and especially to identify Jesus' uniqueness. He describes him as the "only" Son[15] and provides testimonies to him as the Son of God.[16]

Linked with this title "Son of God" is the filial relationship that John emphasizes. Jesus is clearly aware of his relationship with his Father, and John refers to it over one hundred times[17]—more than twice as many times as the synoptists do.[18] Thus, the Son is loved by the Father (10:17) from before the world began (17:24), which results in the Father giving him "all things" (3:35). Because of this unique relationship, the Father reveals to him "all that he himself is doing" (5:20), which culminates in Jesus' claim, "All that the Father has is mine" (16:15). John also refers to the Father entrusting the divine role of Judge to the Son (5:22), and to the honor shared between them both (5:23). Although the Son is sent by the Father[19] and depends on the Father (5:19, 30), this fact demonstrates not the Son's inferiority but rather the unity of purpose between them both.[20] Similarly, the fact that Jesus prays to the Father[21] does not imply that the Son needs the Father, so much as it indicates that he has an exclusive relationship with him. He alone has seen the Father, and therefore only he can truly reveal him.[22] The Son's knowledge of the Father and the Father's of the Son is without parallel (10:15).

The Lord

John uses the term "Lord" (Gk. *kyrios*) much more than the synoptists, and mainly in the context of Jesus' resurrection.[23] Usually "Lord" is a description of him rather than a means of addressing him.[24] The OT uses the term to refer to God and associates it with power. It was an appropriate term for deity and was used in the ancient world of gods and

---

[15] 1:14, 18; 3:16, 18.

[16] 1:34, 49; 11:4, 27.

[17] E.g., 5:19–23; 6:40; 8:36; 14:9–11; 16:27–28; 17:1; 20:17.

[18] The term "father" (Gk. *patēr*), referring to God as Jesus' Father, occurs 43 times in the synoptics and 107 times in John's Gospel.

[19] 3:34; 5:36, 38; 7:29.

[20] 10:20; 14:20; 17:11.

[21] 11:41; 12:28; 17:1, 5, 11, 21, 24, 25.

[22] 6:46; 8:19; 14:24; 15:15.

[23] 4:1; 6:23; 11:2.

[24] 20:2, 13, 18, 20, 25, 28; 21:7, 12, 15, 16, 17, 20, 21.

emperors. When the term refers to Jesus, it indicates an unprecedented relationship of equality and unity with God the Father (10:28–30; 15:9–10). This reaches its climax with Thomas' confession when he saw Jesus after his resurrection, "My Lord and my God!" (20:28).

The Son of Man

To achieve his purpose of exalting Jesus, John also refers to him as the "Son of Man." Daniel 7:13–14 is the most likely source for this title. In contrast to the synoptists, however, John uses the title not in conjunction with the suffering, humiliation, and death of Jesus, but rather to express his exaltation, as seen in his angelic entourage (1:51), his heavenly origin (3:13; 6:62), his supernatural identity (8:28), his saving work and authority to grant eternal life,[25] his judgmental authority (5:27), his right to receive worship (9:35), and his glorification (12:23; 13:31). Each of these elements links the authority of the Son of Man with that of God.

The Messiah

Many throughout John's Gospel affirm that Jesus is the Messiah, including John (1:17; 20:31), Andrew (1:41), Samaritans (4:25–26, 29, 42), Martha (11:27), and Jesus himself (17:3). John highlights Jesus' Jewish nature by presenting him in the context of references to Jewish life and history[26] and OT prophecy,[27] as well as with frequent allusions to the OT.[28] John also helps his readers appreciate the messianic significance of some of Jesus' actions by placing them in an OT context. He uniquely presents Jesus sitting upon a young donkey as he enters Jerusalem (12:15) as a fulfillment of OT prophecy (Zech 9:9). This further evokes themes of covenant, peace, and endless rule to which the following verses (Zech 9:10, 11) refer. John also links the title "Messiah" with the term "Son of God" (1:49; 20:31), thereby helping to remove the weight of popular expectation that the Messiah would be a king who would reign in Jerusalem.

---

[25] 3:14; 6:27, 53; 8:28; 12:32–34.
[26] 1:11, 51; 2:16; 3:2; 4:22.
[27] 2:17; 6:45; 7:38, 42, 51–52; 10:11; 12:13, 15, 38; 15:25; 19:24, 28, 36–37.
[28] 2:14; 3:14–15; 5:39, 45–47; 6:31–33; 7:22–23; 8:17, 56; 12:41; 15:1; 16:21.

The Lamb of God

The term "Lamb of God" occurs only twice in the NT (1:29, 36), though John refers to Jesus as "the Lamb" thirty times.[29] The Passover lamb and the gentle, submissive lamb which was willingly sacrificed (Isa 53:7) are possible sources for John's image. The association with sin in 1:29 suggests that the sacrificial reference was in John's mind when he used this term to describe Jesus. The fact that John specifies that Jesus was crucified at the time when the Passover lambs were killed (19:14) further supports this idea.[30]

The Giver of the Spirit

John also identifies aspects of Jesus' authority with reference to the Holy Spirit. Not only does the Spirit specifically witness to Jesus, but he also remains with him—a fact that John mentions twice (1:32–33). The first verse uses the aorist tense, indicating the Spirit's definite association with Jesus. The second verse uses the present tense, indicating a permanent and ongoing relationship. This reference to the presence of the Spirit with Jesus is unprecedented. That the Spirit maintains an ongoing, unbroken relationship with Jesus spoke loudly to first-century readers and raised the question, "What kind of man is this to merit the constant presence of none other than the Spirit?" In 3:34, John moves even closer to his aim of identifying Jesus so closely with God as to warrant the conclusion that he is fully divine. No one can be the beneficiary of an unlimited bestowal of the Spirit unless he is God; the fact that Jesus had such a relationship with the Spirit indicates his supreme status.

As do the synoptists, John records that Jesus would baptize in the Spirit (1:33), but he also notes that Jesus also asserted his authority to give the Spirit to his followers.[31] Elsewhere, John refers to the Spirit being sent by the Father.[32] The fact is that both the Son and the Father were involved in sending the Spirit, for the authority of the Son is iden-

---

[29] Acts 8:32; 1 Cor 5:7; and 1 Pet 1:19 also refer to Jesus as being like a lamb.

[30] It is possible that John is using the term to refer to a victorious lamb, as he does in Rev 5:6, 12; 7:17; 13:8; 17:4; 19:7, 9; 21:22–23; 22:1–3. This concept is also found in Jewish apocalyptic literature (*T. Jos.* 19:8–9; *T. Benj.* 3).

[31] 14:26; 15:26; 16:7.

[32] 14:16, 26; 15:26.

tical to that of the Father. Thus, after Jesus' resurrection, he met his disciples and, having greeted them and commissioned them, as the Father had commissioned him (20:21), he breathed on them and said, "Receive the Spirit" (20:23). This description of Jesus breathing on them does not indicate that the Spirit is some sort of material substance to be breathed out or in. The word, which occurs only here in the NT, is reminiscent of the action of God in breathing life into Adam (Gen 2:7) and life (identified as the Spirit [Ezek 37:14]) into the dry bones of Ezekiel's vision (Ezek 37:9).

This image of new life or restoration after a period of exile is prominent in John's Gospel. In particular, it signifies Jesus' importance—for he has the authority to impart the Holy Spirit to whomsoever he chooses. Jesus makes the same Spirit, who is in ongoing relationship with him, available to others.

The Unique Savior

One of John's aims is to point his readers to Jesus and to introduce witnesses to identify his unique status. John is the only Gospel writer who mentions the Spirit's role in bearing witness to Jesus.[33] Others will also witness on Jesus' behalf, including the author himself (1:14), John the Baptist,[34] angels (1:51), Jesus' own miraculous works (5:36; 10:25), the Father (5:37; 8:18), the Scriptures (5:39), and Moses.[35] "Witness" is a key word for John, and he uses it twenty-seven times with reference to Jesus, thus identifying him as being superior to all. For those readers who are not yet believers, John provides a path to belief in Jesus as the eternal Son of God. For believers, he presents carefully constructed evidence that Jesus is their God. John makes it clear that Jesus has life in himself (5:26); that he is able to relinquish his life and to reinstitute it (10:17–18); and that he has the authority to give life (8:51; 17:2). Although these are not explicit claims to divinity, they are powerful declarations of authority to do that which God alone is able to do.

---

[33] 1:33; 14:26; 15:26.

[34] 1:7, 8, 15, 34; 5:32–33.

[35] See 1:17; 5:45–46; 6:55–58. The people who ate the divinely-provided manna when they were being led by Moses died; those who eat the bread of life that Jesus provides will never die.

Jesus Provides Salvation

Signs of Truth

Miraculous signs dominate John's narrative between 1:19 and 11:45. John 10:38 and 14:11 reveal that one of the purposes of these signs was to enable people to perceive Jesus accurately—*as their Savior and Lord.* John 20:31 states that the signs were recorded so that readers could know that Jesus was the Christ, the Son of God. They functioned as signposts to a more developed appreciation of who he was. They did not force people to believe (12:37–38), and neither did they always have the desired effect,[36] but the signs did often give people a push in the right direction. Thus John reports (6:2) that many chose to follow him "because they saw the signs that he was doing for the sick."

In contrast to the synoptists, who often include discrete miracle accounts, John typically uses them as prefaces to discourses. The miracles often play a minor role in the narrative as the discourses that follow dwarf them in terms of length. The point is that a miracle can function as a springboard for people's faith in Jesus as their Savior and not simply as their healer. Healing, for John, is an incomplete act unless it leads to the development of faith in the one restored or in the onlookers. While a ministry of signs and wonders may not be the only effective way to evangelize, it is significant that the healings Jesus performed did function as potential stepping stones to a more developed appreciation of his person and mission. The transformation of water into wine (2:1–12) is a sign (2:11), therefore, because it demonstrates that Jesus is able to offer something better than the best that people can provide for a lavish wedding celebration. The sign functions as a precursor to deepening trust in Jesus' miraculous ability to meet a special need, enhance celebration, overcome potential humiliation, and demonstrate his willingness to bring joy. Jesus' supernatural authority, like a sign, can point observers to a more accurate appreciation of his status and ability to offer them eternal as well as physical salvation.

---

[36]In response to the feeding of the 5,000 (6:1–14), the people deduced that Jesus was the promised prophet (6:14; 7:40) and concluded that they should make him their earthly king (6:15). They had misunderstood the sign. Instead of coming to faith in him as their spiritual Savior, they decided to make him their earthly Savior—with the result that he left them. Further misunderstandings resulted from these signs. Many sought to kill him (7:1, 19), others were confused (7:12, 40–43), and still others suggested he was demonized (7:20), an imposter (7:47), and they sought to arrest him (7:30, 32, 44).

The cleansing of the temple (2:13–25) is an altogether different kind of sign. Jesus saw it as his right to decide what was acceptable activity in the temple. Jesus raises the stakes higher when he quotes from Psalm 69:9, refers to the temple as "my Father's house" (2:16), and rejects the legitimacy of buying and selling in the temple (with a probable allusion to Zech 14:21, where the prophet looks forward to an era when there will be no trade in the house of the Lord). His most astounding claim is to contrast the destruction of the temple with the resurrection of his body (2:19–22). The people were used to the idea that Messiah would reinstate the pure worship of God in Israel (Isa 9:2–7; 11:1–9). However, Jesus is asserting that he himself is qualified to rule over the temple.

John uses these signs to demonstrate one of his main emphases—Jesus has the authority to give eternal life (17:2).[37] Thus John introduces the reader to Nicodemus, who has been impressed by the signs of Jesus that he has seen in Jerusalem—for they have indicated to him that God is with Jesus (3:2). Jesus and Nicodemus meet as two highly intellectual teachers at the most appropriate time for theological discussion, in the cool of the evening, and they engage in wordplay. Jesus expertly uses words that can have more than one meaning[38] as he questions the basis of Nicodemus' belief in his right to enter the kingdom (3:5–6) and indicates his own divine authority to grant eternal life (3:3, 13–15). John records that Nicodemus' faith in Jesus developed to such an extent that he stood up for Jesus in the Sanhedrin (7:50–51). Nicodemus also requested, with Joseph, that he might bury his crucified body (19:42).

Similarly, Jesus' knowledge of a Samaritan woman's marital situation is a sign of his supernatural nature that encourages her to place her faith in him. Many of her fellow Samaritans also then come to faith (4:1–42). John 4:46–54 describes Jesus healing, from a distance, the dying son of a royal official. The healing confirms to the father that Jesus is more than a healer and, by the end of the narrative, he is ready to acknowledge Jesus at a much deeper level.

---

[37] This is a more prominent theme in John (3:15, 16, 36; 4:14, 36; 5:24, 39; 6:27, 40, 47, 54, 68; 10:28; 12:25, 50; 17:2–3) than in all the synoptics put together (Matt 18:8; 19:16, 29; 25:46; Mark 10:17, 30; Luke 10:25; 18:18, 30).

[38] See John 3:3, where the Greek word *anōthen* can mean "from above" or "from new"; 3:8, where *pneuma* can mean "wind" or "Spirit" and *phōnēn* can mean "voice" or "sound."

In 5:2–9, Jesus heals a man who has been ill for thirty-eight years. The discussion that follows (5:10–47) provides information that demonstrates that Jesus is worthy of trust—not just as a healer but also as the Son of God functioning in the eternal dimension, executing judgment (5:21, 27), granting salvation (5:34) and eternal life (5:21, 24, 39), and operating with the authority of God.[39] This healing acts as the catalyst for the final question, which is a crucial marker in the narrative: "Will you believe?" (5:47).

John records the healing of a blind man (9:1–41) after an extended confrontation between Jesus and the religious leaders concerning his divine identity (8:12–59), in which he identifies himself as "the light of the world" (8:12). He states that they will die in their sins unless they believe in him (8:24, 31–32); he prophesies that they will kill him, the Son of Man (8:28); and he asserts, "before Abraham was, I am" (8:58). The Pharisees, however, saw Jesus only as an ordinary man without pedigree (9:29), a sinner (9:24), and not one sent from God (9:16). They remain unwittingly blind (9:41). The once-blind beggar is the one who comes to acknowledge Jesus as the Son of Man and to worship him as Lord (9:35–38). Immediately following this narrative is the encouraging message for all who have chosen to follow Jesus (and who will thereby be excluded by the Jewish community, 9:34), that Jesus is the shepherd of all. He is "the gate" (10:7, 9), the "good shepherd" (10:11, 14) who knows his sheep (10:14), gives them abundant life (10:10), and lays down his life for them (10:15). Many conclude that he is demonized (10:20), though others are not certain (10:21). However, while many reject him and try to arrest and kill him (10:21, 39) because of his reference to "my Father" (10:29) and his claim to be united with him (10:30), others believe in him (10:42). Jesus' battle for people's hearts continues.

John 11:2–44 records the seventh sign, the resurrection of Lazarus. Once again, this miracle gives those who are present an opportunity to witness Jesus' authority and to decide how to respond to him and his offer of eternal life. Jesus' words here, "Those who believe in me, even though they die, will live" (11:25), do not relate only to Lazarus but to everyone. Although the resurrection benefited Lazarus, its wider purpose was to enable others to develop faith in Jesus. The challenge to the eyewitnesses and to John's readers is this: will they place their

[39] 5:19–20, 27, 30, 37, 43.

faith in Jesus as a miracle worker or one who can resurrect the dead? Or will they recognize that these signs point to the greater truth that Jesus is God?

Death and Resurrection

John's narrative from 13:1 presents the final week of Jesus' life (John 20:1 records the resurrection account). John dedicates nearly half of his Gospel, therefore, to the Passion Narrative and the resurrection, where he gives his readers the opportunity to decide. Will they emulate Judas, who will betray Jesus (13:21–30)? Will they be like Peter, who will deny him (13:36–38)? Or will they stay in close relationship with him, the true vine (15:1–7), despite the attendant suffering?[40]

The Passion Narrative commences with Jesus washing his disciples' feet (13:1–21) and ends with Joseph and Nicodemus laying his body in a tomb (19:42). The first is an occasion of humility, and the latter one of apparent humiliation—for it appeared that Jesus had been a tragic failure, a cataclysmic catastrophe. The resurrection, however, presents the true context for evaluating his life and death. Far from signaling a forlorn message of doom for his followers, Jesus' death and resurrection proved that he is the Son of God who assured eternal life for those who placed their faith in him (20:31).

The final sign of Jesus recorded by John took place after the resurrection (21:1–14). It occurred after a number of the disciples had spent all night fishing with nothing to show for their labors. When they obeyed the instructions of a man standing on the beach, however, they caught more than their boat could carry. At that point they realized that the man guiding them was none other than Jesus, "the Lord" (21:7). After this act of obedience, the reward for which was receiving far more than they had anticipated, Jesus offered Peter a threefold opportunity to accept a personal commission from him (21:15–22). Jesus' final words in the Gospel are, "Follow me."[41] John's Gospel, which begins with a presentation of its subject as the preexisting divine *logos* and which traces the ever-increasing display of his grandeur, thus comes to a fitting conclusion—calling the readers to respond to its message.

---

[40] 15:18–27; 16:1–4, 32–33.

[41] Jesus' words in 21:23 are simply repeating what Jesus said earlier, prior to the final commission to Peter (21:22).

Equipped to Obey

The Gospel defines Jesus in such grand terms that Jesus demands recognition as an authoritative mentor and guide (8:37–47)—though this did not always happen in his lifetime (8:38–59). Those who recognize Jesus' true nature do well to subscribe to his teachings concerning forgiveness (7:53–8:11), truth (8:30–36), discipleship (13:4–17), prayer (16:23–28), and lifestyle issues (15:9–17). Jesus promises to equip his followers to obey his teachings by sending them the Spirit,[42] providing peace (14:27–31), and also by praying for them (17:1–26). Finally, he promises to prepare a place for his followers and return for them (14:1–11); the salvation he offers is comprehensive.

Conclusion

John's revelation of Jesus is a dignified one. In it he demonstrates that Jesus, as fully divine, became a man to point people to God and to provide them with the opportunity for a relationship with him. John presents his case carefully and thoughtfully. He weaves Jesus' teaching together with story in ways that merit sensitive examination. John identifies Jesus as one who relates to people at their level, as individuals. Although he is God, the miracle is that Jesus has time to gently provide signs to the truth concerning himself that will have eternal consequences. As a result, John intends his readers to not only recognize that Jesus is divine but also that he desires to be their divine Savior.

[42] 14:12–17, 25–26; 15:26–27; 16:7–15; 20:22.

chapter 3

Acts

Jesus, Ascended yet Powerfully Present

The book of Acts is not strictly a history in the modern sense, for Luke, the book's author,[1] has been selective. He documents some of the church's important activities during its earliest years, but he does not write a comprehensive record of everything that happened. Luke, though he was a careful historian, was more than that. He was a theologian who sought to present life-changing truth and he was a teacher who was aware of the needs of his readers—those who have come to faith in Jesus and those who may be on the way.

Luke presents Jesus here as the fulfillment of ancient promises and the forerunner of the church that began to take shape following his resurrection. Jesus is central to the grand plan of salvation that spans time. It is no surprise, therefore, that Jesus is foundational to the book of Acts, which mentions him in the first and final verses and many times in between. Luke derived this picture of Jesus from recorded speeches[2] as well as from the actions and ministry of the apostles.

Anointed with the Spirit

Although Luke makes it clear that the Holy Spirit is significant to the book of Acts, the Spirit only comes after Jesus has ascended (1:4–5).

---

[1] Most scholars regard the Book of Acts as the second part of a two-volume work authored by Luke. If this is the case, one would expect a great deal of continuity between the portrayals of Jesus in Luke and Acts.

[2] 2:14–39; 3:12–26; 4:8–12; 5:29–32; 7:2–53; 10:34–43; 13:16–41; 15:7–11; 17:22–31; 20:18–35; 22:1–21; 26:4–23.

Jesus is the one who gives the Spirit (2:33), and people only receive the Spirit after confessing belief in Jesus (2:38; 11:17). The Spirit then facilitates the witness of believers to Jesus (1:8). Although the Spirit is vital to the believers' preaching, the message itself relates to Jesus (4:8, 10). This is a unique and divine partnership. Thus, when Luke describes the Spirit guiding Paul in his mission (16:6), he informs his readers that it was "the Spirit of Jesus" (16:8).

In Acts 10:38, Luke records that God anointed Jesus with the Holy Spirit and power. Because God was with him, Jesus healed all who were oppressed by the devil. Although Luke might be reminding his audience here that the Spirit is the power source for Jesus' miracles, the Gospels only imply this in a limited way. Indeed, most references to Jesus' miraculous power do not also refer to the Spirit. The Gospel writers present Jesus as functioning in his own authority and as delegating his own power to his disciples (Luke 9:1). It is more likely that in Acts 10:38 Luke intends to remind his readers that the Holy Spirit's partnership validates Jesus and demonstrates his authenticity. His anointing with the Spirit indicates the inimitable nature of Jesus' mission, and at the same time, the uniqueness of his mission presupposes a unique anointing. Because Jesus' mission was without precedent, it was important that the Spirit be present in an affirming role. Following the Father's anointing of Jesus with the Spirit, Jesus undertook his mission in conjunction with the Spirit. It is not that Jesus was powerless without the Spirit; indeed, the notion that Jesus could exist without the Spirit is meaningless since they are eternally integrated as members of the Godhead. Rather, the fact that Jesus was anointed by the Spirit proved that he was the one in whose name the forgiveness of sins was to be granted (10:43).

Jesus was not adopted by the Holy Spirit but the Spirit identifies Jesus as the one worthy of his presence. God the Father reveals Jesus to the world as the one who can legitimately initiate the kingdom of God, whose worth warrants both his being partnered by the Spirit and the Spirit partnering him. Jesus was always supreme, but now the evidence is made public as the Spirit accompanies him and affirms him as the divinely designated King of the kingdom. The message is clear. If the Spirit is with Jesus, he must be authentic.[3] Luke reveals

---

[3]In the OT, the Spirit functioned as a "marker," identifying leaders (Exod 33:15, 16; Judg 6:34; 1 Sam 16:13).

the Spirit validating and endorsing Jesus. Although he may look like a mere man, his association with the Spirit tells a different story. No ordinary man could ever enjoy the unique relationship of the Spirit that Jesus experienced.

The Author of Life

Unique

The book of Acts attests the humanity of Jesus throughout. Several verses refer to him as a man (2:22; 13:38) and as Jesus (Christ) of Nazareth.[4] Many witnessed his crucifixion[5] and resurrection.[6] However, many more passages in the book identify Jesus as supernatural. He is the prophet (3:22; 7:37), the stone which has become the corner stone (4:11), "the Leader" (5:31), "the Righteous one" (7:52), and the judge of all (10:42). God affirms (2:22) and glorifies (3:13) him. He fulfills prophecy in his incarnation (7:52), his resurrection,[7] his exaltation (2:34–35), his rejection and death,[8] his role in forgiveness (10:43), and his coming again (3:20–22).

Luke also describes Jesus as being "holy" (3:14). Although the term "holy" (Gk. *hagios*) can mean "sinless" or "perfect," it fundamentally refers to one who has been set apart or identified as being different from others. Luke is not simply saying that Jesus is sinless; he is emphasizing that he is different, one of a kind, unique. Thus, although Luke describes Jesus as God's servant,[9] which suggests his readiness to serve his Father, this description is linked with the word *hagios* in 4:27, 30—and this helps to define the term's significance for Jesus. Luke emphasizes not just the truth that Jesus served, but that he was a unique servant who performed an act of service that no one can emulate. Namely, he provided forgiveness and the power to turn from sin (3:26). Jesus' willingness to serve is all the more remarkable given his kingly prerogatives and his authority to save.

---

[4] 3:6; 4:10; 6:14; 10:38; 22:8; 26:9.
[5] 2:23, 36; 3:13–15; 4:10; 7:52; 10:39; 13:27–29; 26:23.
[6] 1:3; 2:32; 3:15; 4:10; 10:40–41; 13:30–33.
[7] 2:25–31; 13:32–37.
[8] 3:18; 13:27, 29.
[9] 3:13, 26; 4:27, 30.

Messiah

Luke also highlights Jesus' uniqueness by referring to him as Messiah. Although many doubted that he was the Messiah when he lived in Israel, subsequent events proved the validity of the claim and Luke uses the title to further elevate Jesus in the minds of his readers.

Luke reminds his readers, through Paul's words, that Jesus is descended from David (13:22–23). Although this link affirms Jesus' humanity, it is more likely that Luke intended to elevate his pedigree by presenting Jesus in the messianic line of David, whom God described as being a man "after my heart" (13:22). Jesus is the one, furthermore, whom David addressed as "Lord" (2:25–36). Jesus' messiahship is, therefore, a central element of the preaching of the believers.[10] While before his resurrection he was a suffering Messiah, he is now a conquering Messiah. Jesus is clearly identified as the Messiah (2:31; 3:20), even by God (2:36), yet his designation as Messiah is also joined with his depiction as Lord (2:36) and his close association with Yahweh (4:26).

Lord

The regular use of the title "Lord" (Gk. *kyrios*) for Jesus in Acts is significant for a number of reasons. The term *kyrios* is often used as a polite form of address akin to "Sir," but Luke regularly uses it in a divinely regal way.[11] Acts records events after Jesus' resurrection, when the term "Lord" is most appropriate, as it has been proved that he is worthy of the title; the resurrection is the event which conclusively demonstrates this fact. Luke therefore uses the title more explicitly and frequently in Acts. The disciples, as well, refer to Jesus as Lord and in prayer,[12] and, on occasion, they preface the title with the possessive pronoun "our" (15:26; 20:21). He is their Lord and they own him as such, although he is also clearly the "Lord of all."[13]

What makes the use of the title with reference to Jesus all the more significant is that Luke also uses it to refer to God.[14] Jesus is not simply the Messiah, but "Lord and Messiah" (2:36). In his sermon on the day of

---

[10] 2:36; 5:42; 8:5, 12; 9:22; 10:36; 17:3; 18:5, 28.

[11] 2:21, 34, 36; 13:15; 19:10; 20:19, 21, 24; 28:31.

[12] 1:6, 24; 9:5; 22:19.

[13] Given the regular use of the word "Lord" to refer to Jesus in Acts, it is possible that the angel of the Lord is one who answers to Jesus (2:36; 12:7, 11, 23).

[14] 2:20, 25; 3:19, 22; 4:24, 26, 29; 7:31–33.

Pentecost (2:14–36), Peter quotes from Joel 2:28–32, where "the Lord" is identified with Yahweh. In 2:36, however, Peter identifies the Lord as being Jesus. Luke thus develops the central importance of Jesus. He is the Lord, discharging all the functions of Yahweh in the OT by way of revelation, salvation, and healing. God's people in the old covenant called upon the name of Yahweh; in the new covenant they call upon Jesus, the risen Lord.

Son of Man

Stephen refers to Jesus as the "Son of Man" (7:56). This is unique outside of the Gospel tradition, as is the fact that he describes the Son of Man as standing at the right hand of God, as opposed to sitting—a fact he mentions twice (7:55–56). The term identifies Jesus as the exalted Son of Man who vindicates his witness, Stephen. Furthermore, Stephen's final words, "Lord Jesus, receive my spirit" (7:59), reveal Jesus' authority as the one who initiates the transfer of his followers to the next life. This leaves no doubt that the title Son of Man, referring to Jesus, indicates a dynamic, supreme deity rather than an ordinary member of humanity.

Savior

Not only does Luke refer to Jesus as the exalted Savior (5:31; 13:23), but he also identifies Jesus as the unique mediator of salvation.[15] As such, he is declared "the Author of Life" (3:15). The salvation he offers is a result of his grace (15:11). Luke makes it clear that Jesus' crucifixion was not an accident (2:23; 4:10). It was necessary to facilitate the forgiveness of sins,[16] which Jesus promises to those who believe in him[17]—along with the gift of the Spirit (2:38).

The Savior of People

Risen from the Dead

Jesus' resurrection is of central importance to the book of Acts. The disciples decide that Judas Iscariot's replacement must have been

[15] 2:21; 4:12; 15:11; 16:31; 19:4.
[16] 3:19; 5:31; 22:16.
[17] 2:38; 10:43; 13:38.

a witness to the resurrection (1:22). Luke hints at the resurrection's importance at the end of his Gospel when, in the last two verses, he describes the disciples joyfully returning to Jerusalem and continually worshipping God in the temple (24:52–53). The resurrection had transformed them from frightened, forlorn followers into people of public praise, whose role in life was to authoritatively witness to the reality of the resurrection and all that it meant (Acts 4:33). With the crucifixion, it became the central element of the apostles' preaching.[18] As a result of the resurrection, Jesus was "exalted at the right hand of God" and "poured out" the Spirit (2:33). God's plan of salvation hinges on Jesus' resurrection. It not only proved that the sacrifice and death of Jesus had achieved what was necessary to provide salvation, but it also facilitated the bestowal of the Spirit on believers and the elevation of Jesus to his next mission (3:21).

Exalted to Glory

Jesus' ascension is of fundamental importance to the message of Acts, and the initial verses (1:1–11) focus on this event. Jesus, who was marked by a miraculous ministry and unique mission on earth, has inimitably moved to a different plane of activity and ministry. While his focus is still on those he has saved, he has been "lifted up" to another realm (1:9). His ascension is the beginning of a process of exaltation that will result in the completion of the cycle of Jesus' salvation destiny. Although many assumed that Jesus' death proved that he was a fraud and a failure, God saw it as the occasion to exalt him to his right hand. Jesus' exaltation defines him as the "Leader and Savior" of those who would follow him and who would be saved by him (5:30–31). The contrast, in 5:30–31,[19] between "you killed" Jesus and "The God of our ancestors raised up . . . exalted him" is marked. The Father righteously vindicated Jesus in the face of the unrighteous vengeance of those who crucified him. God "raised from the dead" (3:15) the one who was unjustly "handed over and rejected in the presence of Pilate" (3:13). God's act affirms Peter's claim that Jesus is "the Holy and Righteous One" (3:14) and Paul's definition of Jesus as "the Righteous One" (22:14).

[18] 2:24–32; 3:14–15; 4:2, 33; 17:18, 31; 26:23.
[19] See also 4:10; 10:39–40; 13:28–33.

Present with Believers

Acts 1:1 indicates that while Luke's Gospel set forth the beginning of the acts and teaching of Jesus, Acts completes the story. To assume that Luke is focusing on the apostles in Acts is to miss the point. His is a christocentric thesis. Luke records not so much the acts of the apostles as the acts of Jesus through the apostles. Luke presents Paul and Peter in parallel—perhaps to show unanimity of purpose but, more importantly, to point to Jesus as the past model and present mentor for them both.

The healings that Luke records in Acts reveal Jesus' central place in Luke's mind. Although there are fewer healings in Acts, their presence in the narrative is important. Luke does not specify why he includes them. It is possible that he intends to demonstrate their value in evangelistic contexts. He may use them to provide an insight into the earliest expression of Christianity. However, because of the book's clear apologetic intent among Jews and Gentiles on behalf of the fledgling church, it is more likely that Luke intends the healings to demonstrate the superiority of its central character, Jesus. Luke does not, therefore, provide a methodology of healing that others may emulate. Paul will develop these themes, as will James.[20] Instead, Luke has a central motif that he illustrates through the healing ministry of the early church—in order to place Jesus centrally in the minds of his readers. The miracles demonstrate that Jesus is continuing that which he "did and taught from the beginning" (1:1) of his earthly ministry. The healings, therefore, draw attention not to those healed or to those involved in the healings, but to the continuation of Jesus' ministry.

Those who are most involved in healing are those whom Jesus delegated to heal (2:43; 5:12)—mainly Peter[21] and Paul.[22] Similarly, the name of Jesus is regularly referred to when healings occur[23] and those who are ministering healing use their hands[24]—which Jesus himself often did. The apostles often effected healings with a command,[25] as

---

[20] In the apostles' healing ministry in Acts there is no unambiguous reference to sin as a possible cause of the sickness, no request to repent for sins that may have caused the sickness, and no mention of oil—all of which Jas 5:14–18 refers to but none of which are reflected in the ministry of Jesus. See Warrington, *Jesus the Healer,* 112–25.

[21] 4:30; 5:15; 9:32–35, 36–43 (with John [3:1–10]).

[22] 14:8–10, 19–20; 16:16–18; 19:11–20; 20:9–12; 28:3–6, 7–9.

[23] 3:6, 16; 4:10, 30; 9:34; 16:16–23; 19:11.

[24] 9:12–19; 14:3; 19:11; 20:10; 28:8.

[25] 3:6; 9:34, 40; 14:10.

Jesus also did, and the restorations were immediate,[26] as they were with Jesus. In Jesus' ministry there was a strong link between healing and preaching, and the same is true in Acts.[27] The ministries of Peter, Paul, and others who achieved healings in Acts are reminiscent of Jesus. All of these similarities demonstrate that the apostles are messengers following Jesus' example, walking in his footsteps—but they also indicate that Jesus is present among them.

Not only are the apostles imitating the paradigm of Jesus' ministry; they are also demonstrating his present activity amongst them. The interested enquirer asks, "How do these men have the power to heal?" And Luke answers, "It is Jesus." Thus the man who was "more than forty years old" and had been paralyzed from birth (4:22) was commanded to walk "in the name of Jesus Christ of Nazareth." His immediate and complete restoration followed, and on seven occasions[28] Luke identifies Jesus as the healer. Although he is physically absent, the risen Jesus is present and Luke endorses this by using Jesus' name, most clearly in 9:34: "Jesus Christ heals you."

In Charge until the End

The message of Acts is a story of the church on the move, following the example of its leader who has completed his saving objective in order to complete a new directive. The theme of fulfillment, therefore, is of the utmost importance in Acts. Luke refers to the OT in order to demonstrate that these events fulfill ancient promises.[29] It was according to God's plan that Jesus came (13:23), suffered (3:18; 26:23), was crucified (2:23; 13:29), resurrected (1:11), and received into heaven (3:21) in order to "proclaim light both to our people and to the Gentiles" (26:23).

An early prayer of the believers records that the most important political and religious leaders of the day were only able to function according to "whatever your hand and your plan had predestined to take place" (4:28), with reference to Jesus. Jesus is the one who gives the apostles the responsibility to preach "the word of the Lord"[30] to the

---

[26] 3:7; 9:18, 34, 40; 14:10; 16:18; 28:6.

[27] For Jesus, see 10:36–38; for the apostles, see 4:29–30; Peter, 14:8–10; Paul, 19:10–12.

[28] 3:6, 13, 16 (twice); 4:10 (twice), 30 (cf. 4:4, 17, 18).

[29] 2:16; 2:30–34; 3:18, 24.

[30] 8:25; 13:49; 19:10.

Gentiles.[31] Not only does he decide the audience, but the message they are to preach is his revelation—which is of equivalent value to and identified with "the word of the Lord" (13:48). Thus Luke describes Jesus directing Saul (later renamed Paul) to Jerusalem when he was blind (9:5–6) and organizing for Ananias to pray for his healing (9:10–19). The one who arranges for his healing is the one who commissions him for his life ahead (20:24; 22:10), which must (Gk. *dei*) include suffering (9:15–16; 14:22), and which must (*dei*) include his testifying concerning Jesus in Rome.[32] Although the path ahead for Paul is painful, he knows that his sufferings are not an accident or the fault of fate. The supreme cartographer himself has charted his course for him.

Luke's implicit question to his readers concerns whether Paul was expected to fulfill his mission successfully. His success would indicate that the one who commissioned him had supreme authority. Luke begins to make his case when he records the plot to kill Paul (23:12–35). This plot not only failed but resulted in Paul being protected in Herod's Praetorium and conducted to the home of Felix, the governor, where he had liberty to receive friends (24:23) and the opportunity to speak about Jesus to Felix (24:14–21, 24), to Festus (the governor who succeeded Felix), and to King Agrippa (26:1–29). Luke then informs his readers that although the Jewish religious leaders had prepared forty men to ambush Paul and kill him, a Roman guard of nearly five hundred soldiers protected him on the journey (27:7–28:6). It is clear that Paul was not on his own—someone, although he was invisible, was on his side.

Luke concludes his narrative by recording Paul's journey to Rome by sea (27:1–28:31). It is a voyage dogged by difficulties caused by the wind, the indecision and unwise action of the captain, the fierce storm and darkness, the danger of starvation, the potential of the crew abandoning the ship, the shipwreck, the possibility of their being killed by the soldiers, and Paul's snakebite. These were all huge obstacles, but not one of them was sufficient to derail Jesus' plans for Paul to reach his goal and fulfill his commission.

This story is particularly significant in the first-century context. Modern readers must not underestimate the danger of the Mediterranean

---

[31] 13:47; 22:21; 26:17–18.

[32] 23:11; 26:16; 27:24. In our survey of the christology of the Gospel of Luke we saw that Luke frequently uses the Greek word *dei* ("it is necessary") to indicate the predetermined plan of God.

Sea to the ancients. Today's cruise liners and ferries that sail with sophisticated and accurate maritime aids are very different to the primitive and dangerous conditions of first-century sailing. Another reason for remembering the original context of Paul's voyage relates to the fact that two of the main textbooks that schools in that era used were the *Odyssey* (traditionally viewed as being authored by Homer) and Virgil's *Aeneid*.[33] Pupils read, memorized, and dramatized these books, and they identified in these works principles of life and conduct appropriate to becoming model citizens. These stories recounted the lives of heroes battling against the odds to cross the Greek (Mediterranean) Sea, overcoming the strategies of various gods, storms, and natural enemies along the way to achieve their objectives. The gods supporting these heroes proved their supremacy by their ability to support their protégés against all the obstacles facing them.

Luke's readers would have been familiar with such epics and the messages they presented. In his account of Paul's sea voyage, Luke demonstrates that the one who protects Paul is superior to all other gods because he shields him as he crosses the hazardous sea from Israel to Rome. Christian readers can take heart that the one who protected Paul is covenanted to protect them also. The narrative also encourages those whose trust is not in God to transfer their allegiance to the one whose authority is supreme. The last verse of the book of Acts emphasizes this unprecedented authority. Paul teaches about the Lord Jesus Christ "with all boldness and without hindrance (Acts 28:31)." The final word in the Greek text of Acts, *akōlytōs* ("without hindrance"), Luke's final description of Paul's activity, reminds his readers that Jesus, who reigns in supreme power, not only prophesied but also supervised Paul's destiny. Nothing stood in Jesus' way. Jesus overshadowed Paul, guided him, and controlled his destiny even in the most unfriendly of circumstances.

Conclusion

Luke presents the central involvement of the ascended Jesus in the life of the young Christian community. He encourages his readers

[33] The *Odyssey* is a sequel to Homer's *Iliad* and recounts the adventures of the Greek hero Odysseus (or Ulysses, as he was known in Roman myths) and his long journey home to Ithaca after the fall of Troy. In the *Aeneid,* the prize of the sea voyage undertaken by Aeneas and his Trojan companions is Rome.

to recognize that Jesus is still present, though not in bodily form, and that he still functions with authority. To a sophisticated Gentile audience used to the dominating authority of their gods, such authority is a crucial marker. Neither life nor death, the sea nor sickness, are able to impede or even frustrate the one who commissions and accompanies the apostles. The early church will soon struggle with persecution from without and discord from within. The message of the Book of Acts—that the risen Lord is still actively functioning with authority in the midst of his church—thus provides a timely reminder for all believers. Rather than signaling the departure of Jesus from his followers, the ascension ensures Jesus' ongoing presence through the power of the Spirit. The testimony of the apostles that "The hand of the Lord was with them" (11:21) is a message that still brings encouragement to believers today.

chapter 4

The Letters of Paul

Jesus, Savior and Mentor

Paul offers substantial information concerning Jesus, much of which is repeated throughout his writings.[1] Rather than identify commonalities in the following surveys of each of his letters, these have been collected and offered in this introductory section. As such, a composite picture of Paul's central beliefs concerning Jesus is here presented which allows attention to be given later, in the survey of Paul's individual letters, to his more nuanced features relating to Jesus and his mission.

Jesus: Human and Divine

The Man

Paul clearly defines the humanity of Jesus. He describes him being born of a woman (Gal 4:4) in "human likeness" (Phil 2:7). Paul talks of Jesus being a member of the line of David (Rom 1:3) and an Israelite (Rom 9:5), whose brother was James (Gal 1:19). He was poor (2 Cor 8:9), he lived according to the Law (Gal 4:4), and he ministered to the Jews (Rom 15:2). He chose twelve disciples (1 Cor 15:5) and instituted the Last Supper (1 Cor 11:23–25). Finally, he was crucified, buried, and resurrected (1 Cor 14:4; 2 Cor 1:3–4). Paul says that Jesus was obedient to God the Father (Rom 5:19), suffered (Phil 2:9–10), endured (2 Thess 3:5), and lived righteously (Rom 5:18) and sinlessly (Rom 8:3;

[1]Scholars have disputed which of the NT letters attributed to Paul were actually written by him. For the purposes of this book, Paul's writings are identified as Romans, 1 and 2 Corinthians, Galatians, Ephesians, Philippians, Colossians, 1 and 2 Thessalonians, 1 and 2 Timothy, Titus, Philemon.

2 Cor 5:21). In all of this Jesus demonstrated grace (Rom 5:15; 2 Cor 8:9), love (Rom 8:35), and gentleness (2 Cor 10:1).

It may appear strange that Paul did not record stories about Jesus and that he includes limited material about the historical Jesus. This is not because Paul seeks to differentiate between the Christ of history and the Christ of faith. It is, rather, probably due to the fact that Paul takes the historical nature of Jesus for granted—without it, the message of the salvation that Jesus achieved would be meaningless. Jesus' death and resurrection are the basis for believing the good news that he brought (1 Cor 15:5–8). Another factor in Paul's choice of emphasis is his timing—as one who lived in the age of the church, he sought to demonstrate how believers, with the support of the Holy Spirit, were to live out the good news. His writings build on the foundation of Jesus' life and death and offer fundamental lessons that enable people to discover more about their salvation and the one who made it possible.

The Messiah, Son of God and Lord

Paul often uses the term "Christ" (Messiah) as a proper name for Jesus (not as a title, as it was used invariably in the Gospels).[2] Paul does not refer to Jesus in association with the kingdom of God and rarely refers to it as a concept.[3] Where he does speak of the kingdom, he tends to refer to it as a reality that is still to come.[4] Paul also uses the term "Son of God" to refer to Jesus.[5] Although believers in general are God's sons, Jesus is unique as God's own Son (Rom 8:3, 31) and Paul describes him as "God's beloved Son" (Col 1:13).

Paul also regularly refers to Jesus as Lord. Belief in the lordship of Jesus is the basis for entrance into the Christian community[6] and was central to his message (2 Cor 4:5). "Lord" is also the term that Paul uses to identify the fact that those who confess Jesus as Lord do it as a sign of their corporate identity with each other and with Jesus. The pronoun "our" (Lord) enforces this characteristic. The title "Lord" also

---

[2] Paul refers to Jesus as Messiah (Christ) 58 times. For earlier discussions concerning the description of Jesus as the Christ or Messiah, see pp. 21–22, 34-35.

[3] 1 Cor 6:9–10; 15:24–25, 50; Gal 5:21; Col 4:11; 1 Thess 2:12; 2 Thess 1:5; 1 Tim 4:1.

[4] Though see Rom 14:17; Col 1:13.

[5] Rom 1:3–4; 8:3; Gal 4:4–5.

[6] Rom 10:9; 1 Cor 1:2; 8:5–6; Col 2:6.

reflects Paul's theology, for it reflects his belief in the divinity of Jesus. Thus, although it was used frequently to identify God in the OT, Paul uses it to refer to Jesus. Similarly, although the term "day of the Lord" refers to God in the OT, Paul uses it to refer to Jesus.[7]

Jesus the Savior

Substitutionary Sacrifice

Paul identifies Christ's work in relationship to the salvation he provided by means of his life and death (Rom 5:11; 1 Cor 15:3). Paul emphasizes Jesus' death,[8] though he sometimes chooses to refer to it using other words including the "cross,"[9] "blood" (because it represented sacrifice),[10] or "crucifixion."[11] Jesus' death is a powerful expression of his love (Eph 5:25), and Paul reminds his readers of its sacrificial nature.[12]

Jesus died on behalf of sinners, substituting himself for all those who deserved to die for their sins. His death was thus vicarious.[13] Jesus died for others and in their place, choosing to experience separation from the Father so that believers would be spared that isolating event. In that respect, it may be deduced that Jesus experienced something akin to hell for believers so that they need not.[14] Insofar as he was not guilty of any sin (2 Cor 5:21), there was no need for Jesus to die or suffer separation from the Father. He volunteered to do both, however, and believers are the beneficiaries. Although people have a part to play in responding to that which Jesus has done on their behalf, it must not be forgotten that Jesus committed a unilateral act of grace for them—no one has anything to offer that merits this act (Eph 2:8–9). Although believers have responsibilities to live appropriately if they accept Jesus' sacrificial act, salvation remains an objective achievement by Jesus alone (Rom 6:1–4; Gal 2:20). The subjective response and objective act are intertwined, but the latter is primary in time and importance.

---

[7] Rom 10:13; 1 Cor 1:8; 5:5; 2 Cor 1:14; Phil 1:6, 10; 2:16; 1 Thess 5:2; 2 Thess 2:2.

[8] Rom 5:6–7; 8:34; 14:9, 15; 1 Cor 8:11; 15:3; 2 Cor 5:15; Gal 2:21; 1 Thess 4:14; 5:10.

[9] 1 Cor 1:17–18; Gal 5:11; 6:12, 14; Eph 2:16; Phil 2:8; Col. 1:20.

[10] Rom 3:25; 5:9; Eph 1:7; 2:13; Col 1:20.

[11] 1 Cor 1:23; 2:2; Gal 3:1; 2 Cor 13:4.

[12] Rom 3:25; 1 Cor 5:7; Eph 5:2.

[13] Rom 5:8; 8:32; Gal 3:13; Eph 5:2; 1 Thess 5:9.

[14] Gal 3:13; 2 Cor 5:15; 1 Tim 2:6.

Reconciler

Jesus' death achieved a number of important results. Not only is it now possible to engage in a relationship with God on the basis of the forgiveness of sins that Jesus achieved, but his sacrifice also effected a change in the nature of this relationship between God and the person concerned. This expiation of sin removed the offense to God of personal sin so that God and sinner are reconciled.[15] Jesus' sacrifice removed the wrath that God directed to sinful humanity, and sinners have been propitiated.[16] Jesus' death is not simply about granting forgiveness; it is also about establishing friendships between God and believers. It is only the act of God through Jesus that effects this reconciliation—the individual beneficiary plays no part in instituting it. God's judgment of sin (Rom 1:18; 2:5) is based on his righteous justice[17] and is identified as "wrath" (Rom 5:9). Not to punish sin would indicate arbitrariness on God's part and would call into question the significance of the judicial rules that God had established in his moral law. These rules dictated that punishment for sin was necessary. In God's love, however, God ensured perfect justice by suffering the punishment himself—in Jesus.

Redeemer

Closely tied to the theme of reconciliation is the fact that Jesus' death is redemptive (Titus 2:14), or a ransom (1 Tim 2:6). These concepts are related to the Greek terms *lytron* ("redemption") and *antilytron* ("ransom"). Paul uses the latter on a number of occasions, which is particularly interesting because it so rarely occurs in Greek literature (Rom 3:24; Eph 1:7). Paul's use of the Greek term *agorazō* ("I buy") clarifies this notion of redemption.[18] The price of buying people's redemption is Jesus' life and death. Not only is a change of ownership anticipated thereafter, but there is also an ethical dimension to this costly transaction and believers are expected to live righteously in response to this generous sacrifice.

---

[15] Rom 3:24–25; 5:10; 2 Cor 5:19; Eph 2:15–16; Col 1:21–22.

[16] For more discussion concerning this feature see Charles E. Hill and Frank A. James, eds., *The Glory of the Atonement* (Downers Grove, Ill.: InterVarsity, 2004).

[17] Rom 1:32; 2:12; 6:23.

[18] 1 Cor. 6:20; 7:23; Gal 3:13; 4:4.

Justifier

Another term Paul uses is "justification." With its cognate forms, the word occurs over fifty times in Paul's writings. Contrasting his usage of "justification" with the word "forgiveness" and its related terms (which occur only 5 times in relation to the benefits of Jesus' death)[19] emphasizes the significance of this terminology. Paul often uses the term "justification" in connection with the concept of righteousness, which is a common OT term to describe the act of living in conformity to established rules in a community (family or a broader group, including human and/or divine beings). If the accepted rules are broken, a state of unrighteousness exists until justification occurs and the situation is resolved. The terms "justification" and "righteousness" are therefore best understood in the context of relationships. As a result of sin, a state of unrighteousness existed between God and humanity. Jesus transformed this situation through his atonement.

Justification means that when God judges an individual, that person's eternal destiny is affected by Jesus' death on their behalf. If someone accepts the justifying action of Jesus, that person is no longer in a state of unrighteousness. This does not mean that God overlooks their sin. On the contrary, it is because of sin that God initiated the act of salvation. The act of justification, however, results in the person concerned being designated as righteous. This person then exists in a state that is not theirs by right—they are righteous because someone else has done on their behalf what would otherwise have been impossible. Because they are now wearing the "clothes" of another, they are able to enter a new realm (Rom 4:5).

Righteousness, therefore, has been *imputed,* not imparted. While believers must still amend their lives to reflect the character of God and increasing righteousness, it is God who initiates this process. God positions people in this new state where they are acceptable to God and accepted members of God's family. This change of status is a sovereign act of God. God designates as righteous people, who did not previously exist in a righteous relationship with God and who could never achieve a righteous lifestyle by their own efforts (Rom 3:6). The only thing the individual brings to this transfer from enemy to friend of God is

---

[19] Rom 4:7; Eph 1:7; 4:32; Col 1:14; 2:13. For more discussion, see Mark Husbands and Daniel J. Treier, eds., *Justification* (Downers Grove, Ill.: InterVarsity, 2004).

faith—the belief that God will do as he says if the individual affirms the significance of Jesus' death (Gal 2:16). This act of justification occurs immediately and its effects are enduring;[20] what happens in the present has ongoing and eschatological significance.

On the basis of a person's faith (Rom 4:3), God chooses, as an act of grace (Rom 3:24–25), to vindicate that person and acquit him or her of all guilt and punishment relating to their sin. The basis of this acquittal is that Jesus takes penalty of their sin upon himself (2 Cor 5:19, 21). As a result, God no longer counts sin against the perpetrators. God regards them as righteous because he has justified them. This righteousness is not ethical righteousness—any more than Jesus personally owned the sin that he took upon himself. It is real, nevertheless, and this imputed righteousness has dealt with the past and is the basis of a relationship with God that lasts into the future. Thereafter, as a result of Jesus' death, which established victory over evil and demonic forces (1 Cor 15:24–25; Col 2:15), believers experience a new status as conquerors (Rom 8:37) who are free of condemnation (Rom 8:1).

Conclusion

In a rich portrayal of Jesus, Paul explores a diverse range of issues that relate to Jesus' deity as well as to the salvation that he has provided. For Paul, christology and soteriology are integrally linked. In the chapters that follow, the focused portrayals found in Paul's individual letters will be examined more closely.

[20] Rom 5:1, 9, 19; 8:33–34.

chapter 5

Romans

Jesus, Justifier and Reconciler

Paul wrote this letter (1:1) prior to his visit to Jerusalem (15:25), having completed an evangelistic journey in the northeastern region of the Mediterranean (15:19, 23). The readers of the letter lived in a city of around one million people, of whom between forty and fifty thousand were Jews. It appears that the readers were a mixture of Jews and non-Jews.[1]

Why did Paul write this letter? There are a number of possibilities, including his desire to encourage his readers (1:11, 15) and to gain financial support for his planned trip to Spain (15:24, 28). In 1:8–15, he states that he wishes to see them in order to preach the gospel. However, since he has not been able so to do (1:13), it appears that this letter provides him with the opportunity to present, defend, and explain the gospel. He also explains the concepts of justification by faith (5:1–21) and sanctification (7:1–15) and urges his readers to apply these truths in developing a lifestyle that increasingly reflects Jesus. He notes this motivation explicitly in 15:14–33, where he emphasizes his desire to share the gospel with the Gentiles.

His Royal Majesty

It is important to remember what a challenge it was for Paul to present Jesus accurately to his readers. It was also difficult for his readers to come to terms with these new concepts. The traditional beliefs of the Jews led them to assert that there was only one God—Yahweh

[1] 1:16; 2:9–10; 3:9, 29; 9:24; 10:12; 11:13–32; 15:7–12.

(Deut 6:4). Most Gentiles, on the other hand, believed in a multiplicity of gods. Paul's task was to demonstrate to both that Jesus is God incarnate. He walked a tightrope, therefore, to communicate clearly that Jesus was not merely a man who was adopted by God. He also had to be sure that nothing he wrote suggested that Jesus was not completely human. His diverse readership needed to understand that Jesus was authentically human and conclusively divine. Paul acknowledges the unity of God while he also affirms the reality of Father, Son, and Spirit as God (not gods). This is indeed a mystery, but one which Paul prefers to acknowledge and hold in tension rather than seek to comprehensively explain.

Jesus the Lord

Paul presents Jesus to the readers of Romans with significant stress on his regal status. He refers to Jesus using a range of titles that clearly establish his divine credentials and authority for his redemptive mission. Thus, he is the judge of all (2:16); although he is descended from David (1:3),[2] his Father is God (15:6) and he is God's Son;[3] he is also associated with God the Father as the one who provides grace (1:5, 7; 16:20)[4] and peace (1:7).[5] Readers would have found the fact that Paul was greeting them along with God and Jesus sensational. People were not used to deities being interested in their existence and so were amazed to be acknowledged and welcomed by both their Creator and their Savior.

Paul often refers to the OT (LXX) to help him present Jesus to his readers, and he assumes that they will be familiar with it. Most of the references to Jesus relate to the act of redemption that he achieved. In

---

[2] For earlier discussions concerning this concept, see pp. 33–35, 48–49, 61, 70.

[3] See 1:3, 4, 9. Romans refers to Jesus as "Son" 7 times. For earlier discussion concerning this title, see pp. 11–12, 22–23.

[4] Grace describes God's unmerited favor, which is best reflected in the life and death of Jesus. The word occurs over 150 times in the NT and around 100 times in the Pauline literature. Harold W. Hoehner, *Ephesians: An Exegetical Commentary* (Grand Rapids: Baker, 2003), 149, describes it as "the gospel in one word."

[5] The term "peace" was often used in Semitic greetings (Heb. *shalom*), and in Greek it tended to refer to the absence of war. In the OT, "peace" relates more to the concept of well-being—so people could experience peace even in times of war because they believed that God was in control. Paul invests the term with a Christian flavor. He wants his readers not only to enjoy a sense of well-being, but also to recognize that this contentment is due to God's grace, which Jesus illustrates perfectly. In Eph 6:15, therefore, he uses the phrase "the gospel of peace" as a definition of his message.

10:13, Paul quotes a passage from Joel 2:32 which refers to God as the Lord and applies it to Jesus without seeking to defend it. For Paul, it is an indisputable fact: Jesus is the Lord.[6] He also incorporates the term with Jesus Christ.[7] However incongruous this may seem to Jew or Gentile, for Paul it is not an issue for consideration or debate but an irrefutable truth. In a similar way, he presents Jesus' grandeur by describing him as functioning in exactly the same way as did the Lord of Hosts, who was also "a stone one strikes against . . . a rock one stumbles over" (Isa 8:14). Jesus fulfills the prophecy of being a "tested stone, a precious cornerstone, a sure foundation" (Isa 28:16). The tragedy is that while for some Jesus is a rock in whose shadow they find shelter and protection (9:33), for others he proves to be a stumbling stone over which they trip, which leads to their inability to receive that which he has come to offer (9:32).

In Romans 1:1, Paul associates Jesus with God, and he does so again in the final verse (16:27), where Jesus is the one through whom glory is eternally offered. Similarly, the letter to the Romans ascribes the judgment seat to God (14:10) and also to Jesus (2:16). In 9:5, Paul offers the remarkable assessment that Jesus is God.[8] Paul's readers, and especially his Jewish readers, would have found these close links between Jesus and God to be astounding.

Jesus and the Holy Spirit

Paul also makes clear Jesus' intimate relationship with the Holy Spirit. Indeed, he wrote that the Spirit is "the Spirit of Christ" (8:9)[9] who is also the "Spirit of God" (8:9). Paul does not explain these descriptions, but simply leaves his readers with the thought that it is inappropriate to separate Jesus, the Spirit, and God. The three are more

---

[6] See 1:4, 14:6, 7, 8, 9. In Romans, Paul refers to Jesus as "Lord" 34 times. It is his favorite title for Jesus, and in all his writings he uses it over 230 times. For earlier discussion concerning the title, see pp. 8, 29–33, 49–50, 61–62.

[7] 1:1, 4, 6, 7; 5:1, 11, 21; 6:23; 7:25; 8:39; 13:14; 14:14; 15:6, 30; 16:20.

[8] See also John 1:1; 20:28; Rom 9:5; Titus 2:13; Heb 1:8–10; 2 Pet 1:1; see Hurtado, *Lord Jesus Christ;* George W. Knight III, *The Pastoral Epistles: A Commentary on the Greek Text* (NIGTC; Grand Rapids: Eerdmans, 1992), 326; C. E. B. Cranfield, *The Epistle to the Romans: Romans 9–16: A Critical and Exegetical Commentary* (International Critical Commentary; Edinburgh: T. & T. Clark, 1979), 464–70; John Murray, *The Epistle to the Romans: Volume 2* (Grand Rapids: Eerdmans, 1965), 6–7; contra James D. G. Dunn, *Romans 9–16* (WBC; Waco: Word, 1992), 535–36.

[9] See also Phil 1:19, "the Spirit of Jesus Christ"; 1 Pet 1:11.

integrally linked to one another than our finite minds can comprehend. They may be divisible in some respects, but in a more fundamental sense they are also indivisible. Paul does not intend these descriptions to be the basis for ontological debates or discussions of the intricate characteristics of such a phenomenon. Rather, these truths reflect the grandeur of Jesus who is God. Jesus shares a position of priority and precedence in relationship with the Father and the Spirit that cannot be diminished. The fact that Jesus is the supreme authority has implications for his readers in terms of their security and lifestyles. They should bow in worship before him, rejoice and reflect, raise their hands in praise, and fall to their knees in repentance—for without him, they are lost.

Redeemer and Liberator

The salvation that Jesus achieved, Paul reminds his readers, does not simply result in the forgiveness of sins and the provision of a place in heaven. In addition, Jesus, who has enjoyed eternal relationship with the Father, has opened the way for every believer to experience a relationship with the Father.

Jesus Is Better than Adam

Paul contrasts Jesus with Adam.[10] Whereas Adam was instrumental in bringing sin into the world, Jesus became the source of life. Whereas condemnation (5:16), judgment (5:16), and death (5:17) were the consequences of Adam's sin, Jesus provides acquittal (5:18), eternal life (5:18, 21), and the abundant free gifts of grace (5:15, 17, 21), justification (6:16), and righteousness (5:17, 19, 21). What Adam lost, Jesus restored—but he endowed believers with "much more" (5:15) than even Adam enjoyed. This is because Jesus brings believers from a position of helpless hopelessness and raises them to his level as joint heirs, adopted as children of God and saved by grace. Paul assures his readers that Jesus has removed all condemnation (8:1). Whereas Adam left a legacy of death to all his descendants, Jesus has provided the gift of life. Just as the consequences of Adam's sin last for all time, so Jesus' saving act ensures that grace will reign over believers forever (5:21).

[10] Rom 5:12–21; 1 Cor 15:45–47.

Jesus Is United with Believers

Paul mentions this concept of being intimately related to Jesus on a number of occasions. He refers to Jesus having arranged for believers to belong to him (8:9) so that they are now "in Christ (Jesus),"[11] "in the Lord,"[12] and "one body in Christ" (12:5). In the same way, the churches are also "of Christ" (16:16). Believers belong to him (1:6), the one who conquered death (1:4), irrespective of racial identity (1:5). Theirs is an inclusive salvation, for they are owned by, and therefore protected by, Jesus. Believers therefore share the life of Christ—his relationship with the Father, his authority, his destiny, and his status. Furthermore, Jesus has enabled them to be joint heirs with him (and to be privileged with the opportunity to suffer with and be glorified with him). They are also, therefore, heirs of God (8:17) and are granted eternal life.[13] It is imperative that they recognize that all they have is because of Jesus and all Jesus has he gives to them—a remarkable privilege and an awesome responsibility.

Paul also reminds them that this companionship with Jesus is one they share corporately with all believers, and that it carries with it implications for their lifestyle. In particular, the union with Jesus is emphasized by him being described as the firstborn with the implication that others are to follow (8:29). He is not implying that Jesus was the first person to be born or even that Jesus was born. Paul is using the term metaphorically to refer to the honor that was ascribed to the firstborn in a Jewish family. Paul is not asserting that Jesus was born first *in time,* but that he was first *in priority.* He is commenting on precedence, therefore, and not primogeniture.

The OT uses the term "firstborn" with a similar purpose. Proverbs 8:22 describes Wisdom as being God's firstborn, and Exodus 4:22 describes Israel as God's firstborn. The nation of Israel was not the first to inhabit the earth. In the metaphorical sense, however, and with regard to the privileges and precedence that the natural firstborn child automatically owns, the term applies appropriately to Israel. God specially loved and resourced Israel in unique ways. In a similar way, Psalm 89:27 refers to David as "the firstborn, the highest of the kings of the earth."

Paul asserts that Jesus has precedence over all, and thus the term "firstborn" is appropriate—though he is supreme and therefore of higher

---

[11] 6:11; 8:1; 16:3, 7, 8, 10.

[12] 16:2, 9, 11, 12, 13.

[13] 5:17, 21; 6:4–11, 23; 8:10.

status than all the others to whom this title has been ascribed in the past. Jesus also functions as the firstborn of the new era of people who, through him, can have a relationship with God. He is the forerunner, the one who leads the way for all those who follow him. In particular, he is the first to be raised from the dead and nevermore to die. As a consequence of his resurrection, believers will also be resurrected (8:17).

Paul is not simply identifying facts for readers to add to their knowledge. Rather, he is presenting applicable truth that should make a difference in their lives. As Jesus followed a divine agenda that resulted in his fulfilling the plan of God, so also Paul is encouraging believers to recognize that they have been destined to follow a God-ordained path which is to result in their being "conformed to the image of his Son" (8:29). Although later Paul will remind readers that they have a responsibility to ensure that this happens (12:1–2), here in Romans 8 he wants them to understand that Jesus has initiated a divine agenda for believers. God has set them on the path that Jesus walked. Although some might accuse Paul of downplaying the believer's personal responsibility in achieving this destiny, at this point in his supercharged declaration of the remarkable nature of salvation (8:28–30) he is affirming that the process of conformity to the likeness of Jesus has commenced. God has pressed the start button and is in charge of the molding process that will result in believers increasingly becoming like Jesus. God has predestined, called, and justified them and, as God has glorified Jesus, God will glorify them.

For Jewish believers, who had been the object of government hostility, this was a heart-warming truth. In AD 19, Tiberius expelled them from Rome. In AD 41, Claudius withdrew their right to assemble and, in AD 49, expelled them again. Jewish believers thus came from a vulnerable group of people. But when they chose to follow Jesus (who had been rejected by official Judaism as an imposter) and lost the social context of their Jewish friends as a result, they became even more vulnerable. The Gentiles who followed Jesus increasingly rejected much that Romans accepted as normal, including religious sensitivities, moral assumptions, ethical traditions, and social practices. As a result, Gentile believers were also vulnerable as they suffered disdain and derision. Many believers were also slaves, which made them even more susceptible to rejection. The fact that Paul does not speak of a single church in Rome and that he offers multiple greetings in Romans 16 suggests that the believers may have met in small house congregations

(16:5, 10–11, 14–15). Their fellowship, therefore, was probably somewhat fragmented. Paul was aware of all of these factors and therefore emphasized the sense of inclusion that Jesus offered. These words were a great encouragement to believers who faced the threat of contempt and marginalization.

Jesus Loves Believers

Undergirding all that Jesus did in his mission on behalf of believers is the fact that he loves them (8:35, 37–39). In 8:37, Paul uses the aorist tense (Gk. *agapēsantos,* "loved") to affirm the completion of that expression of love by Jesus. In 8:38, he affirms his belief in this truth by using the perfect passive tense (Gk. *pepeismai,* "I am convinced"). The force of this tense indicates a belief that existed in the past and continues in and beyond the present. Paul's confidence that Jesus loves him towers above everything that might destabilize him. Jesus makes the same commitment to all believers. Jesus proves this love in the comprehensive resources he offers to believers. Paul describes Jesus providing riches (10:12) and blessings (15:29) and entrusting the apostles with his authority (1:5).[14]

Jesus Prays for Believers

Paul provides a further glimpse into the all-embracing nature of Jesus' commitment to believers when he informs them that Jesus intercedes for them (8:34). In 8:26, he writes that the Spirit also intercedes for them. It is not that the intercession of either one or both are necessary because the Father is not a willing listener. As children of God (8:17), believers already have a relationship with the Father and the opportunity to commune with him. Paul is determined, however, that his readers develop a greater appreciation of Jesus' dedication to them. The portrayal of Jesus taking time to petition his Father on their behalf best reflects this commitment. The clear implication is that Jesus' intercession will be successful, for he has unity with the Father, shares equal dignity "at the right hand of God" (8:34), and will only pray appropriately.

It is important not to lose the principle of this truth in an overly intricate examination of how Jesus, since he is God, can pray. The

[14]The context of this verse indicates that Paul has spiritual resources in mind.

metaphor must be carefully unwrapped. Paul is declaring a truth that is precious and therefore to be appropriated, but it is also a mystery and therefore not necessarily to be completely understood—though we are welcome to explore it intellectually and experientially. The picture is of Jesus, who is God, relating so intimately to believers that, for a moment, it is as if he is closer to them than he is to the Father, which enables him to pray for them. Because of Jesus' union with believers, Paul can repudiate any suggestion that believers can ever be separated from the love of God. It is impossible, because Jesus is bonded simultaneously to believers and to being part of the Godhead.

Paul's exultation (8:31–39) takes him from one stage of enthusiastic ecstasy to another as he articulates the unbreakable nature of Jesus' love for believers. He creates such a breathtaking, impressive portrait of love that he is obliged to pause to affirm that he speaks the truth—it is as if he is worried that readers might think he is exaggerating. However, despite the fact that it seems too good to be true, it is true. Paul draws Jesus and the Spirit into his dialogue as witnesses to the authenticity of that which he writes (9:1).

Jesus Redeems Believers

Most of the discussion in Romans relates to Jesus' mission of salvation and its consequences with reference to the Law and Christian lifestyle. Paul asserts that the prophets had promised Jesus' salvation many years earlier (1:2). His preaching therefore focuses on this salvation,[15] as does his service (1:1). Jesus became a servant, he says, to reveal salvation both to Jews (15:8) and to Gentiles.[16] Paul emphasizes just how humiliating, painful, and costly that service was. The notion of redemption (3:24) explicitly indicates that a cost was involved. In order to forgive and save,[17] Jesus died.[18] The term "redemption" would have made Paul's readers think of a payment to buy freedom for a slave or a prisoner of war. This concept would have reminded Jewish readers of the freedom from Egyptian slavery that cost the lives of sacrificial lambs. Indeed, the concept of redemption permeates the OT and God's dealings with the Jews.[19] The good news

[15] 10:17; 15:19; 16:25; see pp. 72–74.
[16] 15:9–12, 18, 21.
[17] 5:10; 10:9, 13.
[18] 4:25; 5:8; 14:15.
[19] Exod 6:6; Deut 7:8; 9:26; 2 Sam 7:23; 1 Chr 17:21; Neh 1:10.

that Paul proclaims here is that Jesus has paid the price for the freedom of all those who place their faith in him, thus redeeming them from sin (3:9).

Jesus Justifies Believers

Paul also refers to the fact that Jesus has unilaterally justified believers[20] and identified them as righteous,[21] as a result of which they have been reconciled to God (3:25; 5:10). The notion of acquittal is integral to the concept of justification. When the cause of condemnation has been removed, acquittal is the appropriate consequence. Since Jesus has received the punishment for sin, those who have placed their trust in him may be acquitted. As a result, they are placed in a position with God that, through no act of their own, enables them to have an authentic relationship with him. Sin had previously impeded such a friendship, but now there is nothing standing in the way of this relationship between God and the believer. Not only has Jesus removed the obstacle of sin, but he has also paved the way for reconciliation with God.

Jesus Frees from the Power of Sin and the Law

Paul personalizes sin, identifies Jesus as condemning it (8:3), and describes Jesus freeing believers from "the law of sin and of death" (8:2; 10:4). Because the OT Law could not free people from the grip or guilt of sin, Paul defines it as "the law of sin." It is not that the Law itself was sinful (7:7), for God gave it and it was associated with the Spirit (7:14). It is because the Law revealed sin that he refers to it as "the law of sin." Similarly, he identifies it as "the law of . . . death" not because it inevitably brought death to all (7:13) but because it identified sin and condemned the Law breaker—the punishment for breaking the Law being death. If people had been able to keep the Law and thereby avoid the consequences of disobedience, Paul could have described it as the law of life. But the weakness of the human condition and will resulted in no one being able to fulfill its requirements.

Before they became believers, their sin had condemned them. They were sinners and, try as they might, they could not erase sin's stigma. Nor could they develop the ability to defend themselves against sin's

---

[20] 3:24, 26; 4:25; 5:1, 9, 15–16; see pp. 73–74.

[21] 3:22; 4:22–24; 5:17, 21; see pp. 73–74.

powerful pull and stranglehold on their lives. Even the Law was powerless in this regard. At best, the Law could identify what sin was, declare that it was heinous, and point out the penalty. But the Law could never enable people to overcome sin. People needed a savior to release them from a law that determined the rules but did not conclusively help the rule breakers. Jesus removed the condemnation of guilt from people when nothing and no one else could.

Paul also describes how Jesus made it possible for believers to fulfill the Law (8:4). Paul is not stating that the Law is to be fulfilled by obedience but that the commandments have been fulfilled in the believer in the sense that believers base their relationship with God on faith that Jesus has done everything necessary to provide the righteousness for believers that the Law could not. Believers acknowledge that they cannot keep God's laws but they come, in faith, to receive God's grace and forgiveness. In response, they are reckoned as righteous and thereby achieve the goal of the Law. Because of Jesus, God has bestowed the status of righteousness on those who otherwise would never have been able to attain it.

Jesus' mission was to destroy all that sin had created in people's lives, reverse sin's effects, stop its eternal consequences, and replace its shroud of death with a garment of praise. He achieved this with his free gift of salvation. Jesus condemned sin in the sense that he broke its power over people. He destroyed the power of sin that worked like a malignant virus in sinful people and took advantage of their weakness like a malevolent parasite. Jesus did this by accepting sin's punishment as an innocent man on behalf of those who deserved its condemnation.

Jesus, in his life, death, and resurrection, not only provided forgiveness for sins, but he also removed people from the sphere or reign of sin as a dominating force. In addition, he placed them in the realm of life and grace where they could live in God's family, benefiting from all of God's resources. Prior to their salvation, believers had few resources to resist sin—now they have all they need.

Paul reminds his readers that the Law no longer governs their lives. Their new partner, the Holy Spirit, has replaced their old partner, the OT Law. The Law kept the Jews in a state of bondage, always reminding them of their sin but never enabling them to improve. The Spirit is a life-giving influence, creating within the believer the power to live the new life he or she desires. Paul's view is that the Law has served its purpose. The time had come for the next stage in the plan of salvation, in which the Spirit comes to live in the believer. As a result of Jesus' successful mission, God has granted believers this transforming influence and mentor.

Practical Deliverer

Paul's presentation of Jesus serves a practical purpose as well. It functions as a pastoral and didactic message to direct the lifestyle of believers. Rarely does Paul extol Jesus' qualities without also emphasizing the practical application. Paul's theology is not merely a systematized framework of belief concerning a truth. His is a theology on the move, providing the education of a coach and mentor rather than that of a scholar and academic. Although his writings are often scholarly, his driving force is not to be erudite but edifying. He concentrates not on teaching facts that fill one's mind but rather on truths that transform one's life.

Paul regularly identifies characteristics of Jesus in order to teach his readers lessons relating to how they are to conduct themselves, and Romans is a good case in point. Believers are to welcome each other as Christ has welcomed them, thus bringing glory to God (15:7). This imperative is grounded in the remarkable fact that Jesus has welcomed believers who have been marginalized by their respective people groups, families and friends. While this timeless message of welcome has practical application, Paul also uses it to urge believers to recognize their central place in relation to Jesus. Jesus did not send an angel—Jesus himself is the one who welcomed them into the family of God. This is not a welcome, furthermore, that will come at the end of their lives—it has already occurred. The aorist tense ("Christ has welcomed you") indicates an event that happened at salvation.

It appears that there were divisions developing among the Jewish and Gentile Christians (11:17–25; 14:1–23) as well as other kinds of division.[22] Paul anticipates that, when they more fully understand the remarkable redemption Jesus achieved for them, his readers will develop a greater appreciation of each other (15:7) and will increasingly

[22] 12:3, 16; 14:3; 15:7; 16:17.

reflect the character of their mentor, Jesus. It is no accident that Paul regularly links believers with Jesus by using body imagery. Believers are members "in Christ."[23] He is "*our* Lord Christ" (16:18), "*our* Lord,"[24] "*our* Lord Jesus Christ"[25] who has died for "*our* trespasses . . . and *our* justification" (4:25), and through him "*we* have now received reconciliation" (5:11). Paul's intention is to encourage his readers so that "*together* you may with *one* voice glorify the God and Father of *our* Lord Jesus Christ" (15:6).[26]

It is significant to note that the only occasion where Paul clearly identifies Jesus as God is in the context of unity. He encourages believers to recognize that the one who calls for harmony amongst his people is none other than God, who was incarnated in Jesus (10:13). Where Paul addresses divisions caused by different opinions concerning lifestyle, he refers to Jesus being "Lord" eight times and "Master" once. He thereby reminds his readers that the one who has saved them is also the Lord who demands that they apply his standards of inclusion, grace, and love to their relationships with other believers (14:1–12).

In his desire to offer applied theology, Paul presents truths about Jesus that should effect transformation. He instructs believers confronted by a desire to sin to "put on the Lord Jesus Christ" (13:14). He views Jesus' relationship with believers as a cloak that can protect from the insidious and invasive nature of sin. Believers, however, have to act on this responsibility and "make no provision for the flesh, to gratify its desires." Paul offers a different picture but a similar message in 15:5, encouraging them to live "in accordance with Christ Jesus." In this way, he is again reminding believers that they have an active part to play in reflecting on their lives and checking to see if they are modeling the character of Jesus. As he came "in the likeness of sinful flesh" but did not sin, so they are to seek to emulate him (8:3). At all times, they are to remember that they belong to the Lord (14:8). As he was a servant (15:8), so they are to be his servants (14:18). They are to be distinct from others who follow a different pattern of life (16:18), taking Jesus, who "did not please himself" (15:3), as their example.

---

[23] 12:5; 16:3, 8, 9, 11–13.

[24] 1:4; 4:24; 5:21; 6:23; 7:25; 8:39.

[25] 5:1, 11; 15:6, 30; 16:20.

[26] Italics have been added in the previous five citations for emphasis.

Conclusion

Paul's rich presentation of Jesus in Romans highlights a number of prominent issues. Each of his emphases would have had specific value for the original readers, but they are also timeless. In a world, then and now, dominated by practices and principles that have little, if any, reference to the beliefs and ethics of Jesus and his followers, it is important to remember the fundamental privileges and responsibilities resulting from Jesus' mission to achieve salvation. Undergirding all of Paul's teaching in this letter is the remarkable fact that Jesus has divine credentials for all that he says and does.

chapter 6

1 Corinthians

Jesus, Lord of the Church

Paul spent eighteen months in Corinth establishing a church but, when he left, it quickly fell into disarray. Lifestyles and worldviews that were alien to Jesus' message dominated Corinth, and the city had many temples with countless priests and priestesses who peddled religious practices that were foreign to Christianity. The fledgling community of believers had not yet renounced many aspects of their ungodly lifestyles and, when they began to feel an elevated sense of their own wisdom (2:1–16; 3:18–23) and self-importance,[1] disaster ensued.

By the time Paul wrote to them, they were disunited (1:10–17), boasting that their spirituality was such that they were able to accommodate extremes of morality that even the Gentiles shunned (5:1–13). They took each other to court (6:1–11), assumed that sexual sins were legitimate (6:12–20), were mixed up with regard to marriage (7:1–40), selfishly put their liberty before selfless love (8:1–13; 9:1–27), were in danger of engaging in idol worship (10:1–33), misunderstood gender distinctives (11:1–16), despoiled the Lord's Supper (11:17–34), were charismatically chaotic (12:1–14:40), and were confused about the details and the implications of the resurrection (15:1–58).

Paul wrote his corrective letter with the intention of providing teaching that would result in the believers being transformed. His goal was for these young Christians to begin to reflect Jesus practically—in their lifestyles and in their worship. Since such a letter requires a high level of authority, Paul regularly refers to Jesus in his literary dialogue with the Corinthians—beginning in the very first verse. Not only does he declare that he is an apostle of Jesus (1:1), but he also reminds readers

[1] 1:18–31; 3:1–17; 4:1–21.

that God has set them apart to serve and call on Jesus and receive his grace and peace (1:2, 3). They have a responsibility, Paul tells them, to live up to their calling.

One God and One Lord

Although he recognizes Jesus' humanity,[2] Paul concentrates on his divine characteristics and their potential impact on the lives of his readers. Jesus' authoritative nature is of consummate importance for Paul.

The fact that Paul most commonly refers to Jesus as "Lord" (Gk. *kyrios*, 64 times) demonstrates his emphasis on Jesus' supremacy. This is significant because while the OT regularly applied the term "Lord" to God, Paul readily applies it to Jesus. He does not offer support for this practice, which indicates that it is a well-grounded feature of his theology and of early Christian confession. He simply states that the Holy Spirit is behind the assertion that "Jesus is Lord" (12:3). No higher authority exists to affirm Jesus' exalted nature. The lordship of Jesus is an encouragement to believers, and it is also a spur to service and sacrifice. For although the Lord is the judge of the world, he will also be their judge (4:4–5) when he returns (11:26). He is defined as possessing divine authority over his kingdom. As the judge over death, he will ultimately destroy sin and death, for he is superior to all that has been created (15:24–28).

The timing of these judicial events is of little importance to Paul. It is their reality that is important, as well as their implications for a more elevated appreciation of Jesus. Jesus' power is supreme—over all other deities and the highest human authorities including the Roman Senate and the emperor. Paul wants his readers not to fret about when Jesus will destroy these powers, or the consequences, or the aftermath. He wants them to realize the incomparable nature of the one who is on their side. Jesus is, after all, "our Lord" (15:31) who reigns now in majestic authority.

Paul further establishes the fact that Jesus (and the Holy Spirit) are an integral part of the Godhead in 12:4–6, where he identifies the simultaneous involvement of God, Jesus, and the Holy Spirit in distributing gifts and commissions to the church. Indeed, on occasions,

---

[2] 1:23; 9:1, 5; 15:3–8.

it is difficult to determine if Paul is referring to God or Jesus,[3] or Jesus or the Spirit (6:11), as the subject of an action. Their divine dignity is often indistinguishable.

Somewhat shockingly, especially for Jewish readers, Paul develops monotheism to incorporate Jesus. Thus, although he asserts that there is "one God, the Father" (8:6), he also notes that there is "one Lord, Jesus Christ" (8:6). Paul emphasizes his belief that Jesus and God are one (8:6) in his reference to and emendation of the *Shema*, the foundational Jewish confession of faith ("The Lord our God, the Lord is one." Deut 6:4 [ESV]). Paul acknowledges (as does the *Shema*) that there is one God and that there is one Lord but, while he acknowledges that the former is the Father, he identifies the latter as Jesus. Furthermore, he asserts that both are involved in creation and are therefore preexistent. He also demonstrates their complementary roles. The Father is the source ("from whom") of all things, while Jesus is the channel "through whom" all things come into existence (8:16).[4] The change of preposition is not intended to differentiate their roles so much as it is to identify the fact that they are inextricably linked in the creation process itself. It is not that they have separate roles but that they perform the whole operation together.

Paul is not offering a flowchart of divine responsibilities in the act of creation, nor is he seeking to exhaustively explicate the roles of the divine persons in creation. His goal is more practical and constructive than cerebral and analytical. He wants his readers to be so impressed with the truth that Jesus is the Lord that they will be motivated to change their lifestyles; this goes beyond encouraging them to probe the complexity of such a truth in order to understand it.

Furthermore, Paul is not teaching dualism but the equivalence of authority. He is not fusing the Father and Jesus into one being but asserting the identification of Jesus with God.[5] He is not suggesting that Jesus has taken God's place or is the only representation of God. Rather, Paul is asserting that the term "Lord," which the OT legitimately used to refer to the supreme deity, may now also be used to refer to Jesus. The

---

[3] 1:3; 4:5; 8:6; 10:9, 26.

[4] He reverses the wording in Rom 11:36 and identifies the Father as the one "through" whom all things have come into existence—in addition to noting that they come from him. Elsewhere he describes creation as occurring "through him and for him" with reference to Jesus (Col 1:16).

[5] N. T. Wright (*The Climax of the Covenant: Christ and Law in Pauline Theology* [Minneapolis: Fortress, 1992], 132) describes this as "christological monotheism."

implications, as Paul realizes, are momentous. Jesus who saved them is also the Lord (1:2, 3).

Again, Paul is not writing to the Corinthian church as a theologian offering a critical and logical analysis of the interrelationships within the Godhead. His theological perspectives are valuable to him largely because they have practical implications related to the lifestyle of believers. Thus, since Jesus' authority is equivalent to that of the Father, to take an action that undermines the salvation Jesus provides (for example, by destabilizing a young Christian, as in 8:9) is as heinous as undermining an action of God. Paul therefore emphasizes the deity of both the Father and the Son, but he does not attempt to explain the complex nature of the interrelationship between the two divine persons. He doesn't want to distract his readers from the significance and purpose of the truth he reveals, which is intended to develop their spirituality and lifestyle.

Similarly, it is instructive to note that Paul often uses OT references to the Lord (God) and relates them to Jesus. In doing so he indicates that, although they are different, they also have a shared identity.[6] Indeed, he often refers to "the *Lord* Jesus" as the authority for his declarations.[7] Events associated with God in the OT are also now associated with Jesus. Thus, Paul writes of "the day of our Lord Jesus Christ" (1:8) in a way that echoes the OT prophets' references to the Day of the Lord—occasions when God would be present (Ezek 13:5; Joel 2:31). The latter was often a day of judgment, but Paul indicates that believers will be acquitted, not judged, on "the day of our Lord Jesus Christ" (1:8).

On other occasions, Paul transfers attributes or responsibilities that were previously associated with God to Jesus. The OT frequently links glory with God, but the NT associates it more often with Jesus (2:8), who is also the Lord of glory. In the OT, God assigned commissions to people (Ezek 30:1), but now Jesus also has the authority so to do (3:5), including Paul's mission (4:19; 16:7). Sometimes Paul also points out that Jesus is in partnership with God (7:17). Similarly, the judgment and power of God reflected throughout the OT are now also prerogatives of Jesus. Paul exerts judgment, therefore, because he believes he is acting in the authority that belongs to Jesus.[8]

---

[6] 1:2 (Joel 2:32), 8 (Joel 1:15), 31 (Jer 9:24); 2:16 (Isa 40:13); 8:6 (Mal 2:10); 10:22 (Deut 32:21); 15:25 (Ps 110:1), 27 (Ps 8:6).

[7] 1:10; 5:4; 7:10, 12; 9:14; 14:37. Italics added for emphasis.

[8] 5:4; 11:32; see also 2 Thess 3:6.

Although some verses (3:23; 11:3) may appear to indicate Jesus' inferiority to the Father, readers need to understand them in the context of the many occasions when Paul identifies the interdependence and equal honor within the Godhead. Any language of subordination is valuable only in order to identify different functions. There is no difference in essence. So it is best to understand both of these verses as expressions of the role of Jesus as Savior rather than assessments of his being. In 3:23, Paul is simply identifying that Jesus, when on earth, lived his life in complete devotion to the will of his Father. In a very real sense, Jesus was God's presence on earth. Many scholars have explored 11:3 ("God is the head of Christ") and come to a variety of conclusions, most of which side with the notion that Paul is referring to issues of leadership or origin. The Greek term *kephalē,* which has caused the dissension, is generally translated "head," though this translation is not without complications and there is a range of different possible interpretations.[9] As far as the relationship between Christ and God is concerned, there is little reason to assume that Paul has eternal subordination or submission in mind. He is probably describing the Father's priority in establishing the plan of salvation that Christ achieved in his incarnation. Thus, again, it is best to understand Paul as referring to the historic Jesus and not his preexistent state.

Neither should the reader assume that the references to Jesus handing "over the kingdom to God the Father" (15:24) or being "himself... subjected to... God" (15:28) indicate a form of timeless subordination of Jesus to the Father. Paul has been at pains to affirm the equivalence of authority between the Son and the Father. It is more likely that he is attempting to identify the Son's role in his mission on earth than that he is making a statement concerning the eternal relationship between them both. Of particular significance to Paul is the fact that these authoritative events relating to Jesus were prophesied of the Messiah (Pss 8:6; 110:1), and Jesus is now fulfilling them (15:27).

As he does in all his letters, Paul presents christology in close association with soteriology. He is more interested in explaining the salvific and ethical implications of his christology than he is in exploring its ontological characteristics. The truths that Jesus sends, saves, and provides authority have christological import for Paul. The consequences are also

[9]David E. Garland, *1 Corinthians* (BECNT; Grand Rapids: Baker, 2003), 512–16; Fee, *Pauline Christology,* 143–47.

significant for him. Believers belong to Christ, he asserts, and it is more important to experience this privilege than it is to rationally explore what it means to "belong." Jesus' resurrection reveals something about his status (15:42–57), but Paul also emphasizes its relevance for the behavior and destiny of believers. Paul's high christology provides an astounding portrait of the remarkable nature of Jesus the Savior, and this should motivate believers to recognize that the behavior of those who own him as their Lord is important (15:33–34, 58). Compared with Greco-Roman deities, Jesus is peerless. He shares characteristics owned by God and thus those who have placed their trust in him should obey him.

For believers, these truths about Jesus carry practical implications and sobering responsibilities. Thus, according to "Christ's law" (9:21; also Gal 6:2), the law of the one Paul describes as Lord, believers must display unity (1:10), rapidly deal with sin (5:4–5), and practice obedience in marital (7:10, 12), financial (9:14), and charismatic issues (14:37). While embracing their freedom in Christ, believers must be sensitive to one another (8:6, 11). They must not follow the example of those in the OT who "put Christ to the test" (10:9).

Crucified Christ and Risen Lord

The Crucified Christ

Early in this letter, Paul asserted that Jesus was crucified (1:23). To suggest to Jews that the Messiah was crucified was outrageous—not only because Messiah was not expected to die, but also because to die on a tree resulted in the victim being cursed by God (1:22–23). Such punishments were reserved for those who had committed heinous crimes (Deut 21:22–23). Non-Jews would have found it ludicrous and illogical that someone who claimed to be the envoy of God would die in such a humiliating fashion. Not only did Jesus' shameful death undermine the Christians' claims to honor, status, and power, but it also meant that anyone who chose to believe in their assertions was likewise foolish. Because the proposition was assumed to be preposterous, people would conclude that their faith was baseless and laughable. Paul, however, identifies the manner of Jesus' death as another sign of the fact that God's wisdom is different from that of all others. While it may seem ridiculous to many, it is in fact an expression of God's eternal wisdom (1:24–25).

The clamor for wisdom that permeated first-century society and that provided a preconceived framework into which all authentic experience must fit also influenced the Corinthian Christians. Jesus' crucifixion did not easily cohere with such wisdom (1:26–3:23), but Paul assures them that this event is the result of divine wisdom, not folly.[10] He warns that those who persist in declaring that Jesus' crucifixion was a reckless act of idiocy are in terminal danger. An absence of love for Jesus, the Lord, he says, results in that person being cursed (Gk. *anathema*) (16:22).

The Passover Lamb

Paul also describes Jesus as "our paschal lamb" (5:7). The reference is to the Passover lambs that the Israelites sacrificed in Egypt—an act of obedience that marked the beginning of their journey to liberation from slavery and that the Jews commemorated every year at the Feast of Passover. Paul's Jewish readers would have understood the graphic nature of this bloody act, and in turn the connection with Jesus' sacrificial death. He also died after his blood had been shed. Passover was celebrated to honor "the Lord" (a reference to God in Exod 12:48), but now the celebration honors Jesus whom Paul also refers to as "the Lord" in the context of the Lord's Supper (11:26, 27, 32).

The Second Adam

Paul also identifies some of the consequences of Jesus' mission that should give believers greater confidence as they consider the future. Although their common ancestor is Adam, who left them weak and with physical bodies that will die, Jesus, as "the second man," promises them power, glory, endless life, and the Spirit (15:42–45). He repaired the spiritual damage that Adam caused and replaced Adam's legacy of death with eternal life (15:21–22). But this is not a mere replacement of that which was lost. Jesus has provided something that is far superior. Paul illustrates this by quoting from Genesis 2:7, "The first man, Adam, became a living being (Gk. *psychē*)" and, with this wordplay, he reveals that "the last Adam became a life-giving spirit (Gk. *pneuma*)" (15:45).

The difference, Paul explains, is twofold. First he contrasts Adam's having life with Jesus giving life. Second, while Adam was merely alive,

---

[10] 1:22–25, 30–31; 2:2, 8.

Jesus' life was associated with the Spirit. Although some translations render *pneuma* as "spirit" with a lower case "s" (15:45), when Paul uses the term he is almost always referring to the Holy Spirit. The implication is that the life Adam experienced is of a different quality. The superior life that Jesus offers is infused with the Spirit.

The Risen Lord

Paul's explanation of Jesus' resurrection in 1 Corinthians is also significant (15:22), particularly because of its implications for the resurrection of believers. Because of the reality of Jesus' resurrection, believers may have confidence that their faith is authentic (15:14, 17) and that they will also be resurrected (15:12, 21, 22). As his resurrected body is incapable of becoming corrupt, so also will theirs be immune to decay. Believers will share in Jesus' glory and power and in the Spirit's life and presence.[11] Paul is painting a portrait of the believer's resurrected body with broad brushstrokes. He is not attempting to convince the skeptic but to encourage the believer. Rather than trying to explain the central characteristics of this mystery, he is pointing to Jesus and asserting, "You will be like him."

Paul is assuring the Corinthian believers that their faith in Jesus is not a forlorn piece of fiction and that their preaching about the resurrected Jesus has validity. Jesus' mission to "hand over the kingdom to God" and destroy all opposition is predicated on his resurrection (15:12–28, 44–49, 57), after which the divine consummation of the plan of salvation can be fulfilled (5:5). Paul encourages his readers to remember that Jesus assures them of continual sustenance—as a result of which they, who were guilty, will be presented guiltless when he returns (1:7–8).

The Church's Foundation

The fact that Jesus is the foundation of the church (3:11) has significant implications. Thus, those God entrusts with developing the church must do so skillfully and carefully, recognizing that their commission and ability both result from God's grace in granting them this role (3:10). God will hold them accountable for what they have done and confer reward or loss accordingly. They are not to be individualistic entrepreneurs but must recognize, at all times, that they are following the agenda that Jesus himself determined.

---

[11] 15:42–45; also 1 Cor 14:37; Gal 6:1; Eph 1:3; Col 1:9.

Lord and Source of Life

Believers Belong to Jesus

As a result of their salvation, believers belong to Jesus. This fact carries significant privileges, including the authority to call on his name and, thus, to invoke his protection and power.[12] There is an implicit assumption that those who call on the name of the Lord have a relationship with the Lord that authorizes the use of his name. At the same time, although it is a special concession for believers to enjoy such a relationship with Jesus, it carries with it a responsibility to live up to the standard expected for those who use his name to declare a special friendship with him.

Privileges and Responsibilities

Paul's christological declarations emphasize the privileges and responsibilities of believers. It is an extraordinary honor for believers to be set apart to him (1:2) and enabled to serve his purposes, and so the onus is on them to exhibit aspirations and lifestyles that are different from those of unbelievers. This is a challenge and an opportunity for the Corinthian believers who live in a city that is contaminated by corruption and full of hopeless people who are being swept away on a path to destruction.

Believers must understand that the fellowship they have with Jesus (1:9) obligates them to actively pursue fellowship with all others who similarly relate to Jesus. Division threatens the internal fabric of their community, undermines Jesus' foundational work in uniting them, provides a counterproductive portrait to the unbelieving community, and calls Jesus' salvific mission into disrepute. Fellowship with Jesus may be personal and precious, but it also has corporate significance.

Paul stresses to his readers that Jesus has died for their sins, in fulfillment of OT prophecy (15:3–4). This is the only gospel that will save them, and therefore believers need to adhere to it (15:1–2). This good news should also have a practical and sanctifying impact on their behavior, especially with regard to relationships that may be harmful to them and the Christian community.[13] Paul uniquely identifies this

---

[12] 1:2, 10; 3:16; 4:10, 17.

[13] 5:7, 8; 8:11, 12; 6:11.

transformation as occurring "in the name of the Lord Jesus Christ and in the Spirit of our God" (6:11). Their dual involvement in this act of renewal demands a rapid lifestyle reformation. Although God has achieved salvation for them, individuals need to apply and live out the implications of this salvation (see Isa 1:16–17).

Thus, believers who "belong to Christ" (1:12; 3:23), who exist "in the Lord" (16:19) and "in Christ Jesus" (16:24), need to adopt his lifestyle and imitate Paul, his apostle, who himself imitates Jesus (11:1). Being "members of Christ" (6:15; 12:12, 27), "united to the Lord" (6:17), and part of "the body of Christ" (10:16) has consequences for their relationships with others. They are to reject immoral liaisons (6:18), refrain from marrying unbelievers (7:39), avoid any relationships that may result in demons influencing them (10:14–22), abstain from abusing each other in the context of the Lord's Supper (11:20–32), and abandon all forms of elitism (12:4–26). Illegitimate affiliations with others and inappropriate behavior harm not only the believer, but also the sanctity and unity between the believer and the one who has chosen to be with them forever. Believers are only supposed to be "infants in Christ" (3:1) for a short time, until they mature and become "spiritual people" (3:1)—that is, people of the Spirit, whose lives are influenced by the Spirit who resides in them. Paul articulates the view that believers can (and therefore should) please Jesus by dedicating their lives to his interests (7:32, 34).

Divine Resources for Believers

Finally in 1 Corinthians, Paul identifies Jesus as being "from heaven" (15:47), which is probably a reference to his future return, not only indicating that he lives there now, but also that he embodies the very character of heaven, its incorruptibility, perfection, and the presence of God. Paul also insists on the significance of the fact that Jesus existed before his incarnation. Jesus is not circumscribed by time or his incarnate body (10:4). In this verse, Paul refers to occasions when God supernaturally provided water for the Israelites from a rock.[14] Not only did this rock follow the people, Paul says, but "the rock was Christ." Rather than assume that Paul believed Jesus to be the literal rock, it makes more sense to understand that he is identifying Jesus as the source of their provision.

[14] Exod 17:1–7; Num 20:1–13.

The one who is the source of all they need as believers has a proven track record of supporting those who need supernatural aid. He proved it in the wilderness by faithfully and graciously providing for the needs of thousands of people over an extended period of time. In the OT, God was often described as a rock—a metaphor reflecting God's strength, permanence, stability (Deut 32:4), and redeeming power (Pss 19:14; 78:35). There are similar associations here as Paul identifies Jesus as a rock. Believers are encompassed by a divine envelope that provides protection, direction, and positive aspirations. In response to his care for them, they are encouraged to function as servants to achieve his will.

Jesus is the source of every believer's being (11:3), and each one should use his resources for the benefit of all. Paul affirms that Jesus has enriched believers, particularly by granting them speech and knowledge (1:5). More fundamentally, Jesus, together with the Father and the Spirit, grants grace, peace (1:3, 4; 16:23), and opportunities for service (12:5) as well as divine aid (15:58). Jesus commissions believers, engaging them to work for him (16:10). Thus, Jesus called Paul to be an apostle (1:1; 9:2) and sent him to preach the gospel (1:17). Similarly, Jesus accepts all believers as servants ("slaves," 7:22) and stewards of God's mysteries (4:1). Even though others may decide that believers are foolish (4:10), Paul affirms that they are authentic channels through whom Jesus is pleased to move. Believers also benefit from having "the mind of Christ" (2:16), which probably refers to the ability to act, speak, and think as he would. The readers are encouraged to embrace and develop this remarkable capacity in order to make substantial, individual lifestyle changes.

Conclusion

Although Paul wrote 1 Corinthians to a first-century church that was experiencing unique challenges, Paul's letter and portrait of Jesus have timeless significance. In particular, the complex interrelationship between christology, soteriology, and ethical transformation provides a sober reminder that mere knowledge of the facts concerning the status and mission of Jesus is insufficient. Having this information needs to result in lifestyle transformation, a more authentic spirituality, and relationships with Jesus and other believers that are increasingly deeper and filled with integrity.

chapter 7

2 Corinthians

Jesus, Agent of Transformation

Second Corinthians is one of the most personal letters that Paul wrote. In it he reveals his vulnerability and private concerns. Rather than addressing a list of issues that needed to be resolved or corrected, as he did in 1 Corinthians, Paul here explains some of his previous recommendations and offers a defense of his ministry and teaching (2:17–3:3; 4:2–15). The majority of references to Jesus, therefore, emphasize his authority, the salvation he provides, and his deity. Paul writes about Jesus' humanity on a limited number of occasions in this letter, mainly with reference to his life, death, and resurrection, though he also refers to Jesus' gentleness and meekness (10:1).

Radiating God's Glory

Jesus Is the Son of God

Paul identifies God as the Father of Jesus[1] and affirms that Jesus is "the Son of God."[2] The use of these terms does not imply that Jesus, as Son, is subordinate to the Father. Rather, the terminology speaks

---

[1]See 1:3; 11:31; Rom 15:6; Col 1:3; Eph 1:3; 1 Thess 1:1. The NRSV translation, "Blessed be the God and Father of our Lord Jesus Christ" (1:2; see also 11:31; Eph 1:17), is potentially ambiguous, indicating not only that God is the Father of Jesus, but also his God—so Murray J. Harris, *The Second Epistle to the Corinthians* (NIGTC; Grand Rapids: Eerdmans, 2005), 142–43, 818–20; and Hoehner, *Ephesians*, 164–65. Revelation 1:6 offers support for this concept. However, the writer's point is not that Jesus is outside the Godhead so as to own God as his God and Creator. Rather, it is a reference to Christ's status in his incarnate, mediatory mission, during which time Jesus refers to God as "his God" (John 20:17).

[2]1:19, also 1 Thess 1:10.

of relationship, rapport, bond, and affiliation between the Father and the Son—and not superiority or inferiority. They are part of the same family with the same aspirations and equivalence of authority. They reign simultaneously and harmoniously. Paul indicates that Jesus lives in a superlative setting (5:6, 8), which elsewhere he identifies as heaven.[3] Jesus and the Father coexist in the same sphere. The description of Jesus as God's Son also indicates uniqueness. Nowhere does Paul speak of an individual believer as a son of God (he refers only to "sons" in the plural form), for this is a term applied exclusively to Jesus, *the* Son of God.

Jesus Is Lord and God

As he does in 1 Corinthians, Paul often refers to Jesus as "Lord" (the usual term to describe God in the OT).[4] Similarly, Paul attributes to Jesus characteristics that were previously assumed to belong only to God. Thus, while the OT refers to God as the husband of his people,[5] Paul identifies Jesus as the bridegroom of the church (11:2). While God is the judge of all,[6] the judgment seat also belongs to Christ (5:10). Deuteronomy 8:20 commands God's people to offer obedience solely to God, and Paul asserts that believers are to obey Jesus as well (10:5). Jesus is the one who commissions Paul in 1:1, and in 1:21 Paul identifies God's role in this. It is clear that it is impossible and unnecessary to differentiate their responsibilities, for both are centrally involved.

Similarly, the Father and Jesus jointly offer grace and peace (1:2; 13:14). Believers are to fear God—and Jesus as well (5:11, see v. 10 as the most obvious referent). Revelations from and of the Lord now refer also to Jesus (12:1) and not solely to God (2 Sam 7:27). Believers communicate with God in prayer (1 Kgs 8:28) and with Jesus as well (12:8). To pray to Jesus, Paul says, is to pray to God.

Paul's clever play on words in 3:13–16 clearly presents this truth. Paul elevates Jesus by demonstrating that he achieves much more for believers than God granted to Moses. Whereas the LXX translation of Exod 34:34 describes Moses repeatedly entering the Lord's presence and removing his veil, Paul describes believers turning to the Lord once and

[3] 1 Cor 15:48–49; Phil 3:20.
[4] 1:2; 5:6, 8; 8:5, 9; 12:1.
[5] Isa 54:5–6; Hos 2:19–20.
[6] Pss 7:11; 50:6; Rom 14:10.

having the veil removed permanently, indicating that they are constantly in the presence of God. Exodus refers to God as the Lord, and Paul identifies Jesus as the Lord and as the one who is the agent in transforming believers (3:14).[7] Not only does Paul modify the wording to indicate a conversion experience (Moses "went in" to God's presence [*eiseporeutō*], whereas believers "turn" [*epistrepsē*] to the Lord), he also amends the tense (from imperfect to aorist) to indicate the immediate change of status that takes place at conversion in contrast to Moses' repeated returning to God. Finally, whereas Moses is described as removing his own veil, Paul uses a passive verb, indicating that believers are the recipients of the Lord's work of removing the veil of blindness that hindered them from seeing God's glory.

The use of the term "Lord" to refer to Jesus in 3:13–16 strongly indicates that its use in verse 18 similarly relates to Jesus. Thus "the glory of the Lord" that believers reflect, or radiate, is the glory that belongs to Jesus. In Exodus 40:34, the glory that filled the tabernacle belonged to God. Here, this glory belongs to Jesus as well (see also 4:4). Although Paul does not explore the identity of this glory, the significance of the text is far-reaching. God, who alone can truly be described as glorious, shares that characteristic with Jesus (8:23). Another remarkable fact that Paul shares here is this: whereas Moses was not allowed to see (unveiled), or reflect, God's glory, Jesus' glory is available to all believers.

Paul also identifies Jesus as being "the likeness (Gk. *eikōn*) of God" (4:4; see also Col. 1:15), the glory of God being revealed in Jesus (4:6). Although Adam was created in the image of God,[8] it is obvious that the character of God in Jesus is greater than it was in Adam—principally because Jesus was not created.[9] Even in his incarnate form, however, Jesus perfectly radiates the character, ethos, aspirations, priorities, and being of God the Father. God, who by definition cannot be seen, since he has no visible form, is seen in Jesus. They share the same "likeness" and, even though they are distinct persons, they also own the same identity. Paul is not simply saying that Jesus was like God. Rather, he is

---

[7] So Fee, *Pauline Christology,* 179. Harris (*Second Epistle to the Corinthians,* 308), however, prefers to interpret it as a reference to Yahweh.

[8] Gen 1:26–27; 1 Cor 11:7.

[9] See Fee (*Pauline Christology*, 317–25) for discussion of the background of the Greek term *eikōn* in Jewish literature (where it refers to divine revelation or Wisdom) and in Greek literature (where it refers to the cosmos), both of which were identified as reflecting the divinity concerned.

saying that Jesus was the visible manifestation of God. The transcendent God becomes available to people in the person of Jesus.

Paul also links Jesus to events associated with God in the OT. Paul writes of "the day of the Lord Jesus" (1:14) in a way that echoes the OT prophets, who also spoke of the day of the Lord (meaning God, e.g., Ezek. 13:5). Moreover, Paul speaks of this day as a more positive occasion for believers than it is in most of the messages the OT prophets delivered.[10]

Jesus and the Spirit

To ensure that his readers recognize the supreme and divine dignity of Jesus, Paul asserts that Jesus is the Spirit (3:18; see Phil 1:19). In this he indicates that the one represents the other.[11] Jesus is identified not only with the Father but also with the Spirit, though readers should not understand this to mean that Jesus is personally absorbed by or into the Spirit. The transformation of the believer is simultaneously the work of Jesus and the Spirit.[12] Paul's confidence (3:4), hope (3:12), and ministry (4:1) thus rest on a very sure foundation. In preaching "Jesus Christ as Lord" (4:5) he proclaims the one who is inextricably linked with the Spirit and the Father. Remarkable though these christological statements may be, Paul offers them with a soteriological application. The obedience that believers offer to God is now the appropriate response to Jesus as well (10:5).

Becoming Sin for Sinners

The most significant act that Jesus achieved, of course, relates to his death (5:15), as a result of which the believer is now "a new creation" (5:17) and reconciled to God through Christ (5:18–20).[13] The phrase "he made him [Jesus] to be sin who knew no sin" (5:21) encapsulates the cost of this transaction. Although it may not be possible to plumb the depths of this concept, it is clear that, in order to achieve salvation,

---

[10] Isa 13:6, 9; Jer 46:10; Ezek 30:3.

[11] See also Gal 4:25.

[12] Fee, *Pauline Christology,* 178.

[13] Harris (*Second Epistle to the Corinthians,* 451) describes this as "one of the most profound mysteries in the universe."

it was necessary for Jesus to be associated with something that was not only distasteful and malignant, but that was also foreign to his character and experience. He who was sinless became associated with sin so that believers might become righteous.

It is possible that this identification with sin refers to Jesus' incarnate life, which he lived out in the context of sin in the people around him and their malevolent responses to him. It may also relate to the fact that he lived a human life—with restrictions and weaknesses that sin initially caused. It is more likely, however, that it refers to the crucifixion—and especially because of the relationship between Jesus' sacrifice and the sin offering of the Passover (1 Cor 5:7).

The OT prophesied that the Messiah would bear the sins of his people.[14] Paul, however, appears to go beyond this and identifies Jesus not just as a sin bearer but as sin itself. Clearly, Jesus suffered the punishment that sinners deserved. He was uniquely separated from the Father before he died, resulting in his cry that he was forsaken. In that respect he was treated as if he were a sinner himself. Paul's personification of Jesus as being sin itself inextricably links his identification with sinners and their sin. Jesus is counted as sin so that sin is not counted to them (5:19). He becomes their substitute and representative, dying on their behalf and in their place.

It is possible that Paul is using hyperbole or metaphorical language to demonstrate Jesus' willingness to identify with those for whom he died. He is not stating that Jesus became a sinner or that sin was actually transferred to Jesus—any more than the sacrificial lamb (Lev 4:24, 28) became a sinner or took on the literal transfer of the people's multiple sins. This is clearly a mystery, and it may be inappropriate to assume that it may be understood. Paul's purpose is less to offer an abstract, philosophical, or merely creedal affirmation and more to provide a theological concept that helps to identify the intimate relationship between the Savior and those saved, between the sinner and the one who absorbed the penalty, punishment, curse, and even identity of the sinner's sin.

Paul is not indicating that Jesus is sinful in an ethical and subjective dimension, neither is he purporting, on this occasion, that believers are made righteous in a subjective manner. Rather, they are made righteous by God in the same sense as Jesus is made sin. There has been a change of status, not a transfer of properties (5:21). As Jesus becomes the sin of

---

[14] Isa 53:6, 10, 11, 12.

the sinner, so the redeemed sinner becomes the righteousness of God. As Jesus receives something that he does not deserve, so believers receive something that they do not merit. As Jesus is assigned the sin of others, so believers are assigned the righteousness of God.

However many words are used to seek to explicate this truth, it remains a mystery—inexplicable, sacred, awesome, humbling, and overwhelming. It calls believers to sensitively consider the depth of Jesus' commitment to them, to fall before him in wonder and praise. This truth inspires believers to resolve never to embarrass him or dishonor him by living in such a way that would discredit or disgrace the one who has willingly chosen to so closely align himself with them at such great cost.

Paul affirms that, although Jesus "was crucified in weakness," he functioned "by the power of God" (13:4), for he "always leads us in triumph" (2:14). Not only does God assure victory in all that Jesus does, but it is also the believer's privilege to participate in that process. Weakness is the catalyst that results in the power of God being activated through Jesus.

Paul describes the riches that God has granted to believers as a result of Jesus' gracious sacrifice—he became poor (8:9), which is "the gospel of Christ" (9:13; 10:14) and "his inexpressible gift" (9:15). This fact is particularly important to Paul—not as a theological or creedal pronouncement, but as the basis for a call to his readers to emulate Jesus' generosity and support those who are experiencing hardship and poverty (8:1–15, 24; 9:1–15).

One of the challenges to believers is to ensure that their deep-seated relationship with Jesus is not harmed as a result of sin, deception, or false teaching (11:3, 4; 13:5). Believers must be careful not to enter into any illegitimate relationships because of the harmful influences that may result from such interaction (6:15–17). Similarly, Paul recognizes the responsibility that comes with the privilege of a relationship (5:10, 21). He knows that Jesus' forgiveness is real because he is "in the presence of Christ" (2:10), and Jesus' lavish love motivates him to respond in love and to seek to be controlled by him (5:14).

Living in Christ

The only direct quote from Jesus that Paul records, it is significant to note, is one in which Jesus says that he grants believers grace and power (12:9). Paul stresses the fact that believers are inextricably linked with Jesus (10:7), and he uses a number of phrases to affirm this union (believers are "in Christ,"[15] 1:21; 12:2, 19; "Jesus Christ is in" believers, 13:5). Most remarkably, Paul describes believers as being "betrothed . . . to one husband . . . to Christ." Their destiny is to be presented to Christ at the end of their lives as "a pure virgin" (11:2). This is an extraordinary privilege that carries with it a responsibility not to dishonor that relationship.

Paul's readers were filled with uncertainty about events in this life as well as the next, and so Paul's reminder that they are united with Christ (1:21; 13:5) was particularly encouraging. They also drew strength from the guarantee that they would be resurrected just as Jesus was resurrected (4:14). Because believers are beneficiaries of, and participants in, Jesus' victory (2:14), they can testify to that success. Paul describes them as "the fragrance . . . the aroma of Christ" (2:14–15) that will draw others to appreciate what Jesus has achieved for them. Believers have been "captured" by the triumphant Jesus and now give him honor and are a pleasant fragrance for the benefit of others.[16]

Another implication of the fact that believers belong to Jesus is that each of them exists as a letter "from Christ." It is their responsibility to ensure that they reflect his character in their lives so that, when people "read" them, they will be authentically discovering truth about him (3:3). Similarly, Paul describes himself and his colleagues as "ambassadors for Christ" (5:20). Believers are channels through whom Christ chooses to speak (13:3), and this has obvious repercussions for how people are to respond to their divinely inspired messages. Furthermore, they are "apostles of Christ" (1:1; 11:13) and "slaves" and "ministers" of Christ (4:5; 11:23) and must deliver their commissions with sincerity and integrity (2:17). Thus, in speaking for Christ, Paul is conscious that he is also "in the Lord's sight" (8:21;[17] 12:19) and must live honorably,

---

[15] Paul uses the phrase "in Christ" over 160 times in his writings. It is a central motif in his theology and affirms the believer's status. Although he does not clarify the description, it indicates an intimate relationship between the believer and Christ. Given the unique relationship between Christ and God, being "in Christ" is remarkably beneficial for believers.

[16] Incense was burned, perfume sprinkled, flowers scattered, and spices displayed as part of Roman victory processions.

[17] Fee (*Pauline Christology*, 189) identifies the even more significant fact that "Paul borrows a κύριος phrase from the LXX and applies it to Christ" (Prov 3:4).

pleasing Jesus at all times (5:9, 11) and even being prepared to suffer for him (1:5; 4:10–11). It is not fear that motivates him, for Jesus, the one in whom believers place their confidence, has promised to be on his side (3:4). The fact that Jesus, who has commissioned him, is worthy of his obedience and service and deserving of his respect and devotion (10:5) stimulates Paul to live with integrity and passion for his mission.

Conclusion

In 2 Corinthians, Paul reinforces many of his central themes concerning Jesus. He demonstrates that Jesus is supreme and that the salvation he has provided is comprehensive. He offers his readers the opportunity to be in awe of the dignity of their Savior, who has chosen to grant to them such a remarkable salvation, despite the terrible cost to himself. As he does in all of his letters, Paul clearly presents the implications of such a gracious sacrifice for the personal and ethical transformation of his readers.

chapter 8

Galatians

Jesus, Liberator from Legalistic Slavery

Galatians 1:1 identifies Paul as the author of this letter. The original readers lived in the southern part of the province of Galatia, where Paul and Barnabas established churches—in Pisidian Antioch, Iconium, Lystra, and Derbe—on their first missionary journey.[1] Paul wrote this letter to refute those who had been undermining the gospel by suggesting that believers had to undertake certain actions, including circumcision and adherence to certain Jewish practices, to complete its effectiveness. Paul stresses the significance of justification by faith for a relationship with God and elaborates on the authenticity of his message and the authority of his apostleship (1:1–2:19). In defending the gospel, he elevates the significance of the person of Jesus who provided it and who is central to its message. His aim is to assure his readers that they need nothing else to receive salvation. Such a superior Savior needs no supplemental action by anyone, least of all by those he came to save.

God's Supreme Son and Savior

Paul emphasizes Jesus' supremacy by clarifying that "Jesus Christ" as well as "God the Father" (1:1) determine his service (1:10) and apostleship. Indeed, it is striking that here, and elsewhere, the reference to Jesus precedes the reference to God. Sometimes Paul even mentions Jesus alone as the one who authorizes him to be an apostle.[2] Both the Father and Jesus give the divine provisions of grace and peace

[1]Acts 13–14; 16:6; 18:23.

[2]2 Cor 1:1; Eph 1:1; Col 1:1; 1 Tim 1:1; 2 Tim 1:1.

(1:3) to believers.[3] Paul identifies Jesus most often as the Messiah (38 times)—probably because of the Jewish opposition to Jesus' mission. He is the Messiah, but he is not the merely anointed man many Jews expected. Jesus is the preexistent Son of God (1:15–16; 4:4). Paul also refers to Jesus as the Lord,[4] asserting that Jesus is exalted to such a degree that the title normally ascribed to God also defines him.

The reference to the Galatians welcoming Paul "as an angel of God, as Christ Jesus" (4:14) is curious. It is possible that the terms are intended to be considered separately as two distinct examples of the honor that the readers afforded to Paul when he was with them. However, it is also possible that he may have placed them in apposition to each other to indicate that there were similarities between the two. If Paul was referring here to just any angel, it would have the effect of reducing Jesus' status to that of an angel, and this would contradict his representation of Jesus elsewhere. As he does elsewhere, however, he might be echoing OT passages that refer to "the angel of the Lord" as the messenger of God (Gen 31:11) and even as God himself (Exod 14:19, 24). Perhaps, then, Paul is indicating not that Jesus has an angelic nature, but rather affirming his capacity as God's *messenger* and, more importantly, even that he himself is God.

Liberator from the Law's Curse

Paul presents his christology with a soteriological ambition: to ensure that his readers realize that their salvation is secure and complete. As elsewhere, Paul refers to the historical Jesus and illustrates an awareness of his humanity, but he always does so to emphasize his soteriological significance. Thus, Paul reminds the Galatians that Jesus died on a cross (2:21; 3:1; 6:14), was wounded (6:17), and resurrected (1:1).

He also refers to Jesus as the offspring of Abraham, though this is not about identifying his humanity as much as it is about highlighting his status as *the* descendant of the great Jewish hero Abraham (3:16). In what appears to be tortuous logic, Paul identifies Jesus as the singular offspring of Abraham on the basis of the (collective) singular "your offspring" (Gen 13:15–16). He thereby identifies Jesus as being the fulfillment of the promise to Abraham (3:16). Jesus is the one who grants life

[3] It is interesting to note that Paul refers to the grace of God (1:15; 2:21), but he also writes of the grace of Christ (1:6).

[4] 1:6, 19; 6:14, 18.

to all who follow him. He is the promise given to Abraham and he gives himself to all those who believe in him as the promise of God.

Paul's flow of thought follows a legitimate exegetical process with which his original readers would have been familiar. God promised Abraham countless descendants and Abraham accepted this promise, even though in human terms its fulfillment seemed impossible. Paul identified Abraham's readiness to believe the word of God as faith (3:9). That faith was sufficient for God to reckon to him the status of being righteous (3:6). Therefore, 430 years before God gave the Law to the Israelites, God categorized Abraham as righteous on the basis of his readiness to believe that God's promise was trustworthy (3:17). Paul wanted his readers to understand that faith, as the basis for being reckoned as righteous, preceded the giving of the Law. Obedience to the Law, therefore, was never intended to be the grounds for achieving righteousness.

Paul also describes Jesus as being God's Son (1:16; 4:4) when he describes the mission of salvation that Jesus undertook. In his capacity as Son, he most comprehensively reflects the Father. As a son was assumed to best reflect a father, so Jesus, in his capacity of son, reflects the mercy of God in seeking to save the world from its hopeless destiny. This gracious act is incongruous, however, in that the one who reflects God the Father was the brother of James and "born of a woman, born under the law" (4:4). The level of willing humiliation by Jesus is incomprehensible, but the realization of God's goal to provide the possibility for people to have an eternal relationship with him is certain and complete. It is for this reason that Paul castigates all attempts to undermine Jesus' perfect consummation of this ambition.

Crucified with Christ

Although 2:20 is a personal confession to the effect that Paul has been "crucified with Christ," this applies to all believers. Because of Jesus' sacrificial death, believers now "live to God" (2:19) and Christ lives in them.[5] The concept of being crucified with Christ graphically portrays the central involvement of believers in Jesus' death. Although Jesus was the one who died, it is as if believers were there also. Paul presents these christological statements in order to develop some soteriological consequences. He is not suggesting that believers also bore the punishment

---

[5]2:20; Rom 8:10; 2 Cor 13:5; Col 1:27; Eph 3:17.

for their own sins or that they experienced the wrath and absence of God, as did Jesus. Rather, he is asserting that the consequences of the crucifixion apply to the believer. That which Jesus gained, they also have gained; what he won on the cross, they also won. Jesus has passed on to his followers the transaction from death to life that he achieved.

Justified by His Grace

Paul asserts that those who believe in Christ, who invest their lives and futures in a relationship with Jesus, are justified (2:16–21). Belief is not merely a mental assent to some facts about Jesus. It is a determined readiness to follow him and to be changed by him to reflect his character and aspirations. Justification is God's acknowledgement that those who trust in Jesus are righteous, guiltless of all charges that they have incurred as sinners. Ethical righteousness is not in view here, but rather the unilateral action of God who, as a result of his Son's death, accords to sinners the status of righteousness. They have changed their identity—once they were unrighteous but now, miraculously and because of God's grace, they are righteous.

Redeemed from the Curse

Jesus became "a curse for us" (3:13; Deut 21:23) at his crucifixion, thereby achieving redemption. Because he died as if he were a Law breaker, God the Father cursed him as he would anyone who had broken God's laws. The Jews in particular found the notion that the Messiah was crucified to be scandalous. As Paul explains, however, this is the basis for redemption because it was in this form of sacrificial death that an exchange took place. The judgment on the people was that they would be separated from God because they had broken God's laws. But Jesus, who had not broken God's laws, died on behalf of those who had. In so doing, he experienced separation from God. Because he bore this punishment himself, God validated him as the one who could grant life to those who deserved to die. His death was therefore the price of their freedom. In that way, he redeemed them.

Children of God

It is a remarkable piece of evidence for this transformation that believers have become "children of God" (3:26). In the previous two verses, Paul uses the first-person plural pronoun "we" three times, but here in verse 26 he uses the second-person plural pronoun "you" to identify that his readers are God's children. This is too important a fact to be missed, and so he makes this truth very clear. Those who are "in Christ" are children of God.

The reference to "children" is due to the fact that earlier he had identified Christ as the descendant of Abraham (3:16); in order to maintain the flow of thought from the era of Abraham, to whom was granted the promise of having a family of countless descendants, he identifies all who are in Christ as children of Abraham but much more importantly also children of God—as is Jesus (1:16; 2:20). Although the OT described angels (Gen 6:2; Job 1:6) and the Israelites (Deut 32:8) as children of God, this term refers to believers, irrespective of their lineage or gender.

Just as God "sent" his Son (4:4) to make adoption possible, so also he "sent" the Spirit of his Son (4:6) to activate it. The adoption process and the sending of the Spirit are simultaneous events that both occur at salvation. As a result of their salvation, believers are able to refer to him intimately as "Abba, Father." This was Jesus' distinctive address to the Father; now it is theirs. Believers now share the unique sonship that the Son of God himself experienced (also Rom 8:14–17). Paul is not anticipating a theological enquiry as to how this can be. Instead, he is anticipating an emotional response as believers try to take in this reality and its positive consequences for spirituality and self-awareness.

Equipped with the Spirit

Believers receive the privilege of salvation because "God has sent the Spirit of his Son into our hearts (4:6)."[6] In 4:5, Paul asserts that God's son was born specifically "to redeem those who were under the law." After the Son achieved redemption for others, God sent "the Spirit of his Son"[7] into the hearts of believers to facilitate their relationship as children of God. The term "spirit" (Gk. *pneuma*) could relate to some spiritual component of Jesus, but it is more likely that it is a reference to the Holy Spirit, who partnered with Jesus in his earthly ministry. The

[6] See also 3:18; Phil 1:19.

[7] The description "Spirit of his Son" occurs only here in Pauline literature.

Spirit is so intimately linked with the Son in Paul's mind that it is not unusual that he speaks of him equally as the Spirit of the Son. Not only does this elevate Jesus, as the one who is associated with the Spirit, but it also enables Paul's readers to have a greater appreciation for the commitment of both Jesus and the Spirit to them. The one who is centrally involved in their lives is none other than the Spirit of the incarnate Jesus who, a few decades earlier, lived on earth. Jesus has ascended to heaven, but he is not absent. His Spirit is present with them. Wherever they are, the Spirit is with them and, because the Spirit is inextricably linked with Jesus, so Jesus is also with them (3:14).

Believers receive the Spirit by faith, and not by keeping OT laws. Thus God grants the Spirit to Gentiles as well as to Jews. Jesus, as a consequence of his death, grants them the Spirit to accompany them from the commencement of their relationship with God (3:2). In addition to Jesus' provisions of the forgiveness of sins, the opportunity to serve God in this world and an eternal home in heaven, he also gives the Spirit. With the Spirit comes a variety of vitally important gifts that flow from the redemption achieved by Jesus.

God sends the Spirit of his Son "into our hearts" (4:6), fulfilling the prophecy in Ezekiel 11:19 concerning a time in the future when God promised to "put a new spirit" in his people. To readers in the first century, the heart indicated the seat of the emotions and the center of one's moral, spiritual, and intellectual life. The heart represented the central core of one's life. Jesus is as centrally and intimately present in the life of the believer as possible.

Baptized into Christ

One metaphor Paul uses to highlight the tightly developed relationship between the believer and Jesus relates to being "baptized into Christ" (3:27; Rom 6:3). Those who were baptized into the name of someone else were expressing their desire to enter into the destiny of the other and to adopt that person's aspirations as their own (1 Cor 10:2). It is possible that this referred to the act of water baptism. It is more likely, however, that Paul is speaking of the moment when a person comes to faith (1 Cor 12:13) and is thereby moved from death to life, from loneliness to partnership with Jesus. In this they are, metaphorically, "clothed" with Christ (3:27), as they take on the destiny and more of the character and lifestyle attributes of Jesus.

Freed from the Law

Paul describes Christ as the one who has "redeemed us from the curse of the law" (3:13), an act that manifested his grace (1:6) and love, insofar as he "gave himself" to achieve it (2:20). Another consequence of the salvation Jesus provided for all who are "in Christ Jesus" (3:14) is freedom from the Law (2:4; 5:1, 13). The Law was associated with bondage (2:4) and slavery (5:1). Although the Law functioned as the guide for the Israelites, Christians now have "the law of Christ" which, as a result of the Spirit's dynamic presence in them, facilitates their spiritual growth. In 5:1, Paul makes this clear by identifying that "Christ has set us free," and also ensures that such freedom is maintained.

He who freed people from the Law as a guide does not expect them to return to the Law in order to retain it as their guide. Indeed, God intended the Law to function only until Christ came (3:24); thereafter, it was to be replaced by the superior "law of Christ" (6:2). The law of Christ is not a new set of guidelines that replaced or were added to the OT Law. Rather, the law of Christ relates to the person of Jesus, who models the lifestyle he expects from his followers. Even more importantly, Jesus enables believers to achieve his ambitions for them through the Spirit he sends (3:14). He is the perfect guide and constant companion who mentors believers personally and powerfully.

Jesus is the one who, Paul asserts, is the comprehensive answer to the needs of humanity. His resources, including the Spirit who has been given as a result of his salvific mission (3:14), are more than enough to both redeem (3:13) and transform (4:19) his followers.

Conclusion

Having explored the quality of Jesus and, particularly, the supremacy of the salvation he has procured, Paul anticipates that his readers will, once and for all time, maintain and develop their relationship with Jesus, the one who has done so much to ensure that their eternal destiny is secure. In Jesus, they have a personal, life-transforming and guiding influence who is superior to the Law in all respects. It is not a stress on its different rules that is to determine their Christian commitment but on an intimate and dynamic relationship with Jesus.

chapter 9

Ephesians

Jesus, Cornerstone of the Church

The identity of the community to whom this letter was addressed is not certain, since the words "in Ephesus" (1:1) are missing from the oldest Greek manuscripts. All versions include these words, however, and the predominant view of the early church was that Paul had sent the letter to the city of Ephesus, a metropolis that was cosmopolitan, deeply religious, and intellectual, but that also had a pervasive criminal undercurrent. After commencing the work in Corinth, Paul traveled to Ephesus (Acts 19:1), where he established a church (Acts 19:2–6; 20:31). It was a time of extraordinary miracles (Acts 19:11, 12) and teaching (Acts 20:27, 31), but it was also a time of significant suffering (1 Cor 15:32; 16:9). When Paul left, he prophesied that divisive opposition would destabilize the believers (Acts 20:28–30).

The letter to the Ephesians is replete with encouraging information about Jesus' mission, as a result of which believers have significant resources available to them to enable them to complete their missions as his followers. Here again, Paul's christology, which emphasizes the exaltation of Jesus and his relationship with the church, undergirds his soteriology. His presentation of Jesus serves as a motivation to encourage the development of his readers' quality of life and spirituality.

Exalted Lord and Cornerstone

The Sovereign Lord

Paul identifies God as the Father of Jesus (1:3) and as the Father of glory (1:17). However, as elsewhere in the Pauline corpus, he also regularly calls Jesus "Lord,"[1] and his final reference in this letter is to the "*Lord* Jesus Christ" (6:24, emphasis added). As in Romans and 1 Corinthians, this is a remarkable designation for Jesus since the OT uses the term to refer to God. The reference to Jesus and God in 1:2[2] indicates that both are responsible for distributing grace and peace, and Paul's concluding doxology identifies the Father and Jesus as the joint source of peace and love (6:23). Jesus is intimately associated with the God of glory, who is also his Father.[3] As God is "true" (1 Thess 1:9), so also Jesus is "truth" (4:21); as God is light (Isa 60:19), so Jesus is associated with light (5:8, 14). Paul also connects Jesus to OT verses that refer to God. Psalm 68:18, for example, declares that God is the victor, while in Ephesians 4:8 the victor is Jesus.

Paul develops Jesus' supremacy in his description of his authority (1:20–23). His resurrection from the dead is but the preface to further exaltation by God.[4] Thereafter, Paul describes Jesus as authorized to sit "at his right hand in the heavenly places" (1:20). The "right hand" indicated supreme power, as the heir to a throne took this position. Being seated "in heavenly places" indicates that although he is absent from earth, Jesus is present in another realm, heaven. Jesus' specific association with heaven is that he dwells in the presence of God the Father and shares his regal dignity. He shares the Father's honor and owns a place of equality with him. Paul clarifies the exalted nature of his position with a short list that is intended to represent every possible (cosmic) contender. Paul elevates Jesus "far above" them all (1:21; cf. Col 1:16). Paul nuances each term to distinguish them from one another, but the cumulative effect is to demonstrate that no one (angelic, demonic, or

---

[1] 1:2, 3; 2:21; 4:4; Paul refers to Jesus as Lord 24 times in this letter.

[2] Several of Paul's letters have similar greetings. See pp. 76, 89, 100, 107, 125.

[3] See footnote 1 on p. 99 for further comment on the phrase "God and Father of our Lord Jesus Christ."

[4] Paul revisits this topic in 4:9–10, where he presents the exaltation of Jesus by referring to his ascension. In passing, he refers to Jesus descending "into the lower parts of the earth." Although this may be a reference to his becoming human or to his going to Hades, it more likely reflects his death and, particularly, his burial (so Fee, *Pauline Christology,* 358). It is an unnecessarily extended description if it was intended to refer to his living on earth, and there is little evidence that Paul was referring to Hades. Hoehner (*Ephesians,* 530–38) prefers a combination of the incarnation and death of Jesus. Andrew T. Lincoln (*Ephesians* [WBC; Waco: Word, 1990], 244–48) sees it as a reference either to the incarnation or to the descent of the Spirit at Pentecost.

human) is outside Jesus' permanent, sovereign authority and control. Finally, Paul asserts that all things are under Jesus, for he is the head over all (1:22);[5] he dominates them, actively subjecting them to his rule and authority. Although there may be an allusion here to Psalm 8:6, where the psalmist describes God putting "all things under" the feet of human beings, Paul elaborates on this description and presents it in a superlative fashion so that it can only relate to Christ.

Startlingly, Paul then identifies the significance of this information. In addition to providing a christological reflection for his readers, it also offers another opportunity for Paul to highlight the significance of their relationship with Jesus. Regardless of the challenges they face, Christ is in control and no one controls him. Therefore, because of his commitment to them, they can trust him with their lives. Christ, who is superior to all, has taken the central place in the church (1:23)—as a result of which the church manifests his grandeur. Paul concludes with the inexplicable and astounding revelation that the church is the unique beneficiary of *all* of Christ—his resources, person, and presence. In order to present this truth as graphically as possible, with its attendant consequences for lifestyle transformation, Paul precedes it with a portrait of the superlative nature of Jesus, who is above everything and everyone (1:20–22).

The Precious Cornerstone

Paul identifies Jesus' central importance to the church by asserting that he is "the cornerstone" on which the church is built (2:20). The word "cornerstone" is rare and only occurs once in the LXX (Isa 28:16, which is also quoted in 1 Pet 2:6) and never in classical literature. The reference in Isaiah relates it to the foundational stone of a building, and this fits the context well here in Ephesians 2:20, where Paul describes the apostles and prophets as foundation stones for the church. More significantly, however, the cornerstone was the first of the foundation stones to be laid and was the one against which all the other stones in the building were to be aligned or measured. As such, Jesus is the starting point for the church as well as its stabilizing force and the standard to which all the other components must conform.

---

[5] See Hoehner (*Ephesians,* 282–90) for an exhaustive exploration of this verse.

The Beloved Bridegroom

Paul encourages his readers to recognize the integral union between each individual believer and Jesus by asserting that Christ dwells "in your hearts" (3:17). Using other physical metaphors, he continues to impress upon them the close bond between Jesus and the church by calling it "the body of Christ" (4:12, 16; 5:30) and describing Jesus as its "head."[6] Whereas Paul described the church in 2:21 with the static and religious term "temple," the emphasis here is on vitality and dynamic growth. The context suggests that the reference to Jesus being the head of the church probably relates to his being its energizing source and resource, or the goal of its development. He is the one who facilitates growth in the body, enabling it to achieve its potential (4:16).

Later, Paul writes of Christ nourishing (see also 6:4, where the same word is translated "bring up" with reference to raising children) and cherishing the church, using terminology that would indicate that Christ is functioning as a lover of the church (5:29). In 5:31, Paul applies Genesis 2:24, "they become one flesh," referring to the physical relationship between man and woman, to the relationship between the church and Jesus. Rather than reducing this to romantic connotations, the emphasis is on the continuous, loving, dedicated, and personal care Jesus provides for the church. Paul speaks of this as a profound mystery (5:32) and one that is ultimately inexplicable.

The allusion to marriage, with its deep relational properties, is appropriate as a metaphor for the relationship between the church and Jesus because it points to the extremely close union between the two. When Paul quotes from Genesis 2:24 in 1 Corinthians 6:16, he is reminding readers that such a relationship has serious consequences for personal behavior. Here, he is highlighting the intense and intimate care that Jesus offers to his church. Paul seems untroubled by mixing varied metaphors in celebrating the union between the church and Jesus, for his motivation is to assert the unbreakable relationship between them. If Jesus is the leader of the church, Paul says, then it must submit to him (5:24)—freely, but also with dedication.

Paul also asserts Jesus' commitment to prepare the church so that he can present it "to himself in splendor" (5:27). In verses 26–27, Paul combines three purpose clauses, each introduced by "so that" (Gk.

---

[6] 4:15; 5:23; see also 1:21.

hina), which develop a sense of continuity. Jesus has given himself for the church and cleansed it[7] *so that* it might be set apart (consecrated)[8] to him *so that* he can present it to himself in purity *so that* it might be different and glorious. This is the eschatological culmination of the divine plan—that the church be spiritually and morally resplendent. In order for this to occur, Jesus sets it apart to himself and then undertakes to transform it ethically. This is not for the purpose of presenting the church to someone else, but so that he can take it to himself as his possession and for his pleasure. In the ancient world, the practice was that the bride would prepare herself for her bridegroom. Then the bridegroom would join her and present her to her father. Similarly, Jesus (the bridegroom) prepares the bride (the church), so that she can be presented to him. Thereafter, as in 1:18, Paul describes the church as the inheritance of God for his possession.

In Ezekiel 16:1–14, the prophet describes the way God transformed his people, represented by Jerusalem. God washed her with water to cleanse her (16:4), set her apart as "mine" (16:8), and beautified her (16:10–14). Paul uses similar language for the church being chosen, transformed by, and prepared for, Jesus. Although this will reach its consummation in the Parousia, it is a present reality because of the "one flesh" relationship that already exists between Jesus and the church (5:31). It is also a foregone conclusion because of Jesus' dedication to the task. This promise stands in stark contrast to the conclusion of Ezekiel's prophecy, where those who had received so much from God utterly reject him and are consequently judged by God (16:15–52).

The consequences of Paul's christological presentation are many. Because of Jesus' superlative dignity, Paul is prepared to be "a prisoner for Christ Jesus" (3:1; see 4:1). Jesus is worthy of praise and worship (5:20) and of dedication to the transformation of one's character (1:4; 4:15–21). Because Jesus loves the church, Paul says, believers should love others (5:25, 28–30), submit to each other (5:24), and obey those

[7] In the context, the word translated "cleansing" (Gk. *katharizō*) refers to the spiritual, moral cleansing of the church that Jesus achieved in his death and by the proclamation of the gospel (6:17). See Hoehner (*Ephesians*, 750–57) for a full and helpful discussion of the verse.

[8] The word translated "sanctified" (Gk. *hagiazō*) generally means to be set apart or consecrated. It is not fundamentally related to the concept of ongoing sanctification as a life-transforming act but rather to being set apart for a particular vocation or destiny.

in authority (6:5). In particular, they should be united as "one body" because he is "one Lord" (4:3–5).

Transformer and Reconciler

It is difficult to explore Paul's christology without seeing the clear association with his soteriology. From the first few verses of his letter to the Ephesians, Paul points readers to the glorious salvation Jesus provides.

Redeemed in Christ

The NT refers to the concept of redemption ten times, and seven of those references occur in Paul's letters. Redemption has to do with the notion of deliverance and/or a price paid to purchase or release someone or something which results in freedom being granted (4:30). Ephesians 1:7 says that the purchase price is Jesus' blood (2:13). His (sacrificial) death grants believers freedom from, or forgiveness for, their sins (1:7; 4:32). The present tense, "we have redemption," indicates a continual state of being redeemed. Jesus has redeemed believers, and the significance of that act in the past is that it is also continuous. The word Paul uses for forgiveness (Gk. *aphesis*) occurs elsewhere to mean "released" and "forgiven," both of which are appropriate translations in this context also. All of this is the result of a lavish expression of Jesus' unfathomable grace (1:8) and extraordinary, incomprehensible love (3:19; 5:1, 25). This catalogue of blessings has resulted because he has taken the initiative and given himself for others.[9] He has also provided insight into divine mysteries with reference to the will of God (1:9, 10) and has appointed believers to "live for the praise of his glory" (1:12).

Finally, because of what Jesus did, the love of God has been "freely bestowed on us in the Beloved" (1:6)[10] and we are called "his children" (1:5). Paul's use of familial terms, which are also used of Jesus' relationship to his Father, emphasizes the significant honor granted to believers in their relationship with Jesus.

---

[9] 5:25; John 10:11, 15, 17–18.

[10] The phrase "in the Beloved" refers to Jesus only here in the NT. Elsewhere, Paul uses the word "beloved" to refer to believers (Rom 9:25; Col 3:12; 1 Thess 1:4).

Sealed with the Spirit

Jesus has authorized the sealing of believers with the Spirit (1:13), who also functions as their guarantee that they are God's eternal possession (1:14).[11] The one who arranged for this sealing, namely Jesus, owns those who are sealed. Christians living in an increasingly inhospitable society were encouraged to know that God had chosen to own them and had affirmed this by the presence of none other than the Holy Spirit. Paul emphasized that, far from being an impersonal religion worshiping an absent deity, Christianity celebrated the central and eternal presence of the ascended Jesus.

Transformed into His Likeness

From Ephesians 2:1 on, Paul explores the radical change that has occurred in the lives of believers because of their salvation. They have been transferred from spiritual death to spiritual life (2:1, 5). They no longer follow the prince of the power of the air (2:2) but are heirs of Christ's kingdom (5:5). Instead of being influenced by an alien spirit, they are now "in Christ" and their purpose is to achieve "good works" (2:10). They were "children of wrath," but now they are the recipients of God's rich mercy (2:3–4). Jesus has raised up believers to sit "with him in the heavenly places" (2:6, as he also was raised up and sits in the heavenly places [1:20]) and to share all the benefits of such a status. Paul's list of negative concepts describes the isolation of believers before they were in Christ. They were "without Christ . . . aliens . . . strangers . . . having no hope and without God . . . far off," but now they have "been brought near" (2:12–13). They were "darkness, but now . . . are light" (5:8). The transformation is not just from being *in* darkness to living in the light. It is also, more graphically, a transformation from *being* darkness to being light.

Alive in Him

Paul asserts that believers are "in Christ Jesus" (2:7) or "in the Beloved" (1:6). This status entails inestimable benefits for believers, and so it is not surprising that Paul is fond of the phrase "in Christ," for it reflects the position, potential, privileges, and responsibilities of

[11] For more on the concept of "sealing" and the reference to "guarantee," see Warrington, *Discovering the Holy Spirit,* 144–47.

believers. The phrase "in (Jesus) Christ" occurs elsewhere in this letter to the Ephesians,[12] and it refers both to what believers achieve through Christ as well as to the benefits that belong to Christ that they enjoy. Because believers are united with Christ, they are able to benefit from all that he has achieved for them and all that belongs to him.

Gentiles are now "fellow heirs" with Jewish Christians and "sharers in the promise in Christ Jesus" (3:6). The text does not specify exactly what this promise entails, but it is clear that its fulfillment is based on the recipients being "in Christ." The promise probably relates to all that is associated with salvation, summed up in the themes of "this gospel" (3:7), "grace" and "the boundless riches of Christ" (3:8). Furthermore, because of their union with Christ, God manifests his wisdom through the church (3:10) and they have "access to God in boldness and confidence" (3:12). The transfer is complete and comprehensive, and believers are heirs to "immeasurable riches of his grace in kindness toward us in Christ Jesus" (2:7).

Reconciled to God

One of the most significant features of the salvation that Jesus provides is the believer's reconciliation with God. Because of the believer's relationship with Jesus (2:13–14), there is no division between the believer and God. Jesus has not only facilitated peace (2:15) and "proclaimed peace" (2:17), "he is our peace" (2:14). His life, death, and resurrection ended all hostility (2:16). Neither is there division between Jews and Gentiles. Because of Jesus, in association with the Spirit, all believers have access to the presence of God (2:18, 3:12). Paul wants his readers to fully appreciate the implications of their relationship with Jesus. He wants them to learn to experience and enjoy constant fellowship with God and with others, including those from different people groups.[13]

Living in Love

The remarkable salvation Jesus offers has significant consequences. Because believers have experienced such kindness, they should seek to do good works for others (2:7, 10). Ephesians 4–6 recommends many

---

[12] 1:1; 2:6, 7, 10, 13; 3:6, 21.

[13] For more on the significance of the concept of "access" to God (2:18), see Warrington, *Discovering the Holy Spirit,* 148–49.

ways whereby readers can respond practically to the privilege of being Jesus' followers and recipients of his grace. Jesus has granted gifts to believers that he expects them to use and develop (4:7–16). Since "truth is in Jesus" (4:21), believers are to adopt his lifestyle characteristics of integrity and authentic behavior (4:22–32; literally, they are to have "learned Christ" [4:20]). As Jesus forgave them, so believers are to forgive others (4:32). They are to "live in love, as Christ loved us" (5:2) and to "be subject to one another out of reverence for Christ" (5:21; 6:5–6).

All of this also has larger implications for the church. Ephesians 3:21 presents God as the one to whom believers should offer glory "in the church and in Christ Jesus." The church has come into being as a result of God's work through Jesus and is dependent on him while also manifesting his glory. Believers are to praise God for facilitating the birth of the church through Jesus' work. The startling revelation is not that Jesus radiates the glory of God, for Paul has demonstrated this intimate relationship throughout his writings, but that the church should be privileged to show forth the glory of the Godhead.

Giver of Every Spiritual Blessing

In Ephesians 1:3, Paul identifies believers as being "blessed . . . in Christ with every spiritual blessing in the heavenly places." A more appropriate translation than "spiritual blessings" for the Greek phrase *eulogia pneumatikē* is "blessings that are mediated by the Spirit." Believers who are "in Christ" (also 4:32) receive these blessings. Paul is not simply stating that they benefit from spiritual (and thus not necessarily material) blessings. Rather, he is identifying the source of all the blessings—the Spirit. Christ's greatest blessing to believers, the one from whom all other blessings flow, is none other than the Spirit himself. Because of him, they have all they need. Believers receive the Spirit because of their union with, and incorporation in, Christ. Their challenge is to take advantage of the blessing of the Spirit.

The fact that Paul uses the phrase "heavenly places"[14] does not indicate that God will grant these blessings to believers when they enter

---

[14] Paul does not use these two words together elsewhere in his writings, though he does use the phrase on four other occasions in Ephesians (1:20; 2:6; 3:10; 6:12). Ancient cosmology assumed that heaven was the region above the earth where deities existed.

heaven in the afterlife. Rather, Paul is describing present blessings that are associated with heaven; they are not derived from the earth, for their source is heaven. His readers were used to spiritual forces that existed in heavenly places (6:12; see also 2:2). However, service to these gods was often associated with fear because they were assumed to be arbitrary in their dealings with people. As a result, fearful servility to capricious gods was the common experience of many people. Service to Jesus is completely different. Although he is also associated with heavenly places, his legacy to his followers, to those who are "in him," is not fretful uncertainty, but a collection of blessings.

In 4:7, Paul refers to "Christ's gift" to each believer. He does not identify this gift, and it could refer either to Christ, who is the gift, or to a gift that Christ has given. If it is the latter, it could refer to the Spirit, who is Christ's gift to the church and who in turn grants gifts to believers. Here, however, it is more likely to be a reference to Christ himself as the giver of gifts and as the one who determines the measure of the gift to be granted. Although Paul writes of the gifts of the Spirit elsewhere (esp. 1 Cor 12:1–11), here the center of attention is Christ. The verses that follow identify Christ, who has ascended and gives gifts to people (4:8)[15] for the development of the church (4:11), as the fulfillment of Ps 68:18. Paul identifies Jesus' resurrection as an example of God's remarkable power (1:19–20) and, on the basis of this, he deduces that such "immeasurable" power is also available to believers.

In 5:14, Paul identifies Christ as the one who provides light for the believer. Believers are, therefore, light "in the Lord" (5:8). Having once been (in) darkness (5:8), they now own the potential to "live as children of light." The one who is Light facilitates believers to walk in light—with regard to their speech, actions, and thoughts (5:15–16). Jesus is the one who enables believers to "find out what is pleasing to the Lord" (5:10).

The final resource that Paul points out to the believers in Ephesus is the ability through Christ to "come to . . . knowledge of the Son of God" (4:13). The fact that he uses this title "Son of God" when all other references to Jesus in this section are to "Christ" (4:7, 12, 13, 15) is of

---

[15] Paul amends the verse, which in Ps 18:18 reads "receiving gifts from people," to "he gave gifts to his people." This fulfills his purposes in identifying Christ as the one who gave gifts rather than the one who received them. Paul develops this further in the verses that follow. See Hoehner (*Ephesians*, 523–30) for a valuable discussion of Paul's use of Ps 68:18.

interest. It is certainly a thrilling prerogative of believers to be able to engage with the Son of God, and it may be that Paul prefers this phrase here because of its association with the eternal God (see 1:2, 3), whereas the more common reference to Christ may have carried the connotation of the earthly Messiah. The exciting promise to believers is that they can develop knowledge of the Son of God—which is identical to knowledge of God himself.

Conclusion

In this theologically rich exploration of Jesus' personality and saving work, Paul explores the divine dignity and exalted status of the Savior. Jesus is presented as the beloved bridegroom who comes to beautify his bride with salvation. In describing the Lord in this way, Paul seeks to inspire wonder in his readers and to lead them to the highest form of admiration. Additionally, Paul highlights some of the remarkable consequences of the salvation Jesus has provided for believers, including reconciliation with the Father. He clearly is convinced that when his readers are struck with awe at the astonishing nature of their salvation and their relationship with Jesus, ethical transformation and a greater self-awareness of their status as believers will result.

chapter 10

Philippians

Jesus, Humbled to Exalt Others

Paul wrote this affectionate letter towards the end of his life and while in prison, probably in Rome. The original readers were part of the first church he established in Greece (Acts 16:11–40), where he had initially spoken to the Jews at the place of prayer. One of the first converts was Lydia, and thereafter her home became their base. The only exorcism that Acts records in narrative form occurred in Philippi, after which Paul was arrested, flogged, and imprisoned. While Paul was in prison there, God used an earthquake to bring about the conversion of the jailor and his family through Paul's witness. After he was released from prison, Paul returned to Lydia's home and then moved on to Thessalonica.

As in his other letters, Paul's concentration on christology in Philippians is the basis for his appeal to believers to lead transformed lives. In addition to informing them of his situation in prison, he warns them not to adopt or return to Judaism but to stand firm in their faith in the gospel. He thanks them for their gift to him in prison[1] and exhorts them to rejoice in whatever challenges they may face and also to maintain unity.

The Name above All Names

Jesus Is Lord

Again, Paul reiterates here that Jesus and the Father both offer grace and peace (1:2; 4:23). In an expression that is reminiscent of the OT "Day of the Lord," he refers to "the day of Jesus Christ" when the

[1] 1:12–14, 19–26; 2:17; 4:10–20.

salvation of believers will be consummated and final judgment delivered.[2] These references not only exalt Jesus as the one who is central to that day, but they also provide readers with the motivation to be prepared for that occasion when they will be presented to him. Paul identifies Jesus as the goal and prize awaiting believers in the eschaton (3:14).

Humbled and Exalted

The well-known section (2:6–11) which explores the exalted status of Jesus from which he stooped in order to identify with and redeem humanity is worthy of much greater development than is possible in this overview. As we explore the salient elements of these pivotal verses, we will limit ourselves to Christological and soteriological implications.

Paul describes Jesus as being "in the form of God" who "did not count equality with God a thing to be grasped" (2:6, ESV). Precisely because Jesus was God, he did not need to clasp his divinity tightly to himself. The phrase, and especially the rare word "form" (Gk. *morphē*),[3] has been the subject of much discussion. O'Brien summarizes the main options.[4] In this context, the word is less likely to refer to "shape" or "external form" and more probably refers to God's internal characteristics and substantial attributes. This is not only because God has no external form, but also because the word *morphē* was used with these meanings in the ancient world. It is thus best to interpret the word as referring to the divine essence[5] that Jesus enjoyed before the incarnation. Furthermore, the words, "he did not count equality a thing to be grasped"[6] indicate that this status rightly belonged to Jesus. He had

---

[2] 1:6, 10; 2:16. Paul refers to this concept elsewhere as well (1 Cor 5:5; 2 Cor 1:14; 1 Thess 5:2; 2 Thess 2:12).

[3] Outside of Phil 2:6, 7 it only occurs elsewhere in the NT in Mark 16:12. Cognate forms are present in Pauline literature (Rom 2:20; 12:2; 2 Cor 3:18; Gal 4:19; Phil 3:10; 2 Tim 3:5), where the meaning often has to do with "form" or "shape."

[4] Peter T. O'Brien, *The Epistle to the Philippians* (WBC; Waco: Word, 1991), 206–11; see also Gerald F. Hawthorne, *Philippians* (WBC; Waco: Word, 1991), 81–84.

[5] It was that which identified him as God, his "godness." Hawthorne (*Philippians*, 84) says, "outside his human nature Christ had no other manner of existing 'in the form of God,' that is, apart from being in possession of all the characteristics and qualities belonging to God."

[6] The words translated "to be grasped" are an attempt to translate the Greek word *harpagmon*, a rare word not used in the LXX and used only here in the NT. For a full discussion, see N. T. Wright, "ἁρπαγμός and the Meaning of Philippians 2:5–11," *Journal of Theological Studies* 37 (1986): 321–52.

no reason to hold on to it as if it did not belong to him, or for fear that it might be taken from him. Although many take advantage of their positions to achieve selfish ambitions, Jesus, who owned the highest status, chose not to do so. Instead, he gave to others in order to save them, despite the cost to himself.

As a result of his willing humiliation, service, and death, God "highly exalted him" (2:9). This exaltation is not a reward, nor is it indicative of a divine law that all who are humbled will be exalted. Rather, it is reassigning to Jesus that which already belonged to him. He had previously been exalted, and after completing his mission of salvation God the Father welcomed him back to the place of supremacy. The description "highly exalted" does not indicate that God assigned him a status superior to that which he previously enjoyed. Rather, since he was in the form of God and therefore enjoyed the most prestigious position, this expresses the fact that not only has Jesus been (re)-exalted, but to the highest location imaginable. This supreme location belongs to God alone (Ps 97:9), and now Jesus shares that position once again.

In his exaltation Jesus received a special name, one that is "above every name" (2:9).[7] This most probably refers to the name that identifies him with the highest status available, that which is also enjoyed by God.[8] The name above every other name is God's name (Exod 3:13–15). The title "Lord" is thus an appropriate appellation for Jesus (2:11). The NT often refers to Jesus as "Lord," even though (and probably because) the OT uses the title to refer to God (see esp. Isa 42:8, "I am the LORD, that is my name; my glory I give to no other"). The ancient world understood that a person's name was invested with the qualities and character of the name bearer. Calling Jesus "Lord," therefore, assumes that Jesus owns the properties associated with such a name.

The evidence of the superlative authority that Jesus owns is that every created being will be obliged to honor him as "Lord."[9] Again, an OT text (Isa 45:23) that refers to God describes Jesus here (2:11). It is important to recognize that this is not merely a prospect for the future but an astonishing statement concerning the current status of Jesus who, although he functioned as a man for thirty-three years, now

---

[7] Fee (*Pauline Christology*, 397) refers to it as "*the* name-above-every-other-name Name."

[8] Thus, even though "Jesus" is the name ascribed in 2:10, it is unlikely that this is the title intended by Paul as, in itself, it did not represent divine, supreme dignity.

[9] 1:2; 2:11; 3:1, 8; 4:1, 4.

reigns supreme. His authority is such that everyone and everything is subservient to him. He is truly the Lord.

Because of Jesus' exalted status, Paul is prepared to be his servant (1:1), endure imprisonment for him (1:13), count everything else "as loss" for him (3:7), and share "his sufferings" (3:10). Similarly, Paul says that Epaphroditus is prepared to die "for the work of Christ" (2:30). In partnership with himself, Paul encourages his readers also to be prepared to suffer for Jesus (1:29–30; 3:10) and to boast "in Christ Jesus" when they experience joy (1:26), as part of their ongoing experience as believers (3:3). The word translated "boast" (Gk. *kauchēma*) often refers to the basis or content of one's boasting. Jesus, Paul says, is the one of whom believers should feel proud. It is appropriate to boast about who Jesus is and what he has done.[10]

Emptied in the Incarnation

Supreme Self-Sacrifice

Paul refers to Christ as the subject of the gospel (1:15, 17, 18, 27). He graphically portrays Jesus' sacrifice when he describes how Jesus, being "in the form of God" (2:6), voluntarily "emptied himself" (Gk. *ekenōsen*, 2:7). Commentators have endlessly sought to plumb the depths of such a selfless act on Jesus' part. What is at stake is the extent to which Jesus emptied himself, whether Paul intended this to be understood literally or metaphorically, and what it was that Jesus was divesting.[11]

One of the main interpretations relates to the possibility that Jesus divested himself of some divine attributes (such as omnipresence, omniscience, glory, or majesty), or that they remained latent during his incarnation. Fee sounds a note of caution, however: "Historically, far

[10] See also 1 Cor 1:31; 2 Cor 10:17. Both of these passages quote Jer 9:24, which refers to God.

[11] On the basis that 4 of the 5 verses that use the Greek word *kenosis* (Rom 4:14; 1 Cor 1:17; 9:15; 2 Cor 9:5) are clearly metaphorical, O'Brien (*Philippians*, 217) argues for the latter here also. He identifies the main possible interpretations: Jesus gave up the form of God; he allowed himself to be subjected to demonic powers; he functioned as the Servant of the Lord; he became the righteous sufferer; or he became a slave/servant to God. O'Brien critiques each of these possibilities and concludes that the latter is closest to the truth (217–24).

too much has been made of the verb, as though, in becoming incarnate, he literally 'emptied himself' *of something*."[12] A metaphorical interpretation of the verb removes the need for this kind of speculation, which the NT does not confirm elsewhere. Furthermore, any link between the words "emptied himself" and "the form of God" is most unlikely, given the literary separation in the flow of the passage. The Gospels present Jesus functioning in divine power over demons and sickness and portray him as possessing a status and authority that were previously attributed exclusively to God. The Gospel narratives, therefore, do not reflect Jesus emptying himself of divinity.

It is possible that, as Hawthorne says,[13] Paul is describing Jesus as "pouring out himself" in an act of self-humiliation. In other words, Paul may be asserting that Jesus put others before himself when he was, in truth, before all others in time and precedence. Thus, he became a servant so that others could have freedom; he became a child of humanity so that others could become children of God; he died so that others could have life; he went to the cross so that others could go to heaven. Thus, it is probable that Paul is describing Jesus' divine selflessness, and not a self-emptying of any element of his divine being.

Given Jesus' high status (equality with God) in 2:6 and his different lifestyle (the form of a servant) in 2:7, it is clear that Paul is exploring the momentous step down that Jesus took to become a servant (Gk. *doulos*, literally "a slave").[14] It is possible that Paul was describing Jesus as a servant to God the Father in achieving the divine agenda (Heb 10:7), but practically, in so doing, he also became a servant to humanity, and specifically to the people to whom he ministered. In becoming a servant, Jesus added an activity to his previous experience. Remarkably, and inconceivably, the process of redemption resulted in a fundamental change in the Godhead. The Creator added a new dimension of servanthood of those he had created. Certainly Paul's original readers would have understood the concept of "slavery," and the complete loss of rights by the one enslaved. This portrayal of Jesus makes an astonishing statement: he willingly accepted this demeaning status and, while

---

[12] Fee, *Pauline Christology,* 384 (italics original).

[13] Hawthorne, *Philippians,* 85–86; Gk. *ekenōsen* may mean "poured out" as well as "emptied."

[14] Fee (*Pauline Christology,* 386) cautions against assuming that Paul is identifying Jesus as the slave of the Lord, since this would be the only place one would find such a definition of Jesus' relationship to God in his writings.

he continued to possess a divine nature, he chose to live as a servant instead of as a sovereign.

Paul clarifies that this act of self-abnegation, manifested in his being a servant, involved his taking the form[15] of a human being and dying as a criminal on a cross (2:7–8; 3:18). This verse identifies Jesus as a human being who bore resemblance to others, though the word "likeness" (Gk. *homoiōma*) clarifies that there were differences. It does not mean that Jesus was not fully human or that he merely resembled a man. Neither was he simply a copy of a man, for he was incarnated completely as a man. Paul is attempting to put into words that which is ultimately inexplicable—Jesus, who is at all times God, also, at a moment in time, becomes man. He was similar to people in that he became a human being, but he was dissimilar in that he remained God. His obedience to the plan of salvation, which involved his incarnation and death, as well as his acceptance of the manner of that death, which was degrading, shameful crucifixion,[16] are evidence of his servanthood. Jesus was born to die, and he was a willing participant in that divine agenda. The cross was not an accident. The only one who could bring about spiritual freedom freely entered into enslavement to accomplish it. In enabling believers to achieve the highest place possible, Jesus plummeted to the lowest position imaginable.

Owned by the Savior

Again in Philippians, as elsewhere in his writings, Paul defines the believers' central position "in" Christ.[17] This refers to the believer's intimate union with Christ. Using different terminology to affirm the same fact, he asserts, "Christ Jesus has made me his own" (3:12). In this verse, Paul uses the same word twice and a cognate form once. "Not that I have already obtained (Gk. *lambanō*) this or have already reached the goal; but I press on to make (Gk. *katalambanō*) it my own,

---

[15] The word translated "form" (Gk. *skēma*) in v. 7b occurs only here and 1 Cor 7:31 (and once in the LXX, Isa 3:17); it refers to the outward form or shape of that which it refers to, here relating to the outward appearance of a man.

[16] O'Brien (*Philippians,* 230) writes, "Here the rock bottom of Jesus' humiliation was reached." Crucifixion was administered to slaves and to the worst of criminals. It was associated not only with massive pain, but also with cruel humiliation. The Jews linked crucifixion with divine curse (Deut 21:22–23). Cicero famously recommended that even the word "cross" should be far removed from the mind of a Roman (*Pro Rabiro* 5. 10, 16).

[17] 1:1, 14; 3:9; 4:21.

because Christ Jesus has made (*katalambanō*) me his own." The term *katalambanō* often refers to the acts of taking (Isa 10:14) or grasping (Job 5:13; 1 Thess 5:4), while *lambanō* is a very common word meaning "I take." The context determines if the action of "taking" is hostile or friendly, but the word implies a force on the part of the one taking the initiative. So although Paul has not yet *owned* the prize that awaits him, he is determined to *own* it and is confident that this will happen because Jesus has chosen to *own* him first. Using these words enables Paul to confirm that any divinely promised goal is achievable because Jesus partners with believers so that they can attain that which would otherwise be out of their reach. Paul graphically expresses Jesus' unconditional, unilateral expression of love, and again the soteriological challenge is clear. The result is that he is "straining forward," "forgetting" the past. He is determined to "press on toward the goal for the prize of the heavenly call of God in Christ Jesus" (3:13–14), and he encourages his readers to follow his example (3:15).

The notion of belonging to Christ and benefiting from his astonishing act of salvation has ethical consequences. Thus, because of their status "in Christ," believers should exhibit a deep love for others and humility (2:1–2, 5). They are to reflect this in the way they welcome and honor Epaphroditus (2:29), in developing friendship and reconciliation between Euodia and Syntyche (4:2), and in their greeting of every believer (4:21). Fundamentally, Paul's ambition is to honor Christ at all times (1:20), not to shame him, and to concentrate on those issues of importance to him (2:21).

Intimately Related to Jesus

Paul desires to "be with Christ," a phrase that is unique to Paul here.[18] He describes being with Christ as "far better" (1:23)[19] but operates on the basis that "to live is Christ" (1:21). In other words, his

---

[18] See similar references in 2 Cor 4:14; 13:4; Col 2:13, 20; 3:4; 1 Thess 4:17; 5:10. See O'Brien (*Philippians,* 130–37) for a full exploration of the concept. Paul could be referring to his being spatially with Christ, but he is more likely referring to being in relationship with Christ—a relationship that will be enhanced after the limitations of this life have been removed.

[19] Here Paul offers two Greek comparative adverbs—*mallon kreissōn* (lit., "more better") in order to accentuate the superlative option of being with Christ in comparison with any other.

relationship with Christ dominates his life. Christ is his motivation, his inspiration, and his goal. Furthermore, Paul reveals that a fundamental consequence of believers following Jesus is that they are granted the opportunity to know him (3:8, 10). Although the concept of knowledge (Gk. *gnōsis*) was common in the Greco-Roman world and referred to intellectual achievement and the value of knowledge in philosophical apprehension of religious ideas, Paul is more likely taking advantage of the meaning of the term as it relates to his Jewish background. There, it related to the knowledge that God had of his people, which was equated with his choosing them (Exod 33:12) and their experiential relationship with him (Jer 31:34). Similarly, Paul anticipates that an intimate relationship with Jesus is available to believers, based on his love for them.

Jesus also enables them to resource the power (Gk. *dynamis*) that is available to him—the supernatural power that resulted in his being resurrected (3:10). It is possible that Paul is referring to the power of resurrection that awaits believers at the end of their earthly lives. Although this may be part of it, however, it is more likely that he is also referring to the dynamic power available to believers in this life (as in Eph 1:19–20). In an unusual reference, Paul describes "the Spirit of Jesus Christ" helping him (1:19). Elsewhere he describes the Spirit as "the Spirit of God."[20] Paul does not explain the phrase, one that he has used elsewhere,[21] but assumes that it is an acceptable reference for the Spirit.

Readers should not assume that the Spirit belongs to Jesus or that they are one and the same. Paul links both persons of the Trinity naturally and without explanation. He has no difficulty in associating the two, for they own equivalent authority. Therefore, although there is a difference in identity, there is significant interdependence between them. Paul's language may be best appreciated if one remembers that he is writing primarily in a pastoral role, and not as a systematic theologian. He informs his readers that the one who will function as their helper is none other than the Spirit who partnered with Jesus when he was on earth. In 2:13, he asserts that "God . . . is at work in" believers. The fact is that each person of the divine triad is fully committed to the believer. Paul does not feel the need to identify the different responsibilities of each of the persons of the Trinity with regard to the development of believers, for their ministry cannot be easily fragmented and

---

[20] Rom 8:9; see Gal 3:18; 4:6.

[21] Rom 8:9; 2 Cor 3:17; Gal 4:6.

deciphered. Paul's central message is not to distinguish who does what but to emphasize that each one is fully committed to all believers and that together they work tirelessly to resource and transform them.

Paul also attributes to God the authority to provide that which believers need, based on "his riches in glory in Christ Jesus" (4:19). The clearest expression of God's lavish giving is Jesus, who, in his person and in his mission, sums up all the wealth of God. Since Jesus is united with believers, they are able to benefit from his unique resources. Paul describes his wealth in terms of glory, a word that reaches its fullest expression in association with God. God is the most exquisite of all beings, and that which is integral to him is uniquely glorious. God's glory is that which identifies him and marks him as different to all others. Because of Jesus, believers can benefit from God's inexhaustible being both in this life and in the next. Paul therefore identifies Christ as the one who increases his capacity to love others (1:8) and also enables him to live a righteous lifestyle (1:11). Hope and confidence are available to believers because of their relationship with Jesus (2:19, 24), as are joy (3:1; 4:4) and peace (4:7).

Not only is a consummated relationship with Jesus the apex of Paul's aspirations, but that same Jesus who is "Savior"[22] and "Lord" will take the initiative and "transform the body of our humiliation that it may be conformed to the body of his glory" (3:21). Here, Paul elevates Jesus by identifying this eschatological authority as belonging to him while at the same time reminding readers that this is their destiny. Jesus will deliver them from the weakness of the physical form and will destroy those who have rejected them (3:19–21). Although believers are "being saved," there will come a time when the process of salvation will be completed—when Jesus returns.

Conclusion

Again a deeper appreciation of the person of Jesus helps to inform the readers of the supreme dignity of their Savior, the personal cost of

[22] The only other place in Pauline literature where this occurs is in Eph 5:23. It was of particular value to readers who were used to the title being ascribed to the Caesar who, though claiming to be a deliverer, was no match for that role in contrast to Jesus. At the same time, as Fee (*Pauline Christology,* 403) notes, Jesus is given the same title as that which belonged to God (Deut 32:15; Ps 25:5).

the salvation he has procured for others, the unilateral nature of his self-sacrifice, and the inexplicable love that motivated his mission. In order to protect his readers from reverting to Judaism, succumbing to temptation, or sliding from their commitment to Christ, Paul reminds them of the remarkable sacrifice of Jesus on their behalf that makes even his imprisonment as a Christian pale into insignificance.

chapter 11

Colossians

Jesus, Fullness of God

It appears that Paul did not establish the church at Colossae (1:4; 2:1). According to the evidence of the letter itself, few if any of the Colossian Christians were Jews; it is clear that they were predominantly, if not exclusively, Gentiles. Yet Paul became involved with the church as a result of a heresy that threatened to undermine the church's understanding of the person of Jesus. Some were teaching that people could only gain salvation by adopting practices that included Jewish rituals (circumcision, diet laws, and the observance of special days). The focus of Paul's letter to the Colossian church, therefore, is Jesus and his exalted status.

God Incarnate

United with the Father

At the beginning of the letter Paul describes God as "the Father of our Lord Jesus Christ" (1:3). Jesus is also the one who channels thanksgiving to the Father (3:17). It is not that Jesus is merely a conduit through whom gratitude streams to God the Father. Far from Jesus being in an inferior position, this is a confirmation of Jesus' proximity to the Father. Jesus and the Father receive praise simultaneously. Jesus is not the servant presenting praise on a plate to the Father but the one who enjoys receiving it with the Father. After all, Paul has just identified "the name of the Lord Jesus" as the basis for all Christian activity (3:17), and Jesus is associated with glory (1:27; 3:4), an attribute that is most often associated with God.

Creator God

In 1:15–20, Paul provides a detailed description of Jesus that elevates him to such a height that there can be no doubt he is portraying him as God. In the verses before this portrait, however, he reminds readers that Jesus owns "the kingdom"[1] and is the "beloved Son" (1:13). Paul's purpose in this depiction is to identify Jesus' precedence and supremacy over everyone and everything else. Paul deliberately uses language, therefore, that is normally associated with God and clearly identifies Jesus' central role as motivator and fulfiller of God's plan of salvation.

He calls Jesus "the image of the invisible God" (1:15). Second Corinthians 4:4 also explores this notion of Jesus being the image (Gk. *eikōn*) of God. Further, Paul describes Jesus as "the firstborn of all creation" (1:15), an image Paul uses in Romans 8:29 as well. In both contexts, the emphasis is on precedence, not primogeniture. He is stating that Jesus is supreme over creation, not that he is the first created thing.

Paul further explains his description of Jesus as "the firstborn of all creation" by asserting that "in him all things . . . were created . . . through him and for him" (1:16). The phrase "in him" could refer to the notion that creation was caused by him or that it depends on him. Clearly, Paul is not saying that creation exists spatially inside Jesus. Rather, he is stating that nothing else exists without Christ's involvement in its creation and in sustaining it to its appointed end. He is not a distant creator, nor is he an absent landlord. Rather, he is intimately involved with his creation. Furthermore, Paul reveals, "in him all things hold together" (1:17). Creation completely depends on Jesus, who gives it coherence and continuity. He is not just a divine architect or cosmic designer but the very basis of creation's existence and destiny. He initiated creation, but he is also the one for whom everything was created and the goal of creation as well. Because he is the Creator and therefore precedes creation (1:17; "he is the beginning," 1:18), he is superior to everything he has created.

Paul repeats the fact that Jesus is the Creator twice in verse 16 and also stresses that he is the Creator of "all" (a word used 6 times in

[1] Although elsewhere the NT describes the kingdom as "the kingdom of God," here Paul refers to it as belonging (also) to Jesus. The NT does not often say that the kingdom belongs to Christ (Matt 13:41; 25:31), though it is of interest that in Eph 5:5, which refers to "the kingdom of Christ and of God," Paul asserts that it belongs to them both.

1:15–20). He develops this concept in 1:16, where he demonstrates that Jesus created everything that has ever existed. People and powers, friends and foes, visible and invisible—all are part of the creation that Jesus initiated, controls, and supervises. Jesus' involvement in creation demonstrates his divinity, since creation is an act of God.[2]

The Fullness of God

In 1:18, he adds the phrase "from the dead" (see also Rev 1:5). The implication is not, of course, that Jesus was the first person to be raised from the dead since he himself raised people from the dead in the course of his ministry. The idea is that he is a pioneer, the first to be raised by God to a new era and existence. Whereas every other person who was raised from the dead subsequently died, Jesus' resurrection is eternal and therefore vastly superior. God raised him from the dead so that he might be manifested as having "first place" (1:18).

Paul asserts that "in him all the fullness of God was pleased to dwell" (1:19; 2:9–10). Jesus' status and person are so exalted, he says, that in his incarnate form, Jesus expressed all of God's character. He is the face of God who comprehensively radiates God. When God wanted to visit humanity, he came as Jesus. While many in the Greco-Roman world assumed that divinity existed in creation, including in people, Paul clarifies that God dwelled uniquely in Jesus. Because God cannot be truly revealed in anyone other than himself, Jesus was the authentic reflection of God. He radiates God's being with integrity, accuracy, and completeness because he is none other than God. Jesus is, indeed, the repository of "all the treasures of wisdom and knowledge" (2:3). He is the source for all wisdom and he is intimately involved with believers. Each of them, therefore, is able to tap those divine resources. The OT associated such wisdom uniquely with God, but now Paul asserts that Jesus is also the source of all wisdom.

The Head of the Church

Paul also describes Jesus as "the head of the body, the church" (1:18). The metaphors "head" and "body" demonstrate that Jesus is as important to the church as the head is to a physical body. The church depends

[2] Gen 1:1; Job 38:1–42:6; Isa 33:6.

on him and benefits from his supreme resources and power. The fact that the one who created everything is particularly enamored with the church emphasizes the fundamental significance of the church. In 2:10, Paul also identifies Jesus as "the head of every ruler and authority." His supremacy extends beyond the church to everything.

Paul's assertions in Colossians concerning Jesus' preeminence seem to confer a new dignity upon Jesus' servants. With a solemn sense of calling Paul identifies himself as an "apostle of Christ Jesus" (1:1), Epaphras as a "minister of Christ" (1:7) and "servant of Christ Jesus" (4:12), and Tychicus as a "minister, and a fellow servant in the Lord" (4:7). He also mentions that Archippus has been granted a "task . . . in the Lord" (4:17). Each of them functions with integrity in the church because of what Jesus has achieved for them (4:1). Thus, Paul prays that his readers will "lead lives worthy of the Lord" (1:10), serving (3:23, 24) and pleasing him as their model and mentor (1:10; 3:20).

Christ the Victor

United with Believers

Again, here in Colossians, Paul uses his favored term to refer to believers as being "in Christ" (1:2; also "in the Lord" [3:18], and "with him" [2:13, 20; 3:3, 4]). The point is that their sphere of existence is in relation to, and with, him in an intimate union. Their behavior should reflect this central truth about their identity "in Christ." Paul also reverses the metaphor and describes Christ as being in them,[3] his presence being the guarantee that they will experience his glory. They have "received Christ Jesus the Lord" (2:6) and, although it is difficult to conceptualize, Paul is declaring the divine immanence in believers. They cannot be anywhere other than in the presence of Jesus or he in them. This applies not only to the gathered community or corporate church but to the individual believer as well. Their salvation is based on their "faith in Christ Jesus" (1:4; 2:5). When Paul asserts that Jesus is "your life" (3:4) he is characterizing this intimate relationship that believers enjoy with Jesus. The life of Jesus pulsates through believers—they breathe the same spiritual breath.

---

[3] 1:27; see also Rom 8:10; 2 Cor 13:5; Gal 2:20.

Transforming Believers

Paul also lists some of the consequences of salvation. Because of Jesus, believers are continually experiencing renewal (3:10). Jesus has "rescued" them "from the power of darkness" (1:13) and "transferred" them "into the kingdom of his beloved Son" (1:13). The diabolical authority of darkness no longer dominates them as believers experience a life enveloped by love.

Believers have received a superior "circumcision" to that of the Jews in the old covenant (an act which confirmed their membership in the people of God) through Jesus' death (2:11).[4] They have been "buried with him in baptism" (2:12)[5] and "raised with him" (2:12; 3:1).[6] Although previously they were spiritually "dead in trespasses," God made them "alive together with him" (2:13).[7] God has cancelled the legal accusations of guilt against them (2:14). Paul graphically describes these allegations being nailed to the cross, as if their proximity to the place where Jesus died results in their automatic and immediate removal.[8] Such a description of the salvation Jesus procured demands not only a greater appreciation of his dignity but also of his demands on his disciples.

Forgiving Believers

As a result of what Jesus achieved, believers have been redeemed, or released (1:14), and have received forgiveness (1:14; 2:13). Although

---

[4] Paul contrasts the act of physical circumcision, which resulted in a Jewish boy being welcomed officially as a member of God's community, with God welcoming believers into the new covenant community as a result of Jesus' death. That which people once achieved, God has replaced with a brand-new and superior surgery of initiation "without hands."

[5] This is probably a reference to water baptism, though it is related to the union with Jesus that is symbolized by baptism rather than indicating that baptism itself brings about such union with Jesus. Rather than an exposition of the significance of water baptism, this is part of a list of graphic and memorable metaphors which indicate the intimate relationship with Jesus that believers enjoy.

[6] Again, this reference to sharing in Jesus' resurrection is a vivid way of expressing the fact that believers benefit from all that Jesus achieved when he was raised from the dead; it is as if they died and rose with him.

[7] The word translated "made alive together with him" (Gk. *sunezōpoieō*) only occurs elsewhere in Eph 2:5. The sense is more that believers share Jesus' life than that Jesus grants them life or gives them his life.

[8] There may be an allusion here to the practice of attaching to their crosses the crimes of those crucified (John 19:20). There may also be an echo of the ancient practice of writing down one's debts. The script was destroyed once the debt had been paid.

forgiveness was central to Jewish belief, the forgiveness that Jesus provides is superior, for on the basis of his forgiveness believers can enjoy a relationship with him and benefit from his resources. The fact that Paul does not mention repentance here is perhaps because he assumes its presence in the process of granting and receiving forgiveness. It could also be that Paul is emphasizing Jesus' grace in granting forgiveness and redemption, rather than focusing on the activity of the individual concerned. That which is remarkable is not that forgiveness should follow repentance but that forgiveness should be granted at all.

Reconciling Believers

Having clarified Jesus' divine supremacy, Paul states that God, through Jesus, has reconciled everything to himself (1:20). Because of Jesus' supreme excellence, believers may confidently place their faith in the one who has promised to grant them salvation. It is not a mere human being or even an angel who has facilitated the process of salvation, but God himself in the person of Jesus. The one with whom believers need to reconcile is the one who initiates it. Since Jesus created all things and all things were created for him, he has also made reconciliation with God possible.

Believers who were once "estranged and hostile" and "doing evil deeds" (1:21) have now been reconciled (1:22). Paul says that the act of reconciliation that Jesus' death achieved established "peace through the blood of his cross" (1:20). One man's death has resulted in cosmic harmony. Jesus' death has replaced the clamoring cry of "guilty" with peace, the noise of hostility and opposition with tranquility and friendship. In some ancient texts, 1:21 reads "he has now reconciled [you]" while others read "you have now been reconciled."[9] Either reading gives the believer cause for rejoicing. The miracle is not only that believers have been reconciled, but also that the one who was estranged from them is

---

[9]The reference to Jesus reconciling "to himself all things" has been the cause of much discussion. Paul's wording makes it clear that Jesus' reconciling role is comprehensive. Some suggest that even the physical creation, which originally existed in its entirety in relationship and harmony with God and reflected his beauty and perfection, will be reconciled in the eschaton as a result of Jesus' death (see Peter T. O'Brien, *Colossians, Philemon* [WBC; Waco: Word, 1982], 53–57, for a discussion of this issue). However we are to understand this passage, we should be impressed, as Paul was, by the comprehensiveness of Jesus' work in making all things new. Thus, in the final act of the drama of the world, Jesus will provide an outcome of cosmic perfection.

the very one who has achieved that reconciliation. Indeed, the Father and the Son, who are equal in essence, have completed that process together.

Victorious over Evil

While believers have accrued benefits, Jesus has also achieved cosmic victory in that he has "disarmed" "rulers and authorities" (2:15), and when he returns in triumph, believers will appear with him (3:4). The event that 2:15 refers to is probably Jesus' death. Using different metaphors, Paul affirms that Jesus completed this conquest. Not only did he meet these malevolent powers[10] and disarm them,[11] he also humiliated[12] them publicly and defeated them. Jesus has exposed them for what they are—inferior, evil, and powerless in his presence. All of this Jesus achieved in his death (1:22) on the cross (2:14). A death that appeared to be a confirmation of abject failure and humiliating weakness was, in reality, the remarkable means whereby Jesus manifested his divine and supreme authority over all that might try to stand against him. Humiliation awaits all those who seek to humble him.

Not only do believers benefit from the actions of Christ on their behalf, but they are also so intimately united with him that they are no longer bound to the malignant powers that controlled them in the past (2:20). Jesus gained victory over these powers, and so in Christ they participate in that victory.

Saving to the End

Paul also has an eye to the future, however, because what Jesus achieved has an eschatological objective. The aim of this process has been to present believers "holy and blameless and irreproachable" (1:22) and "mature" to Jesus (1:28). Christ is the fulfillment, or "substance," of all that awaits the believer (2:17). In particular, when he appears in

---

[10]2:8, 20; Gal 4:3. Although Paul does not clarify his use of this term, he is probably referring to spiritual, diabolic powers that were manifested in those people who opposed him and that sought to keep people in bondage. Jesus gained a dramatic and total victory over them. For further discussion of the identity of these powers, see O'Brien, *Colossians, Philemon,* 129–32.

[11]The Gk. term *apechduō* often means "disrobe" or "strip."

[12]The Gk. word *deigmatizō* is often translated "to disgrace" or "to shame."

the eschaton he will provide not only fullness of life but also glory to believers (3:4). Every believer will also embrace the glorious existence available only to Jesus as God.

Once again here Paul makes it clear that christological statements have practical soteriological consequences. The exalted Lord who died as a perfect sacrifice did so with the intention of transforming those who believed in him and transferring his blamelessness to them. Not only has Jesus borne the punishment of their sin in his death, but he also transfers his purity to them at the moment they decide to follow him. One of the many benefits of their relationship with Jesus is that they can also experience his peace (3:15). His words provide them with wisdom and are the basis of their thanksgiving (3:16). Such facts have ethical consequences, not least because believers now exist in a community that excludes no class or race (3:11). Thus, the fact that "the Lord has forgiven" them means that they also "must forgive" (3:13). Having received the peace that Jesus provides, they are to behave peacefully (3:15). Since "the word of Christ" dwells in them, they are to teach one another wisely (3:16) and praise God with thankfulness. Having "received Christ," they are to "live . . . in him" (2:6). Having "been raised with Christ," they are to "seek the things that are above" (3:1). They are to no longer engage in behavior that is inappropriate for believers and instead take on attributes that reflect Jesus, especially love (3:5–14).

His salvation enables Paul to rejoice in his sufferings because they become opportunities to more closely identify with Jesus and his sufferings. His intimate relationship with Jesus is such that he views his personal suffering as sharing in "Christ's afflictions" (1:24). Even prison has become a venue for declaring the "mystery of Christ" (4:3). It is as if he was suffering along with Jesus in his anguish on behalf of the church.[13] Paul is writing metaphorically, yet the truth behind the metaphor provides a powerful perspective on Christian suffering.

It does not indicate that Jesus' sufferings were somehow inadequate to achieve salvation. Rather, Paul is teaching that those who follow in

---

[13]This notion has caused much discussion (see O'Brien, *Colossians, Philemon*, 77–81). It is unlikely that Paul is suggesting that Jesus' actual sufferings are somehow also being expressed in his life in a mystical sense. Rather, he is probably reflecting his close relationship with Jesus in that he emulates Christ in a number of respects in his life, including suffering for his mission. Elsewhere, he graphically and metaphorically refers to his dying in, and being crucified with, Christ (Rom 6:3–11; 2 Cor 4:10–12; Gal 2:20) as well as to suffering with Jesus (Rom 8:17; Phil 3:10).

Christ's footsteps and proclaim his message throughout the world will experience suffering, as he himself did. Paul heard the Lord ask him on the way to Damascus, "Why do you persecute me?" (Acts 9:4). Although believers were the ones suffering at Paul's hands, Jesus felt their pain as if it was his. Jesus identified with their sufferings. It is a remarkable but challenging privilege that believers can be involved in the divine drama of salvation that Jesus initiated. This opportunity will bring pleasure but also pain, satisfaction but also suffering, achievement but also anguish.

Conclusion

In Colossians, Paul again portrays Jesus as the supreme deity who chose to redeem and reconcile people who were hopelessly destined for a life without God. By uniting believers with himself, Jesus provided them with the hope of transformation and eternal life. The concise description of Jesus as God in 1:15–20 provides the backdrop to this comprehensive salvation. Any teaching that undermines the integrity or divinity of Jesus is to be rejected. Because of his superlative status, he alone enables believers to enjoy a dynamic relationship with God; he alone has the authority to facilitate such a friendship.

chapter 12

1 and 2 Thessalonians

Jesus, Coming King

The letters to the Thessalonians, dated around twenty years after Jesus' death, might be the earliest NT material to have been written. The first verse of each letter records Paul, Silvanus, and Timothy as the writers. Paul clearly was involved in writing the letters and it seems certain that he approved of both of them.[1] Both letters were probably sent less than a year after the establishment of the church in Thessalonica.[2]

The book of Acts records that Paul had preached to the Thessalonians about Christ's death and resurrection (Acts 17:1–3). There was a significant Jewish community in the city with its own synagogue, although many of the believers were Gentiles (1 Thess 1:9).

The letters are mainly a defense in response to those who opposed Paul's teaching or questioned his courage (2:3–6, 9–10) after he had left the city when opposition occurred (Acts 17:10). Paul also wished to encourage believers in the face of the persecution they were now facing.[3] Because he had been with them for such a short time (Acts 17:2), they needed more teaching. One focus of this instruction is Jesus' return (1 Thess 4:13–5:14; 2 Thess 2:1–12), but these letters also address social responsibility (2 Thess 3:6–15), unity (1 Thess 5:13, 15), practical godliness (1 Thess 4:1–8), and leadership (1 Thess. 4:9–12; 5:12–13). Despite his initial fears concerning their response to persecution and opposition, he is pleased to hear from Timothy of their progress. Their

[1] The first-person singular pronoun occurs throughout (1 Thess 3:5; 5:27; 2 Thess 2:5) and, on two occasions, the name "Paul" accompanies it (1 Thess 2:18; 2 Thess 3:17).

[2] Because the letters were sent in the same time period and because of their similar christological content, this book will explore their contents together.

[3] 1 Thess 1:6–7; 2:14–16; 3:1–5; 2 Thess. 1:5–12; 3:3–5.

faith requires complementing rather than correction.[4] He also notes his pleasure with them in 2:14 and commends them as examples to others in their capacity to love (1:3; 4:9–12).

The Returning Lord

The Lord Himself

Paul's description of Jesus' exalted nature perhaps reaches its pinnacle when he refers to believers being called to experience the glory of God (1 Thess 2:12) and also of Jesus (2 Thess 2:14). He does not differentiate between them as if one form of glory were superior to the other. Because Jesus is divine, the two glories are essentially the same. Similarly, Paul refers to the gospel as being "of God"[5] and "of Christ."[6] It is the same gospel and it derives from God and Christ. Both are centrally involved in its initiation and provision. It is not that Jesus dies on God's behalf. Jesus dies as God. It is not that God sends Jesus to die. Jesus, as God, chooses to die. Instead of thinking that Jesus died on the cross while God watched from heaven, it is more appropriate to recognize that Jesus, as God incarnate, died while angels watched and wondered.

Paul describes the events that surround Jesus' return (1 Thess 2:19) in a way that is reminiscent of OT passages that refer to God returning to deliver his people. Rather than send angels (Matt 24:31), Jesus himself (note the emphatic "the Lord himself") will lead the heavenly entourage to collect believers who are alive (1 Thess 4:16). That this meeting will occur in the clouds (1 Thess 4:17) is a clear reference to a divine appearing. The manner of Jesus' coming, associated with God's work in the past, encourages readers to ascribe divinity to him.[7] Paul also notes that Jesus' descent from heaven (the Parousia[8]) will be majestic,

---

[4] 3:6–10, 12; 4:1, 10.

[5] 1 Thess 2:2, 8, 9; 3:2; 5:13.

[6] 1 Thess 3:2; 2 Thess 1:8; also Rom 15:19; Gal 1:7; Phil 1:27.

[7] Clouds were associated with a revelation of God (Exod 19:16; 40:34) or with a message from God (Matt 17:5). In particular, in Dan 7:13 clouds signal the coming of the Son of Man. Jesus, who ascended in a cloud, would return in the clouds at the Parousia (Matt 24:30).

[8] "Parousia" is a term often used to refer to the "coming" or "appearing" of a dignitary. When an important person was expected in the ancient world, people would go out of their city to meet, welcome, and usher him back into the city (as with Paul in Acts 28:15). What is sensational about the picture that Paul paints here is that Jesus is

accompanied by "a cry of command,[9] with the archangel's call[10] and with the sound of God's trumpet"[11] (1 Thess 4:16). There are clear links here between God's appearance in the OT to rescue his people from their time of exile and Jesus' return to bring his (exiled) people home.

In describing the events that will accompany Jesus' return, Paul notes that his information has come to him as "the word of the Lord" (1 Thess 4:15). Although he has no direct scriptural basis for his claims concerning the return of Jesus as it relates to those who have already died, he nevertheless maintains that they are based on an authentic word transmitted to him by Jesus. He does not discuss how this revelation was given to him, but he is certain that it is authoritative because the Lord (Jesus) has spoken to him. Just as Jesus died and rose again for those he came to save, he will also "bring with him" those who have died in him (1 Thess 4:14–15). Readers need not fear that those believers who have died prior to the Parousia of Jesus will be forgotten in the momentous events of the last days. On the contrary, they will already have been raised from the dead before his return—a fact that will be proved when they return with Jesus at his Parousia (1 Thess 4:14–16).

Those who are still alive when Jesus returns will join all other believers and be forever with him (1 Thess 4:17). Paul's message to believers who are concerned about the destiny of members of their Christian community who have died is clear. Believers are in Jesus regardless of their situation. Being in him means that there can never be a situation where they are separated from him, whether they are alive or dead (1 Thess 5:10). Paul describes those who have died as "the dead *in*

---

the one who descends from heaven (his city) in order to meet, welcome, and usher in believers who will be with him thereafter. The superior takes the place of his inferiors and exalts them by his action.

[9] Not only will the call be public but, because of the status of the one who speaks, it will be authoritative and irresistible. Because of the context of meeting Jesus, it will also be encouraging. Although he does not identify the one who utters the cry, John 5:25, 28–29 refers to the dead hearing the voice of the Son of God.

[10] Jude 9 refers to Michael as an archangel (the Jews identified 7 archangels). This verse does not identify the archangel, but the message is clear—one of the most honored angels supports the call.

[11] The trumpet here probably symbolizes victory (Exod 19:16–17, 19). The OT refers to the trumpet when the day of the Lord was announced (Joel 2:1; Zeph 1:15–16) and, in particular, when the people of God were to be gathered together, returning to him from exile (Isa 27:13; Zech 9:14–17). Matthew (24:31) and Paul (1 Cor 15:52) use it elsewhere with reference to Jesus' Parousia.

Christ" (1 Thess 4:16, emphasis added). At the same time, believers who are alive at the time of Jesus' return will meet him and be united with him.[12]

Although these may well be literal events, the focus is on the OT precedents associated exclusively with God. Paul refers to Jesus' future coming (1 Thess 3:13) in words that described the coming of God (Zech 14:5). While the psalmist referred to God ascending with a shout and the voice of a trumpet (47:5), Paul identifies Jesus descending with a shout and a trumpet (1 Thess 4:16). The prophecy was that Jesus would come from the place of highest honor, heaven. He will also be accompanied by "*mighty* angels,"[13] who form his entourage, serving and following him, as well as "flaming fire" (2 Thess 1:7–8). This fire is not smoldering or flickering but blazing brightly. All of these descriptions of Jesus here also describe God elsewhere.[14]

Here, as in his other writings, Paul ascribes the prerogatives of God to Jesus. He uses the name "Lord" (the name most commonly used to refer to God in the OT) throughout the portrayal of his return[15] and elsewhere.[16] In particular, the well-known phrase "the day of the Lord," which the OT often uses with reference to God,[17] here refers to Jesus.[18] The OT day of the Lord was associated with judgment and also deliverance, as it is here.[19] Similarly, the phrase, "the word of the Lord," often associated with messages from God in the OT (e.g., Isa 1:10; Jer 1:4) is here identified with Jesus.[20] As a result of Jesus' high status, Paul is eager to acknowledge that he is an apostle "of Christ."

---

[12] 1 Thess 1:10; 3:13; 5:23; 2 Thess 2:1.

[13] Italics added. It is possible that Paul is emphasizing that these angels are particularly powerful (F. F. Bruce, *1 & 2 Thessalonians* [WBC; Waco: Word, 1982], 150), thereby highlighting the power of the one they serve. He may, however, be describing Jesus' power, which the angels represent. In this interpretation it is not the angels' power that is celebrated but Jesus' power that they announce by being with him (so Leon Morris, *The First and Second Epistles to the Thessalonians* [Grand Rapids: Eerdmans, 1959], 202; Charles A. Wanamaker, *The Epistles to the Thessalonians: A Commentary on the Greek Text* [NIGTC; Grand Rapids: Eerdmans, 1990], 226).

[14] For angels, see Exod 19:13; Zech 14:5. For fire, see Exod 3:2; 19:18.

[15] 1 Thess 2:19; 4:15, 16, 17; 5:2, 9, 23; 2 Thess 1:9–10; 2:1, 8.

[16] 1 Thess 1:5; 2:15; 3:11; 4:2; 5:23, 28; 2 Thess 1:1, 2, 12; 2:13, 14, 16; 3:1, 6, 12, 16, 18.

[17] Amos 5:18–20; Joel 1:15.

[18] 1 Thess 5:2; 2 Thess 2:2; see also 1 Cor 5:5; Phil 1:6.

[19] Joel 2:31–32; Zech 14:1–21.

[20] 1 Thess 1:8; 4:15; 2 Thess 2:6; 3:1.

What is unusual, though not unique,[21] is that Paul presents Jesus before he refers to the Father (2 Thess 2:16). Though he is not implying that Jesus is superior to the Father, he is certainly indicating that readers should make no distinction between their authority and grace. In his introductions (1 Thess 1:1; 2 Thess 1:1), Paul uniquely describes the church in Thessalonica as being simultaneously owned by or, better, as existing in, God the Father and Jesus. He also emphasizes their joint role in the way they direct (1 Thess 3:11) and welcome believers (1 Thess 2:19; 3:13) and receive prayer.[22]

The Lord Victorious

Paul refers to Jesus being "revealed from heaven with his mighty angels in flaming fire, inflicting vengeance on those who do not know God" (2 Thess 1:7–8). The lawless one will be revealed in order to be destroyed (2 Thess 2:8), and Jesus is the one who has the authority to destroy him. Paul sums up Jesus' superlative authority over the lawless one by recording two ways that demonstrate how he will easily accomplish his victory—by "the breath of his mouth" and by "the manifestation of his coming" (2 Thess 2:8).[23] When Jesus meets the lawless one, the outcome is decisive. No battle is necessary, no drawn-out confrontation, no fight to the death, not even an altercation—the opening of Jesus' mouth is sufficient to dispatch the enemy of humankind, his presence is enough to rid this world of its tormentor. It is little wonder that, when Jesus returns, he will be "marveled at" (2 Thess 1:10).

In 2 Thessalonians 1:7–9, Paul describes Jesus in words that indicate his authority to judge. The image of fire is probably there to support this context of judgment.[24] The judgment that Jesus brings is not only "eternal destruction" but also exclusion from his presence, including his "glory" and "might" (2 Thess 1:9). His presence brings glorious power, and so exclusion from his presence is the most painful and truly awful punishment that awaits those who reject Jesus.

---

[21] 2 Cor 13:14; Gal 1:1.

[22] 1 Thess 3:11–13; 2 Thess 2:16–17; 3:5.

[23] The Gk. word *epiphaneia* described the appearing of a deity or a ruler whose presence was manifested generally by some act of power—often the rescue of a community or person.

[24] See Isa 66:15–16; Matt 3:12; Jude 7. So Wanamaker, *Thessalonians*, 227; also Gene L. Green, *The Letters to the Thessalonians* (PNTC; Grand Rapids: Eerdmans, 2002), 289.

In these verses, Paul appears to be alluding to Isaiah 2:10–19, which refers to the day of the Lord that will bring terrifying judgment on those who have rejected God. Paul indicates that Jesus is the one who has the authority to judge as God did in the OT (Ps 94:1). In so doing, Paul even uses words that, in the OT, describe the judgmental nature of God.[25] Paul is, once again here, clothing Jesus with metaphors and authority that were previously only attributed to God.

In an unusual and rare portrayal, Paul anticipates the future occasion when *Jesus* will be "glorified by his saints" (2 Thess 1:10, 12). Paul is probably citing the LXX (Ps 89:7) here, where God is glorified by angels. Here, however, it is Jesus who is honored in and/or with believers.[26] Paul is probably describing the character of Jesus being reflected in the lives of believers, for the purpose of Jesus' Parousia is to reveal himself graphically through believers.

Vengeance upon unbelievers is not the central purpose for Jesus' return, but rather the revelation of himself through those he has saved. The church will have the opportunity to reveal Jesus' manifold beauty and grace so that all will realize how marvelous he is. People will look at believers and be astonished at the grace of the one who has redeemed them.

Although unbelievers may deduce that a savior who died on a cross is a weak deity, Paul reminds his readers that Jesus' strength is infused with glory. People may mock and abuse Jesus' followers because they cannot see him and therefore do not fear him. But the time will come when Jesus will be revealed to all, and fear will be the overriding emotion that those who opposed his followers will feel. Jesus is hidden but not missing, ascended but not absent, gone to heaven but not gone away.

The Lord Our Life

As in his other letters, Paul's overriding purpose in presenting Jesus is to make some points concerning the salvation of his readers and the implications of that salvation for their lifestyle. He is not exhaustive or systematic but wants to engender transformation in the thinking, morality, and spirituality of believers. There are consequences to

---

[25] Isa 11:4 = 2 Thess 2:8; Isa 66:4, 15 = 2 Thess 1:7–8; Isa 2:10 = 2 Thess 1:9. See Fee, *Pauline Christology,* 58–62.

[26] See Wanamaker (*Thessalonians,* 230–31) for a discussion of the preposition *en* (in . . . his saints) in 1:10.

recognizing Jesus' supremacy. Jesus is worthy of being emulated (1 Thess 1:6). The fact that Jesus has accomplished the Father's will should motivate believers to do likewise (1 Thess 5:18). Paul's final command—that his letter be read to all—is stimulated by his belief that this is in step with the will of the Lord (5:27). Similarly, he prefaces his exhortation that readers distance themselves from lazy believers by saying that this command is "in the name of our Lord Jesus Christ" (2 Thess 3:6). The concept of the name is important because it relates to the name bearer's character and status—here, it is Jesus himself.[27] He anticipates that readers will follow his guidance because of the supremacy of the one who sanctions it (see also 2 Thess 3:12).

The Rescuer from Wrath

It is "the gospel of Christ" (1 Thess 3:2) that motivates Paul and all those who serve Jesus (1 Thess 1:3). Jesus has procured the salvation, as a result of his death (1 Thess 2:15), which provides him with hope (1 Thess 5:9). All believers are in him ("in Christ," 1 Thess 4:16; "in Christ Jesus," 1 Thess 2:14; "in the/our Lord Jesus Christ," 1 Thess 1:1, 3; 2 Thess 1:1). As a result of their salvation, believers are loved and given eternal comfort and hope (1 Thess 1:3; 2 Thess 2:16). Both of these verbs are aorist and therefore indicate a definite occasion when Jesus initiated them.

The salvation that Jesus achieved provides believers with the motivation for their suffering (1 Thess 2:14) and also prescribes their sphere of life, the church (1 Thess 1:1). In these letters, Paul clarifies the elements of salvation. Jesus has delivered believers "from the wrath that is coming" (1 Thess 1:10; 5:9). Elsewhere, the NT associates wrath with God.[28] Although some might struggle with the idea that a loving God has the capacity to feel anger, his judgment is not capricious or arbitrary but central to his being just and righteous. God must judge sin, and those who do not take advantage of his grace must bear the consequences. It is a remarkable truth, however, that Jesus, as God, offers an escape.

Not only does Jesus rescue believers from wrath, but they are also destined to "obtain the glory of our Lord Jesus Christ" (2 Thess 2:14). He delivers them from an awful destiny and then dedicates them to an

---

[27] For a discussion of the names of Jesus, see pp. 8–9.

[28] Rom 1:18; 2:5, 8; Eph 5:6; Col 3:6.

awesome dignity. The noun translated "obtain" (Gk. *peripoiēsis*) refers to a possession. The same word occurs in 1 Thessalonians 5:9, where it has reference to salvation. Not only do believers possess salvation as a result of Jesus' life and death, but they have also obtained the promise of possessing the glory that belongs to Jesus. Glory is best understood as the manifestation of God's essence that radiates from Jesus. The remarkable promise is that those who follow Jesus will also express his glory. This inexplicable honor is not due to anything that believers do, but rather to Jesus' work in them; not to their presence in heaven but to their proximity to him. Belief in Jesus' death and resurrection determines this hope and security (1 Thess 4:14).

The Giver of Grace and Peace

As he does elsewhere in his writings, Paul reminds his readers that Jesus and the Father grant them grace and peace,[29] though he also specifically presents grace as coming from Jesus (1 Thess 5:28; 2 Thess 3:18). These are significant resources, but Paul is also making the point that Jesus and the Father operate together. Paul also writes of Jesus and the Father working together to provide divine guidance in the future (1 Thess 3:11). This grace that believers can expect, Paul says, will be evident in their divinely inspired and resourced love for each other (1 Thess 3:11) in which they will be established, sanctified, and blameless (1 Thess 3:13; 5:23–24). Furthermore, Jesus and God the Father will comfort and enable believers to perform "every good work and word" (2 Thess 2:17). Paul has a confidence for their future based on his knowledge of Jesus, who he is certain will strengthen and guard them from evil (2 Thess 3:3–4). Jesus has dedicated himself to influencing them positively, to helping them realize how much he loves them and how reliable he is (2 Thess 3:5).

Conclusion

As a result of the supreme status of Jesus and the remarkable resources he grants, Paul anticipates that believers should be able to "stand

[29] 1 Thess 1:1; 2 Thess 1:2, 12; 3:16.

firm in the Lord" (1 Thess 3:8). They can be constant and stable, for Jesus is their example and motivation (1 Thess 4:1–2). Although they are suffering for their faith, it is only for a short time; eternity awaits when Jesus, the victorious Lord of Glory, will fulfill his aspiration for them by welcoming them into his presence forever. Such a prospect is the basis for believers to continue in the faith and follow Christ's example in their lifestyles.

chapter 13

1 and 2 Timothy

Jesus, Savior and Lord

The two letters to Timothy and the one to Titus are sometimes referred to as the Pastoral Epistles, since all three are addressed to church leaders dealing with practical issues related to the local church. Although there is ongoing discussion concerning the authorship of the letters to Timothy,[1] it is safe to say that they contain a great deal of information that is reminiscent of Paul. Therefore, we will refer to them as Paul's letters because of the close historical association they have with Paul's life and ministry.

Both letters are addressed to Timothy,[2] Paul's traveling companion and ministry trainee whom Paul left in Ephesus to help combat false teaching. Among other issues dealt with in the first letter, asceticism was beginning to permeate the church (1 Tim 4:3–5). The opposition began in the Jewish community and sought to impose Jewish practices, including circumcision, on Gentile believers. These teachers were also encouraging both Jewish and Gentile believers to retain or adopt the Mosaic Law (1 Tim 1:3–11). The result was that they diminished Jesus' person, authority, and message. The second letter was written later, partly to encourage Timothy to join Paul in Rome, where he was on trial. To enable Timothy to make the trip, Paul sent Tychicus to replace him in Ephesus (2 Tim 4:9–13).

[1] Because of the similar christological content, this chapter will explore the two letters together.

[2] It is possible that Timothy was one of Paul's converts (1 Tim 1:2), and it is certain that Paul mentored him (1 Cor 4:16, 17). Timothy joined Paul on his missionary journeys in Galatia (Acts 16:3–5). It appears that he was also in prison with Paul (Phil 1:1; Col 1:1) and acted as his representative in Macedonia (Acts 19:22; 1 Thess 3:1).

In these letters, Paul speaks clearly of the humanity of Jesus, who came into the world as a man (1 Tim 1:15; 2:5),[3] descended from David (2 Tim 2:8; also Rom 1:3),[4] and spoke with integrity to Pontius Pilate (1 Tim 6:13). He did not merely appear to be a human being; he actually became a member of humanity. At the same time, Jesus is validated as being God, as reflected in the identification of Jesus with the divine title, the Lord.

The Lord of Our Confession

His Glory Encapsulated

The most significant theological statement concerning Jesus in 1 Timothy (3:16) offers succinct assertions relating to his incarnate life and influence. Paul affirms that Jesus was "revealed in flesh"[5] and "vindicated[6] in the Spirit." Jesus was truly human, but the vindication of the Spirit indicates that he was not merely human. Although the term "flesh" (Gk. *sarx*) may suggest a contrast with "spirit" (Gk. *pneuma*), thus referring to the human spirit,[7] it is more likely that Paul is describ-

---

[3] Paul's description of Jesus as a man, rather than as a Jew, helps focus attention on his humanity instead of his racial identity. As a human, Jesus identifies with those for whom he functions as mediator. Philip H. Towner (*The Letters to Timothy and Titus* [New International Commentary on the New Testament; Grand Rapids: Eerdmans, 2006], 181–83) explores Paul's possible allusion to Num 24:7, 17 (LXX), which speak of a man who will rule Israel in the future. Paul's emphasis, therefore, may be on the fulfillment of prophecy as much as it is on the humanity of Jesus. I. Howard Marshall (*The Pastoral Epistles* [Edinburgh: T. & T. Clark, 1999], 431) explores (and rejects due to lack of evidence) the possibility that Paul is drawing a contrast with Adam as the first man.

[4] The reference to David highlights Jesus' messianic credentials.

[5] There is no reason to assume that Paul is identifying any weakness on Jesus' part or bias to sin by his use of the term "flesh" (Gk. *sarx*). Rather, he is identifying his incarnate life as the mode in which he completed his achievements, to which the rest of the verse refers.

[6] The Gk. verb *edikaiōthē* is translated "justified" in Titus 3:7, but here the better and alternative translation is "vindicated" (also Matt 11:19; Rom 3:4). Towner (*Timothy and Titus,* 280) suggests that it refers to a declaration of Jesus' innocence, though Knight (*Pastoral Epistles,* 184) argues that it vindicates Jesus' status as Messiah and Son of God.

[7] So Donald Guthrie, *The Pastoral Epistles* (London: Tyndale, 1957), 89–90. However, it is difficult to see how the human spirit (Paul infrequently uses this concept and, where he does [2 Tim 4:22], he prefaces it with "your") could affirm Jesus' person and mission.

ing the Spirit's role (as in 2 Tim 1:14; Titus 3:5) in affirming Jesus as Savior on earth.

It is not clear just when the Spirit validated Jesus. It is conceivable that it occurred at his birth (Luke 1:35), at his baptism (Luke 3:22), during his temptations (Luke 4:1), at the commencement of his ministry (Luke 4:1), when he set his ministry agenda (Luke 4:18), and/or at his resurrection (Rom 8:11).[8] It is less important to identify a particular occasion when the Spirit affirmed Jesus and more significant to recognize this affirmation as a feature of the Spirit's relationship with Jesus. The one who was truly human, and who could have been assumed to have been merely human, was worthy of the presence, affirmation, and vindication of the Spirit.

While he was human, Jesus was also "seen by angels" (1 Tim 3:16), indicating that the angels had a special proximity to or interest in him. The identity of these angels is uncertain. They could be "principalities and powers" (Eph 3:10) who see Jesus in his glory or who are described as being disarmed by him (Col 2:5). They may have been the angels of God who served Jesus throughout his earthly life (e.g., at his birth, Luke 2:9–14, or during times of temptation, Matt 4:11; Luke 22:43). It is most likely, however, that the reference is to the angels who served Jesus specifically in relation to his resurrection.[9] In his resurrection his victory is made certain (Eph 1:21) and celebrated as the next phase of the plan of salvation, leading to his ascension and the provision of the Spirit to believers.

The fact that he was "proclaimed among Gentiles" (1 Tim 3:16; see also 2 Tim 2:8) and "believed in throughout the world" demonstrates the quality of his message and mission. The fact that he was "taken up in glory," which is a clear reference to his ascension and exalted status following his earthly mission, proves the success and integrity of his mission. To these truths may be added the fact that he rose from the dead (2 Tim 2:8) and will come again (1 Tim 6:14).

---

[8] The association of the Spirit and Jesus' resurrection with reference to his designation as the Son of God in Rom 1:4 (cf. Rom 8:11) provides a possible background to this verse. Marshall (*Pastoral Epistles*, 525–26) and Towner (*Timothy and Titus*, 280–81) conclude that Paul is referring to the resurrection as a vindication of Jesus and his *mission*.

[9] Matt 28:2–7; Mark 16:5–8; Luke 24:4–7; John 20:12–13; Knight (*Pastoral Epistles*, 185) notes that in all the other NT references to Jesus, the Gk. term *ōphthē* ("seen") is used in relation to his resurrection (Luke 24:34; Acts 1:2; 9:17; 13:31; 26:16; 1 Cor 15:5–8).

His Lordship Affirmed

As he does elsewhere, Paul often combines references to Jesus and God in these letters. He says that salvation is due to the Father[10] and also to Jesus.[11] God the Father and Jesus were both involved in calling him to be an apostle (1 Tim 1:1, 12; 2 Tim 2:1) and both are part of his sphere of existence.[12] God and Jesus are both sources for the guidelines he offers (1 Tim 5:21; 6:13–14), though some he attributes to Jesus alone (1 Tim 6:3). He also identifies Jesus as the judge of the living and the dead (a role the OT attributed to God) whose kingdom is the manifestation of his authority (2 Tim 4:1, 8, 14). The one who offers the possibility of reigning with him, who is Lord of all, also has the awesome authority to reject those who reject him.[13]

As he does elsewhere, Paul identifies Jesus with the divine title "Lord."[14] Furthermore, Jesus is the one who, along with the Father, provides grace, mercy, and peace (1 Tim 1:2; 2 Tim 2:2). In 2 Tim 2:1, Paul encourages Timothy to "be strong in the grace that is in Christ Jesus." As the Lord and the dispenser of God's gifts, Jesus deserves the same glory that is also due to God (1 Tim 1:17).[15] In 2 Tim 2:1–13, Paul encourages good behavior "in Christ Jesus" and then gives a number of practical guidelines (2:14–18). He concludes this section with two statements (2 Tim 2:19) that may contain allusions to OT passages: "The Lord knows those who are his" is probably related to Num 16:5; "Let everyone who calls on the name of the Lord turn away from wickedness" is loosely related to Num 16:26 and/or Isa 52:11. What is significant is that Paul draws from OT contexts that refer to Yahweh and uses the concepts in new contexts that apply to the Lord (Gk. *kyrios*) Jesus Christ.

Because Jesus is Lord, Paul encourages Timothy to remember the elevated responsibility that the Lord has granted to him. While the calling itself is important, it is even more so because of the identity of the one who commissioned him (1 Tim 4:6). Paul encourages Timothy to

---

[10] 1 Tim 1:1; 4:10; 2 Tim 1:8–10.

[11] 2 Tim 1:10; 2:10; 3:15.

[12] 1 Tim 5:21; 6:13–14; 2 Tim 4:1.

[13] 2 Tim 2:12; see also Matt 10:33.

[14] 1 Tim 1:2, 12, 14; 6:3; 2 Tim 1:2, 8, 16, 18; 2:7, 14; 4:8, 17, 18, 22. See also 1 Tim 6:15, where the title refers to God.

[15] 1 Tim 3:16; 2 Tim 2:10; 4:18.

be "a good soldier" because his commanding officer is none other than Jesus (2 Tim 2:3). When Paul concludes his second letter, he commends Timothy to none other than the Lord (2 Tim 4:22), the one who has divine dignity and resources essential to his very being.

The Mediator of Our Salvation

Jesus the Savior

In a classic and precise statement, Paul writes, "Christ Jesus came into the world to save sinners"[16]—this was the reason for his incarnation. The emphasis is not on how Jesus came into the world or what this says about his preexistence. The focus, rather, is on the result of his incarnation and, in particular, the salvation of humanity. It is also clear that the source of the plan of salvation is the Godhead, who determined it "before the ages began" (2 Tim 1:9). In particular, Paul relates Jesus to peace (1 Tim 1:2; 2 Tim 1:2), mercy,[17] and grace,[18] as well as to salvation.[19]

Paul identifies two manifestations of Jesus' mercy and lavish grace as being love and faith "that are in Christ Jesus."[20] Paul is probably indicating that faith in Jesus and love for him and others should result from receiving his mercy and grace.[21] Paul may be saying, however, that love and faith are gifts from Jesus, in that he loves people and provides them with faith to believe in him. Thus, as a result of believing in Jesus, and not as a result of working for him (2 Tim 1:9), Jesus promises salvation (2 Tim 3:15) and eternal life (1 Tim 1:16; 2 Tim 1:1).

Jesus the Lifegiver

Paul graphically describes the result of Jesus' mission: he has abolished, or rendered ineffective, death itself (also 1 Cor 15:26). At the

[16] 1 Tim 1:15; see also Mark 2:17; Luke 19:10.

[17] 1 Tim 1:2, 13, 16; 2 Tim 1:2, 16.

[18] 1 Tim 1:2, 14; 2 Tim 1:2, 9; 2:1.

[19] 1 Tim 1:1; 2 Tim 1:10, 15; 2:10; 3:15.

[20] 1 Tim 1:14; 3:13; 2 Tim 1:13.

[21] Marshall (*Pastoral Epistles*, 396; also Towner, *Timothy and Titus,* 142–43; and Knight, *Pastoral Epistles,* 98) argues thus on the basis that this would then enable Paul to contrast Christian behavior with that of his opponents, who have drifted from this lifestyle.

same time, Jesus offers believers instead "life and immortality" (2 Tim 1:10) and "eternal glory" (2 Tim 2:10) in "his heavenly kingdom" (2 Tim 4:18). The fact that believers will "live" and "reign with him" indicates the quality of life that commences when they establish a relationship with Jesus and that reaches its fulfillment in the life to come (2 Tim 2:11–13).

Jesus the Mediator

Paul also refers to Jesus as the only mediator between God and humanity (1 Tim 2:5). The term translated "mediator" (Gk. *mesitēs*) referred in the ancient commercial world to a negotiator who brokered deals. In that context, however, there was no expectation that the mediator's role involved any sort of relationship, friendship, or pastoral concern for either party in the transaction. Jesus' mediation is vastly superior in this respect. It is also significant that Jesus functions as mediator in the sphere of humanity. Even though he is God, he has closely identified with humanity in order to bring them into relationship with God.

Jesus the Redeemer

Paul also describes Jesus as the redeemer who "gave himself a ransom for all" (1 Tim 2:6).[22] These words are reminiscent of God's redemption of the Jews from Egypt (Exod 6:6), but also more broadly of God freeing Israel from the consequences of sin (Ps 130:8). What Paul makes explicit about the redemption that Jesus achieved, however, is the significant personal cost involved. The reference to "himself" reminds readers of the substitutionary nature of this redemption.

Jesus Our Lord

Paul insists that believers should respond to Jesus' grace and mercy with a readiness to serve him (1 Tim 1:12). A believer who claims to be "the Lord's servant" must live accordingly (2 Tim 2:24), exhibiting a life that is dominated by "righteousness, godliness, faith, love, endurance, gentleness" (1 Tim 6:11). Paul wanted his readers to understand that his

---

[22] The Gk. word *antilytron* is found nowhere else in the NT; see p. 72 for further comment.

guidelines are from Jesus (1 Tim 5:21), for they are "the sound words of our Lord Jesus Christ" (1 Tim 6:3) and they are to follow them "until the manifestation of our Lord Jesus Christ" (1 Tim 6:14).

Our Faithful Provider

The grace and mercy provided through Jesus equips them not only for the commencement of their life in him, but also for the continuation of their relationship.[23] Jesus promises to give believers wisdom and understanding (2 Tim 2:7). Because they have these resources available to them, believers can radiate Jesus' life in their character and lifestyle (1 Tim 1:12). Jesus has also promised to protect and guard them until the end (2 Tim 1:12, 18), a commitment that believers should match with a readiness to guard the truth (2 Tim 1:13).

Even when believers are faithless, Paul asserts that Jesus will remain faithful. Indeed, Jesus' faithfulness is central to his character (2 Tim 2:13). Paul encourages his readers to recognize that even when their ability to trust God is being stretched—by destabilizing, false teachers and dubious, inauthentic leaders—they can rely on Jesus to ensure that their status as believers will not be undermined. Jesus is faithful to his promises, and Paul promises that believers are secure "in Christ."

Believers are never to take Jesus' unilateral commitment to remain faithful as an excuse to live in a way that does not honor him. On the contrary, Jesus' dedication to believers should result in increased devotion on their part. Therefore, Paul accompanies this admonition in 2 Tim 2:13 with directions relating to life and spirituality. On the basis of all of the spiritual resources that Jesus offers, Paul says, a believer's life should display certain characteristics, including a readiness to suffer (2 Tim 2:3; 3:12). Paul testifies to the fact that Jesus rescued him on occasions of significant persecution (2 Tim 3:11; 4:17–18).[24] Although Paul's persecutors sought to destroy him and end his mission, Jesus was in control and caring for him and was the one who determined that he would complete his agenda successfully. Jesus' abundant provision fills Paul with gratitude (1 Tim 1:12).

---

[23] 1 Tim 1:2, 12; 2 Tim 1:16, 18; 2:1.

[24] Fee (*Pauline Christology*, 461–62) offers OT parallels (Exod 34:5; Ps 22:21) that identify God as the rescuer. He argues that with such allusions Paul implicitly identifies Jesus as God.

Conclusion

Paul wrote these letters to a young leader he had mentored for a number of years. He seeks to encourage Timothy and successfully does so by reminding him of both the humanity and divinity of Jesus. Because of the former, Timothy is encouraged to recognize that, as an authentic member of humanity, Jesus is able to identify with him in his trials as he seeks to fulfill God's will in his life. At the same time, a recollection of the divinity of Jesus strengthens his belief that not only has he been called by the supreme Savior but also that Jesus has provided everything he needs to fulfill his commission. It is important for all believers to know and remember that the one who has called and commissioned them is capable of supporting them in the fulfillment of their tasks. God has all the resources they need and is personally united with them in their mission. God has not only redeemed them but also functions as their mentor and advocate who is immediately and continually present with them.

chapter 14

Titus

Jesus, Savior from Sin and Error

The Pauline authorship of the letter to Titus,[1] like that of the letters to Timothy, has been disputed by some NT scholars. Nevertheless, because of the letter's close historical association with Paul, for our purposes it will be referred to as Pauline. The letter concerns Titus' responsibility as a church leader to complete unfinished business related to the Christian assemblies on the island of Crete (1:5). It appears that a number of people there were advising believers to adopt some form of ascetic ritualism. Titus also seems to have been faced with a number of strong characters who were prepared to oppose and destabilize him (1:10; 2:15). These people taught error (1:11, 16), ignored the truth (1:14), wasted time in endless controversies (3:9), and exhibited inappropriate lifestyles (1:16). Paul advised Titus to be firm in his response, to rebuke error wherever he saw it,[2] to teach the truth (2:1–15), and to establish reliable church leaders throughout the island (1:5–8).

Our Great God and Savior

Although he identifies himself as a servant of God, Paul also refers to himself as "an apostle of Jesus Christ" (1:1). As he does throughout his writings, he proclaims that grace and peace are available from both God the Father and Jesus (1:4). Similarly, he says that the future

[1] It is possible that Titus was one of Paul's converts (1:4). It is certain that he traveled with him to Jerusalem for the important council (Gal 2:1; Acts 15), represented him in Corinth (2 Cor 7:6, 13), collected money for the poor on his behalf (2 Cor 8:6), ministered in Dalmatia, and was described as his partner and fellow worker (2 Cor 8:16).

[2] 1:9, 11, 13; 2:15; 3:10.

"blessed[3] hope" is "the manifestation of the glory of our great God and Savior, Jesus Christ" (2:13). History is geared to the time when Jesus will reappear with the Father and with the glory that they share.[4] Philip Towner argues that, rather than assume that Paul is referring to God and Jesus separately as the "blessed hope," readers should understand that Jesus is the blessed hope and simultaneously the glory of God.[5] Similarly, Fee concludes that Paul identifies Jesus as being the glory of God, writing, "The coming of Christ is the full and final manifestation of God's glory."[6] Jesus is the fullest expression of God's glory and it is his personal appearance that is the "blessed hope" of all believers. Marshall and Knight, however, argue convincingly that Paul is describing Jesus as God, not just as the glory of God, Marshall writing, "it is difficult to see why the One in whom God is fully manifest should not be entitled to the title of God."[7] This idea occurs elsewhere in the NT.[8]

Our Redeemer from Sin

In three different places in his letter to Titus, Paul describes Jesus as "Savior" (1:4; 2:13; 3:6). The fact that these are three of only four references to Jesus in the letter indicates the importance of this truth. This salvation is lavish—Jesus justifies believers and makes them heirs of eternal life (3:6–7). It is also significant that God is associated with salvation (1:3; 2:10; 3:4) and the Spirit with renewal (3:5). Paul makes clear the Trinity's central involvement in the act of salvation.

Paul also describes Jesus here as the one who redeems believers from all sin (2:14).[9] Jesus gave himself specifically, altruistically, and sacrifi-

---

[3]Although it is sometimes, and inappropriately, assumed to mean "happy," here "blessed" reminds readers that the emotion is due to God's action on their behalf.

[4]See Fee (*Pauline Christology*, 442–46) for discussion on the relevance of the term "glory."

[5]See Towner, *Timothy and Titus,* 756–58. In particular, he notes that the notion of "appearing" or "manifestation" mainly refers to Jesus in the NT. The one definite article that governs both "God" and "Savior" here indicates that the reference is to one person (as the phrase "God and Savior" referred to just one person in Hellenistic and Jewish discourses).

[6]Fee, *Pauline Christology*, 446. See also Towner, *Timothy and Titus,* 752–55, who offers Col 2:2 as a literary parallel (754).

[7]Marshall, *Pastoral Epistles,* 274–82, esp. 282; Knight, *Pastoral Epistles,* 321–26.

[8]John 1:1; 20:28; Rom 9:5; Heb 1:8–10; 2 Pet 1:1.

[9]Mark 10:45; 1 Tim 2:6.

cially in order to redeem or ransom people and purify them, so that he could provide "for himself a people of his own" who are dedicated to good works. Fee notes similar wording in Psalm 130:8 and Ezekiel 37:23, which identify God as the one who will ransom people from their sins, cleanse them, and make them a people for himself. Here, Jesus shares the role by taking it upon himself to achieve redemption, despite the catastrophic cost he paid.

By describing him as the one who gives the Spirit lavishly, Paul further exalts Jesus in the minds of readers. This giving of the Spirit is part of the salvation Jesus offers.[10] It is not that the Spirit is inferior to Jesus, who can dispense him whenever he wishes. Rather than become confused with trying to discern hierarchy in the Trinity, or to separate the members of the Godhead in some philosophical and unhelpful fashion, it is better to catch the flavor of Paul's metaphorical language. The one who many assumed was simply a man has the authority to partner the Holy Spirit in salvation. Furthermore, Jesus grants the Spirit to his followers not drip by drip but as a deluge. Jesus' remarkable generosity to his followers is a significant encouragement for them. They are not on their own—a supernatural Spirit-waterfall is their continual source of refreshment.

Conclusion

Titus faced difficult circumstances in the island of Crete, and his pastoral leadership there involved some arduous tasks. Yet Paul reminds him that he is not expected to undertake them on his own. Jesus, who is God, has saved him and has also granted him the Spirit, who is committed to stay with him and to renew him from his own inexhaustible, immeasurable, and magnanimous resources.

[10] 3:5–6; Acts 2:17, 33 (Joel 3:1).

chapter 15

Philemon

Jesus, Friend of Sinners

Paul wrote this letter to Philemon on behalf of the latter's slave, Onesimus, who had come to faith in Christ and had helped Paul while he was in prison. It is likely that Onesimus had run away from his master (v. 18), spent time in prison with Paul, and was now being released and returned to Philemon (v. 12), despite the fact that Paul would have preferred to keep him close by (v. 11). It appears that Paul may have previously led Philemon to faith in Jesus (v. 19), and now Paul appeals to Onesimus's new status as a follower of Christ in making his case that Philemon should forgive and restore him. This letter is distinctive among Paul's epistles in that in it, he addresses an individual about a personal matter between the two of them.

The Granter of Grace

Although this letter contains only twenty-five verses, Paul refers to Jesus several times. As he does in other places, Paul refers to God and Jesus in the same breath (v. 3) and uses the name "Lord," which so frequently refers to God in the OT, to refer to Jesus (vv. 3, 16, 20, 25). Paul is conscious that his imprisonment is a privilege because it is in the service of such an exalted Lord (vv. 1, 9, 23). Even though he is a prisoner of Caesar, Paul prefers to identify his imprisonment as due to his service to Jesus. Even though the conditions were such that "it is possible to consider captivity and martyrdom inseparable," Paul is not ashamed of this experience.[1]

---

[1] M. Barth and H. Blanke, *The Letter to Philemon: A New Translation with Notes and Commentary* (Eerdmans Critical Commentary; Grand Rapids: Eerdmans, 2000), 244.

Paul makes it clear again here that Jesus and the Father are both responsible for granting grace and peace to believers (v. 3). He also says that Jesus grants grace (v. 25). In an expansive statement, Paul refers to the fact that believers comprehensively benefit as a result of Jesus' provision for them (v. 6). Because Christ, who guides his actions (vv. 8, 20), has motivated his request to Philemon, Paul is sure that Philemon will respond positively. Although they converse as fellow believers, they do so in the knowledge that this is not a dialogue but a trialogue in which their divine mentor is also involved.

Conclusion

In this short yet distinctive letter, Paul demonstrates that appreciating Jesus' supremacy makes a difference in one's dealings with others. Central to the letter is his contention that to own Jesus as Lord has behavioral consequences. Thus, although Paul finds Philemon's faith in Jesus and love for other believers encouraging (v. 5), he exhorts Philemon to direct this love very particularly to Onesimus as a new member of the Christian community (v. 16).

chapter 16

Hebrews

Jesus, Superior Savior

The original readers of the letter to the Hebrews were Jewish Christians who were in danger of drifting away from the gospel and back to their Jewish religious roots. In response, the author (who is unknown) robustly declares that Jesus is better than anything or anyone else associated with the history of the Jews and, as such, Jesus' message is final.

He delivers his thesis in four sections, each of which concludes that Jesus is greater than those with whom he is compared—the OT prophets (1:1–3), the angels (1:4–14), Moses (3:1–6), and the high priests and the sacrificial system (3:7–10:39). The author intersperses warning passages that remind readers of the consequences of cutting their connection with Jesus.[1] Other passages offer motivations and guidelines for developing a relationship with Jesus (11:1–13:25). The letter to the Hebrews presents Jesus' humanity graphically[2]—his prayers and tears (5:7), his readiness to obey the divine agenda that he willingly initiated and followed (5:8), and his moral perfection (5:9). The author also encourages readers to recognize Jesus as the one who is worthy to be followed by highlighting his suffering, trials (2:18; 13:12, 13), opposition (12:3), crucifixion (6:6; 12:2), and resurrection (13:20). Jesus understands the challenges that his followers face, including important life-changing decisions that have to be made.

A Superior Person

Over the Prophets

The OT prophets were very important to the Jews because God had spoken and revealed himself through them. They had prophesied

[1] 2:1–4; 3:7–4:11; 6:1–12.
[2] 2:7, 11, 14, 17; 10:5.

in God's name (Jas 5:10). They had represented God and his values to his people—guiding, correcting, rebuking, encouraging, and forgiving them. They were the people's public mentors who sought to direct them in their relationships with God and each other.

Although the OT prophets and their messages were respected as coming from God, Jesus came to offer a full and final revelation. Although the prophets were successful in accomplishing their God-given mission, they were inferior to Jesus. Their light of revelation was dim in comparison to his. They spoke in the distant past (1:1) while he speaks in the present (1:2). Compared to Jesus, their knowledge of God was inadequate and their ability to represent God was limited. The prophets' messages were infrequent, fragmented, and partial, while Jesus' message is final, full, and perfect. Because the importance of the message rests a great deal on the status, integrity, calling, and authenticity of the messenger, from the outset the writer to the Hebrews elevates Jesus. The message is clear: if Jesus is so much more important than the prophets, then his message must be much more significant than theirs.

The writer elevates Jesus' status and the good news he preached by describing him as "a Son" (1:2). He is not implying that God has more than one son, or that Jesus is merely *a* son or even simply *his* son. He is, rather, stating that God used this superior medium of "son" to reveal himself. God best achieved his objective through the medium of a son. The ancient world viewed a son as the most complete reflection of his father. So Jesus, the son, is the best way to radiate the Father to people. As a son, Jesus is a complete manifestation of the Father.

In 1:2–3, the writer succinctly describes Jesus in order to highlight his superiority over the prophets as well as over the angels with whom he contrasts Jesus in the verses that follow. Thus, he is "heir of all things," which implies dignity and dominion (1:2).[3] The allusion here to Psalm 2:7–8 implies that the inheritance could refer, at least in part, to people—though it probably also refers to all that God owns in the present and the future (a theme that 2:5–9 will develop). Because of Jesus' high status, readers are to regard him as superior to all others.

---

[3]To concentrate on the statement that Jesus has been "appointed" to this role, as if to suggest that he was promoted or granted a status that was not his before, misses the point. It is not that he becomes superior from a position of inferiority. Rather, the emphasis is on the fact that he is heir, with all the implications of such a position. This status was full of symbolism for an ancient reader.

His involvement in creation (1:2)[4] hints at his divinity, since the OT defines God as the sole Creator,[5] but it also reminds readers of his preexistence and coexistence with the Father (1:10). The fact that the author refers to the creation using the Greek plural *aiōnas* (lit. "ages," 1:2) illustrates that his creation involves more than the earth. He is responsible for the total universe, visible and invisible, known and unknown—a tiny part of which is the world. Everything exists because of his central involvement.

Jesus radiates, or reflects, God's glory (1:3). "Radiance" is a better translation of the Greek term *apaugasma*[6] than "reflection." Jesus fully and uniquely manifests the brightness of God's glory (that which best represents him). He also bears "the exact imprint of God's very being" (1:3). His character is identical to God's. They share the same essence. The writer uses different metaphors to exalt Jesus. The word translated "exact imprint" (Gk. *charactēr*), a term that occurs only here in the NT, describes the impression that a stamp or a seal makes on wax. For the image to be of any value, it had to be a perfect representation of the stamp. Jesus is the exact representation and embodiment of God, whose nature (Gk. *hypostasis*) is so uniquely complex and different that nobody can define or explain him.

Furthermore, Jesus "sustains all things by his powerful word" (1:3). The verb "sustains" (Gk. *pherein*) indicates more than the ability to hold an object up. Rather, it refers to the ability and desire to carry an object from one location to another. Jesus directs the universe forward to its appointed end. It is not just that he holds the universe in space. He continually acts upon it as he governs, sustains, and guides events within it. He is not merely a cosmic architect; he is a conscientious supervisor of its destiny "by his powerful word." He functions with ease, as did God the Father when he created the world with a word.[7] In these early verses of Hebrews, the author hints at the remarkable truth that Jesus functions as God did. This, of course, begs the question: "Is he God?" Throughout this letter the author will present readers with opportunities to determine how exalted their estimation of Jesus is. Clearly he is superior to many, but the underlying message that is so radical (especially to monotheistic Jews), is that he is God.

---

[4] See also John 1:3, 10; Col 1:16.

[5] Gen 1:3; Prov 8:22–30.

[6] This word appears only here in the NT and only once in the LXX (Wis 7:26).

[7] Gen 1:3, 6, 9, 11, 14, 20, 24, 26.

In 1:3 the writer reminds readers of one of Jesus' most significant achievements—he has "made purification for sins" (1:3), choosing to forget them (10:17). This, of course, is reminiscent of the cleansing that the Jewish sacrificial system, which incorporated the possibility of atonement for people's sins (Lev 16:30), achieved.[8] Jesus' redemptive death is a completed act of purification—the aorist tense emphasizes this fact. While the Day of Atonement occurred every year, the sacrifice of Jesus was made once and for all. Not only has the sacrifice been completed, the writer affirms, but Jesus also offers more than forgiveness—he has achieved purification.

The writer completes this initial portrait of Jesus by describing him as having "sat down at the right hand of the Majesty on high."[9] It is the symbolism of this picture, and not its literal presentation, that is important. The "right hand" was the traditional place of honor, and rulers ensured that their heirs sat there (1 Kgs 2:19). Jesus' position therefore denotes equality with God and honor. The right hand also symbolized strength (Exod 15:6). The term "on high" illustrates the fact that Jesus is above all others, including his enemies (10:13). That he is seated signifies the completed work of purification, the place of honor (1:13//Ps 110:1), and the posture of rest.

In this tightly-packed portrayal of Jesus that concentrates on his superlative authority, some of which is normally associated with God, the writer to the Hebrews clearly presents Jesus as being better[10] than the OT prophets. Readers, therefore, need to maintain their commitment to him.

Over the Angels

The Jews had an overwhelming and legendary regard for angels that had developed, especially during the intertestamental period, into an elaborate angelolatry. The reference to angels here probably relates to their role in the giving of the Law (2:2), which provided the basis of the covenant with God. In order for readers to accept Jesus' message as being more important than the Law, with which angels were associated, the writer needed to establish Jesus' superiority over them.

---

[8] See Ladd, *Theology,* 423–36.

[9] 1:3; 8:2; 10:12; 12:2.

[10] The word "better" (Gk. *kreittōn,* 1:4) occurs 13 times in Hebrews to elevate Jesus.

The writer supports his case with quotations from and allusions to the OT. First, he reminds readers that Jesus has been given a name which marks him out as fundamentally superior to any angel (1:4). Although he does not identify the name, since the term "Son" occurs in the following verses (1:5, 8; 3:6), and since "Son" was the initial description of Jesus (1:1), it is probable that the author is referring to that term here also.[11] Thus, while angels bear a certain dignity, Jesus is son. The writer then refers to seven OT passages in order to corroborate his argument that Jesus is exalted above the angels.

The author twice refers to Jesus as "Son." Although the OT refers to the angels collectively as sons of God (Job 2:1; 38:7), only Jesus is described as an individual son. He is also "begotten" of the Father (1:5)—which does not imply that Jesus was a created being or that there was a time when he did not exist. It may refer to the incarnation[12] or, in this context of exaltation, to his heavenly enthronement.[13] The emphasis, however, is not on his being begotten but on his relationship with God who is described uniquely as his Father. This privileged relationship as Son of God is unavailable to the angels.[14]

The reference to Jesus being the firstborn[15] indicates his precedence over all and is not a crude description of his being God's first creation.[16] Here, the term "firstborn" refers not to primogeniture but to primacy in terms of dignity, honor, and status. The OT uses the term to refer to Israel, even though the Israelites were not the first people on earth (Exod 4:22; Ephraim also, Jer 31:9). Similarly, Psalm 89:27 describes David as the firstborn, even though he clearly was not the first person to be born—not even in his own family (1 Sam 16:11). What is important is the term's symbolism. As heir, the firstborn received a double portion

[11] See Paul Ellingworth (*The Epistle to the Hebrews* [NIGTC; Grand Rapids: Eerdmans, 1993], 104–6) for a fuller discussion.

[12] Other suggestions include his birth, baptism, resurrection, or ascension.

[13] So Ellingworth, *Hebrews,* 114; see also William L. Lane, *Hebrews 1–8* (WBC; Dallas: Word, 1991), 26.

[14] Although the original text (2 Sam 7:14) relates to King David, as God promises to treat him like a son, the author is not narrowly referring to that event as if to suggest that God will treat Jesus as *if* he is his son. The author of Hebrews does not mention David's name here because he is not seeking a messianic association. Rather, he is contrasting the angels' relationship with God with that of Jesus who, as son, is in all ways superior.

[15] 1:6; 12:23; Col 1:18; Rev 1:5.

[16] If it is intended to refer to an event, it could relate to his birth, incarnation, or Parousia.

of the inheritance (Gen 49:3; Deut 21:17) and was the one most highly honored (Gen 49:3) and sacred to God (Exod 13:2; Num 3:13). It is Jesus, then, who now fulfills the promise of Psalm 89:27.

The next step in this ladder of exaltation is to remind readers that the angels worship Jesus (1:6; Deut 32:43 LXX). Angels are servants of God (1:7, 14; Ps 104:4), while Jesus sits at the place of highest honor (1:13; Ps 110:1). While angels are temporary and intermittent (which the references to wind and fire imply), Jesus "is forever and ever" (1:8). They are ephemeral, but he is eternal.

Of even greater significance here are the descriptions of Jesus as God (1:8, 9) and Lord (1:10). In 1:8–9, the writer quotes Psalm 45:6–7, which refers explicitly to God, and applies it to Jesus. The writer thereby transfers to Jesus the acclamation ascribed to God. This is more than poetic license on the author's part. It reflects his belief that Jesus is not just superior to the angels but is equivalent to God. Jesus is the one anointed[17] above all others, enthroned as God. He reigns in royal dignity and power (as symbolized by his "scepter," the emblem of royal dignity [Esther 5:2]), which is also "righteous" (1:8). God's rule of righteousness and justice, which Psalm 89:14 describes, now refers to Jesus and his kingdom. The kingdom of God, to which both the OT (Dan 7:27) and NT (Mark 10:23–25; John 3:5) refer, is now associated with Jesus also (also 2 Pet 1:11).

As God, Jesus is righteous, creative, and eternal (1:10–12; Ps 102:25–27). While Psalm 102 addresses God, here the reference is to the changeless Christ. The word for "remains" (Gk. *diamenō*, 1:11) is a compound word made up of *menō* ("I remain") and the preposition *dia,* which is intensive. The sense, then, is "to remain permanently." In contrast to the fragile earth, Jesus is strong, permanent, and reliable.

Over the Devil and Death

The writer follows this exalted description of Jesus with the first of his sober warnings (2:1–4). He recommends that readers pay "greater attention" to their Christian heritage and to the one who provided

[17] The Jews regarded anointing with oil as rich in symbolism. It was associated with bestowing honor and affirmation (Matt 26:7; Luke 7:46) and, since it was regarded as precious, the one who was anointed was also deemed to be special. They also used it as part of religious formulae. Anointing with oil separated kings (1 Sam 10:1; 16:1) and priests (Lev 8:12) to serve God, and thus indicated the importance to God of those anointed.

them with a salvation (2:3) that is beyond compare (2:4–18), for Jesus is superior to the angels. The theme of salvation undergirds much of the rest of the letter.

Jesus deals with the people's sin and its consequences (2:17).[18] He is therefore "the source of eternal salvation" (5:9) who through his death has made it possible for people to be "sanctified," or set apart (10:10, 14; 13:12). This "single sacrifice for sins" has achieved all that is needed, "once for all," to deal with the issue of sin (10:10, 12, 14, 17). As a result, believers now have confidence to enter into a relationship with God because of "the blood of Jesus" (10:19; 13:20). Jesus has not only pioneered salvation—he has also perfected it (in the sense of completing it, 2:10; 12:2). He is not only the sacrificial lamb but also the Shepherd who has died and risen again and who has thereby established with believers an "eternal covenant" which cannot be superseded (13:20).

Quoting from Psalm 8:4–6, the writer identifies Jesus as being crowned with glory and honor, such that everything is subject to him (2:7–8; 3:3).[19] Despite this status, he became "lower than the angels"[20] so he could suffer and die for everyone (2:9). He became a member of humanity (2:11, 14, 17) in order to make salvation available (2:10). He chose to set people apart and welcome them into his family (2:11–12),[21] and he gave them the opportunity to share in his glory (2:10). He has become their champion (Gk. *archēgos*, 1:10), their hero who has rescued them and provided them with a security that is inviolable. As a result of his resurrection, he destroyed the power of the devil (2:14) and the fear and power of death (2:15). As the OT described God as the

---

[18] Much has been written concerning the meaning of the Gk. term *hilaskesthai*, which is translated as "propitiation" (the removal of God's anger towards sinners caused by sin; one propitiates a person) or "expiation" (the removal of sin; one expiates a problem, here sin). The salvation that Jesus achieved includes both senses, though most modern conservative scholars prefer to translate the Gk. *hilastērion* (9:5) as "propitiation" and not "expiation." See Mark A Seifrid, *Christ, Our Righteousness* (Leicester: Apollos, 2000).

[19] Psalm 8 refers to people. However, the writer to the Hebrews applies it to Jesus and thus gives it a christological application. His incarnation, then, is the occasion when he was made "for a little while lower than the angels." Of course, it is possible that this quotation may have an anthropological *and* a christological application, though its primary reference here must be to Jesus, since he is the subject of the section.

[20] It is possible that this abasement, if it indeed relates to any occasion in Jesus' life, refers to his incarnation or to the short period after his death but prior to his resurrection.

[21] Lane (*Hebrews 1–8*, 59) writes, "Jesus does not blush to identify himself with the people of God."

divine warrior (Isa 42:13; 49:24–26), so the NT defines Jesus in similar terms. He ejected the tyrant, the devil, and ended his tyranny, which is best identified as death.

Thereafter, Jesus has continued his work by becoming "a merciful and faithful high priest."[22] He helps people to be resilient in the face of their challenges as he himself was in confronting his (2:17–18). His suffering enables him to function constantly as a perfect high priest—to empathize with his followers and to be a victorious protagonist on their behalf (2:10).

Over Moses

The Jews admired Moses for many reasons. He rescued his people from Egypt, led them through the wilderness, and supervised the construction of the tabernacle and all it contained. He talked with God (Num 12:7–8) and was believed to have written the Pentateuch. Most importantly, however, Moses provided them with the Ten Commandments, the basis of the Law that was central to their lives. It is not surprising, therefore, that the writer to the Hebrews seeks to demonstrate that Jesus is superior to Moses.

He does this by asserting that Jesus, like Moses, was faithful (3:2)—but he was also better in a number of ways. Moses was a servant, but Jesus was an apostle, high priest, and son (3:1, 5). Moses served *in* God's house; Jesus was *over* it (3:5–6).[23] The glory that belongs to Jesus is superior to that associated with Moses (3:2–3). The writer follows this passage with another caution to readers to put their trust in Jesus, for the "rest" he offers is superior to that of Moses. The better promise Jesus offers relates to a relationship with himself (3:7–4:13).

A Superior Priesthood

The major section which explores Jesus' superlative status compares the Jewish high priestly system with Jesus (4:14–10:18, see also

---

[22] Although 2:17 mentions this idea of high priest first, it becomes an increasingly important theme of the letter.

[23] If "God's house" refers to the creation of all things (3:5), the author is further distinguishing Jesus from Moses by identifying the former as having supervisory control over the world.

2:17–18; 3:1). This passage includes additional warnings[24] that exhort readers to take full advantage of the salvation[25] Jesus makes available. On the basis of his superior status, the writer encourages readers to "approach" (4:16; 10:22) with boldness and to "hold fast" to Jesus (10:23) in order to "receive mercy" (4:16) and "find grace" (4:16). On the basis of Jesus' commitment to believers, the writer exhorts his readers to encourage other believers to do the same (10:23–25).

The section which concentrates on Jesus' superiority over the Jewish high priestly system begins by saying that Jesus is "a great high priest" who has ascended to heaven (4:14). The section likewise ends with a reference to his being "a great priest over the house of God" (10:21). Jesus does not leave earth because his priestly mission has ended. Rather, he leaves in order to continue his priestly ministry in heaven. He functioned as high priest when he sacrificed himself for sin, but his presence in heaven is a constant reminder that this act has timeless significance and ongoing application. He is, therefore, superior to all of the high priests who functioned in the OT era.

In highlighting for his Jewish readers Jesus' continuing mission as high priest, the author of Hebrews emphasizes a number of features of his salvific care that are important to them. However, they would be mistaken to take his priestly image too literally. Were they to do so, they might get the impression of Jesus presiding over a literal, ongoing sacrificial ministry in an actual heavenly temple or tabernacle. This would, of course, be to misunderstand the analogy that the author is drawing for his Jewish readers. Nevertheless, the priestly metaphor is best appreciated when the Jewish context of the readers is clearly understood. Thus the author spells out the unique role of Jesus as high priest in detail.

Empathy, Mercy, and Grace

Human high priests were able to sympathize with people since they were also sinners (5:2). Although Jesus is without sin, he is also able to empathize with believers (4:15).[26] The author uses a double negative to forcefully assert that there is no possibility of the opposite being true.

---

[24] 3:7–4:13; 6:1–12; 10:19–39.

[25] 3:18; 4:1, 3, 5, 8, 9, 11.

[26] Lane (*Hebrews 1–8*, 114) writes, "he was susceptible to all the temptations that are connected with the weaknesses inherent in the frailty of humanity."

Jesus is not only sympathetic but also actively involved in helping them. He experiences emotions associated with "prayers and supplications, with loud cries and tears" (5:7) and he also "suffered" (5:8). He knows what it is like to live as a human being. Not only did Jesus willingly place himself in the role of a learner, but in order to better relate to believers his path of learning included suffering. As other high priests prayed for their people, Jesus is also committed to praying for believers in accordance with the divine agenda (5:7).

Jesus also provides mercy and grace (4:16). Other high priests could only request that God give these things to the people. Jesus has the authority to provide them himself because he is God incarnate and his priesthood is of a different quality. The call to "approach the throne of grace" (4:16) alludes to the annual Day of Atonement, when the high priest would present himself on behalf of the people to request forgiveness. The writer asserts not only that Jesus has made forgiveness available, but also that it is no longer restricted to one day per year. Rather, it is available "in time of need" (4:16). Jesus does not enter God's presence in the earthly temple once a year, every year. He is in heaven, continuously, once and for all.[27]

The Order of Melchizedek

The writer to the Hebrews quotes from Psalm 110:4 and applies it to Jesus (5:10). He thereby elevates Jesus' priesthood by associating it with Melchizedek. Jesus has precedence because he precedes the Aaronic priesthood, but also because he supersedes Melchizedek. Melchizedek was the "priest of the Most High God" (7:1) who exists as a priest forever (7:3). He was king of Salem (7:2) and king of righteousness and peace (7:2). He has no parentage (7:3) and is eternal (7:3), "resembling the Son of God" (7:3). Abraham gave him a tenth of the spoils of war (7:1), which means that Abraham recognized that Melchizedek was superior to him (7:4, 7). A tenth was the payment that the Jews would later give to the Levites as compensation for their service in the tabernacle and the temple (7:5). Abraham, the ancestor of the Levites, represented them and, as it were, gave Melchizedek a tenth on their behalf (7:9–10). Melchizedek blessed Abraham (7:6), and the significance of this again relates to his superiority—the superior blesses the inferior

[27] 9:24–28; 10:10, 12, 14.

(7:7). Despite Abraham's exalted status as the one who "obtained the promise" (6:13–14), he received a blessing from Melchizedek.

The author then draws a contrast between the Levites ("mortal men") and Melchizedek, whose priesthood is perpetual because he is the one who "lives" (7:8) and has "an indestructible life" (7:16, 17, 23–25). Melchizedek is thus superior to Abraham and his descendants, including the Levites. Since Jesus is a high priest "according to the order of Melchizedek" (6:20), he must therefore be superior to the Levitical priesthood and his message must be of a more enduring quality than that associated with the Jewish priestly system and the Law.

The author is engaging in Jewish exegesis here, and readers should not assume that Melchizedek was the Son of God in a prior incarnation. Genesis 14:17–20 presents Melchizedek as a human being and not as one endued with supernatural status. Nevertheless, the author draws from traditions about Melchizedek that expand upon the OT's limited descriptions of him and uses these traditions to elevate Jesus in the eyes of his Jewish readers. Thus, for example, on the basis of the silence in Genesis with regard to Melchizedek's parentage, he argues that his priesthood is not based on racial or family pedigree. The writer concludes that although Melchizedek preceded the Levitical priesthood, he nevertheless functioned as a high priest of God in a way superior to the Levites. Jesus functions in a similar way (7:14), because like Melchizedek he is not descended from Levi. Fulfilling the prophecy that God would appoint a priest "according to the order of Melchizedek" (Ps 110:4), Jesus' priesthood supersedes and is superior to that of the Levitical priests.

Since Jesus was a high priest of a superior order, the expectation was that a new law code would be instituted in the context of a new priestly initiative (7:11–14). This new law has resulted in the possibility of people being perfected, unlike the old system related to the Levitical priesthood which was described as "weak" and "ineffectual" (7:18–19).

Endless Intercession

Jesus provides believers with "a sure and steadfast anchor," offering "hope" to believers that they can repeatedly[28] enter the presence of God (6:19). He has gone before as "a forerunner" to ensure that all is ready

[28] The verb "enter" (Gk. *eiserchomenēn*) is in the present continuous tense.

for when they need divine help (6:20). Jesus forever applies this "eternal salvation" he achieved (5:9), because his representative, priestly role is superior to that of all high priests who have gone before. Ordinary priests were accepted without having to pronounce an oath, and the Levitical priesthood was initiated merely by a command (Exod 29:35). However, the scriptural promise that Jesus would be "a priest forever" (7:21; Ps 110:4) makes his priesthood superior. With such affirmative backing, Jesus is bound to be a better guarantor of their salvation than anyone else (see also 6:17–18).

Unlike ordinary priests whose intercession was limited because of death, "he continues forever." Thus his priesthood is permanent and his intercession is never ending (7:24–25). Rather than assume that Jesus is constantly engaged in actual prayer on behalf of believers, it is better to appreciate the awesome message that the writer to the Hebrews is presenting here. By his presence with the Father, Jesus is functioning as a constant reminder that believers have the right to engage with God. It is not that the Father constantly needs to be reminded that believers are acceptable to him or that he only allows believers in his presence if Jesus introduces them to him. God (Father, Son, and Holy Spirit) devised the plan of salvation, each pereson of the Godhead was centrally involved in its achievement, and each is integrally related to believers. The picture of Jesus as high priest is not to remind the Father of the identity or acceptability of believers. Rather, it is to encourage believers to remember that the inexplicable facts concerning the intimate union with God are true. Jesus is not protecting believers from the wrath of the Father. Jesus is not the friendly Savior as compared with the frightening Father. On the contrary, God (Father, Son, and Holy Spirit) loves and relates to believers, continuously equips them with divine resources, and surrounds them with his presence.

A More Excellent Ministry

The writer to the Hebrews strongly affirms Jesus' eternal, moral uniqueness. Jesus had no need to offer any sacrifice since he was without sin. His self-sacrifice was solely for others (7:26–28; 8:3–4). Such an exalted description of Jesus is important for a number of reasons. It reminds readers of the superlative status of the one who is on their side (8:1–2) and of the more enduring ministry he has engaged in with them in mind (8:6). Indeed, 8:6 describes Jesus' mediation as "excellent," which indicates care on the part of the one involved in the mediation (9:15; 12:24). This description also clarifies the matchless nature of their salvation and of the covenant Jesus established between believers and God (8:6; 9:15; 10:16). Jesus sacrificed his own blood and granted complete forgiveness (9:14; 10:17–18, 22). In addition, as a result of the covenant he initiated they have received "eternal redemption" (9:12) and an "eternal inheritance" (9:15).

The most remarkable revelation here is that Jesus abolished the need for the sacrificial system that God initiated in the old covenant. It served its purpose, and Jesus has replaced it with his new covenant (9:15; 12:24) based on his life, death, and resurrection. A new relationship is now available to believers (10:10), and the Spirit will be their constant companion as they journey through life with their sins forgiven and their consciences purified (9:14).

He is always with believers (2:17; 4:15), who can place their trust in him and receive everything they need (4:16), for he "is the same yesterday and today and forever" (13:8). He is superior to all others for he is the Lord (1:10; 13:20), the Son of God (1:5; 4:14; 10:29), and God (1:8, 9).

Conclusion

As in other NT letters, it is almost impossible to separate the christology in Hebrews from its soteriological implications. The presentation of Jesus as superior to the OT prophets, the angels, Moses, and the priestly system is valuable as a reminder to readers, but also it provides the reason they should remain faithful to him. Jesus is the one to whom believers must give their allegiance, in the knowledge that he will never change.

Because the believer's earthly and heavenly future is secure (9:28), the writer anticipates a consistent lifestyle that mirrors Christ and reflects an authentic friendship with God. The readiness of the supreme Jesus to enter this world and to demonstrate his status and mission on a route marked by obedience, love, and suffering is a powerful motivation for the writer to expect no less of his readers as they also seek to fulfill God's individual commissions in their lives.

chapter 17

James

Jesus, Glorious Lord

According to church tradition, the author of this letter, referred to in the first verse of this letter simply as James, was the Lord's brother, who became one of the leaders of the church in Jerusalem. Although James the apostle would be another candidate for authorship, he was killed in AD 44 (Acts 12:1–2), prior to the likely date of this letter. James writes to Jewish believers using frequent references or allusions to the OT.[1] He treats ethical problems with stern warnings in the style of an OT prophet (5:1–6) and stresses the importance of the Law (2:9–11; 4:11–12). He provides ethical examples from the OT[2] and uses Jewish terms in his writing (e.g., synagogue, 2:2; Lord of hosts, 5:4). Appreciating the letter's Jewish roots enables us to better understand its contents.

The Authority of His Lordship

James refers to Jesus only in 1:1 and 2:1, where he describes him as the "Lord Jesus Christ." In 2:1, however, he also refers to Jesus as "glorious" (2:1).[3] He is clearly drawing attention to Jesus' glorious and exalted nature. Because of James' knowledge of the OT, he would not have used the word "glory" without being aware of its usage there, where it defines the manifestation of God.[4] He uses the term "Lord" with

[1] OT quotes are found in 1:11; 2:8, 11, 23; 4:6. For OT allusions see 1:10; 2:21, 23, 25; 3:9; 4:6; 5:2, 11, 17, 18. Jewish idioms occur in 1:1; 2:9–11; 4:11, 12; 5:4.

[2] Elijah, 5:17–18; Rahab, 2:25; Abraham, 2:21, 23.

[3] He also uses the term "Lord" (*kyrios*) to refer to God (5:4, 10, 11). On some occasions, it is not clear whether he is referring to Jesus or to God (4:10, 15).

[4] Exod 14:17–18; 40:34–35.

reference to Jesus' coming (5:7, 8) and, in association with this, the reference to "the Judge" in 5:9 is also to Jesus. These references to Jesus affirm his divine authority, for God is the one who receives glory and who alone can judge.

The Power of His Name

James writes of the faith of believers as being "in our glorious Lord Jesus Christ" (2:1). Their salvation is based on trust in Jesus and, in particular, in his mission to save the world. The teachings of Jesus, on which believers base their lifestyles, permeate the letter. Indeed, there are more implicit parallels to Jesus' teaching here in James than in any other NT letter. James does not quote Jesus' words but expresses the ideas that his words reflect. There is a clear relationship between James' allusions to Jesus' teachings and the actual teaching of Jesus that Matthew records.[5]

James also encourages readers to employ the name of the Lord in their prayers (5:14; see 2:7), probably with reference to Jesus, following the example of the apostles in healing scenarios.[6] In the NT, the name of the Lord represents his authority (see, e.g., 1 Sam 17:45; Acts 3:6). Indeed, the Bible often appears to use the "name" of the Lord and the "power" of the Lord synonymously.[7] That James incorporates the name of the Lord undergirds an expectation that believers will experience his power. James 5:14 is the only occasion where "in the name of the Lord" occurs in the context of a prayer for restoration. Here the anticipation is that the Lord will "restore" the believer, who is lacking wholeness (5:15).

The meaning of "Lord" needs to be carefully defined and its appropriate use determined. In 5:10 it occurs in the context of prophets who spoke with the authority of the Lord or, more generally, on behalf of the Lord. The words they spoke were not their own but were initiated by God and thus were in keeping with God's will. In the context of prayer, the activation of the authority to restore a believer is based on adherence

---

[5]See, e.g., 1:2 (Matt 5:10–12); 1:4 (Matt 5:48); 1:5 (Matt 7:7–11); 1:6 (Matt 21:21); 1:20 (Matt 5:22); 1:22 (Matt 7:24–27); 2:8 (Matt 22:39); 2:10 (Matt 5:19); 2:13 (Matt 5:7); 3:1 (Matt 23:8–12); 3:2 (Matt 12:36–37); 3:18 (Matt 5:9); 4:4 (Matt 6:24); 4:10 (Matt 5:5); 4:11–12 (Matt 7:1–5); 5:2–3 (Matt 6:19); 5:9 (Matt 24:33); 5:10 (Matt 5:12); 5:12 (Matt 5:33–37).

[6]Acts 3:6, 16; 4:10, 17, 18, 30.

[7]E.g., 2 Kgs 2:24; Acts 3:16.

to his will.[8] Thus, to pray in Jesus' name is equivalent to praying that his will would be done. It is to offer the prayer that he would pray. It is therefore appropriate to use the name of the Lord when Jesus is sanctioning or commissioning the prayer, for then it will effect a change.

Conclusion

Although the letter of James only explicitly refers to Jesus on two occasions, his deity, influence, and ethos permeate it. Jesus' glorious and exalted authority as the Lord obligates followers to lead lives in accord with his royal law, denying partiality, hypocrisy, slander, divisiveness, and greed. At the same time, he provides forgiveness and wholeness to those who stand strong in faithful prayer.

[8] 1:25; also 1 John 5:14, 15.

chapter 18

1 and 2 Peter

Jesus, Suffering and Victorious Redeemer

The first of the two letters attributed to Peter, one of the disciples closest to Jesus during his earthly ministry, was probably written shortly before Peter's martyrdom during the reign of the Roman emperor Nero (around 62 C.E.). The authorship of the second letter has been disputed by some scholars, who believe its style and contents reflect a later period. For the purposes of this chapter, we will refer to both letters as Peter's. Peter wrote the first letter, and perhaps the second as well, to mostly Jewish followers of Jesus scattered throughout the Roman Empire. Because his original readers experienced suffering (probably localized persecution),[1] Peter refers to Jesus' humanity (1 Pet 3:18) and affirms that Jesus also suffered unjustly,[2] bled (1 Pet 1:19), and died (1 Pet 3:18). Indeed, Jesus' sufferings are an example to his followers (1 Pet 2:21–23). Those who endure hardship are "sharing Christ's sufferings" (1 Pet 4:13; 5:1).[3] When they are "reviled for the name of Christ," they "are blessed" (1 Pet 4:14) and can be confident that they will partake "in the glory to be revealed" (1 Pet 5:1).

---

[1] 1 Pet 1:6, 7; 3:13–17; 4:1, 4, 12–19; 5:10.

[2] 1 Pet 1:11; 2:21, 23–24; 4:1; 5:1.

[3] This does not refer to a sacramental or mystical sharing in his earthly sufferings. Rather, it is a graphic reference to the sufferings that his followers experienced as they encountered similar opposition and rejection.

God and Savior

Sharing Divine Prerogatives

Peter refers to Jesus with the title "Lord," the name the OT used most often for God.[4] In particular, Peter identifies him as "Lord and Savior."[5] Surprisingly, Peter encourages believers to develop their knowledge of Jesus but does not say that they should increase their knowledge of God (2 Pet 1:8; 3:18). This is because to develop one's knowledge of Jesus is equivalent to increasing one's knowledge of God. It is significant that Peter is probably referring to Jesus as God in 2 Peter 1:1 ("our God and Savior Jesus Christ") rather than referring to God the Father and Jesus separately. Although this feature is unusual in the NT, it is by no means unique.[6]

Peter presents Jesus and God interchangeably throughout the letters. The phrase "divine power" (2 Pet 1:3) may relate to God the Father or Jesus or both, since each is powerful. Peter also talks about believers being "called" (2 Pet 1:3, 10). Although God called people in the OT (1 Pet 1:15; 2:9), the Gospels also reveal Jesus calling disciples. The OT associates God with glory, but glory also belongs to Jesus (2 Pet 1:3). Peter describes Jesus' return in language reminiscent of the appearance of God in the OT.[7] Because he is so highly exalted, Peter asserts that Jesus is worthy of glory both now and forever (2 Pet 3:18). Elsewhere, the NT associates the eternal kingdom of heaven with God.[8] Here, however, Peter says that the kingdom belongs to Jesus as well.[9] Peter thus demonstrates the equality of honor that Jesus shares as a member of the Trinity.

In 1 Peter 1:25, the quotation which includes the words "the word of the Lord endures forever," which in Isaiah 40:8 clearly refers to the word of God, is applied to Jesus and, in particular, to the "good news" of his mission.[10] Similarly, the quotation from Psalm 34:15–16 (which

---

[4] 1 Pet 1:3; 2:3; 2 Pet. 1:2, 8, 11, 14, 16; 3:8, 9, 10, 15, 18.

[5] 2 Pet 1:11; 2:20; 3:2, 18.

[6] John 1:1; 20:28; Heb 1:8–9.

[7] 2 Pet 3:8 is an allusion to Ps 90:4; see also "the day of the Lord" in 2 Pet 3:10. See R. J. Bauckham (*Jude, 2 Peter* [WBC; Waco: Word, 1983], 306–10) for a full description of the meaning of these verses.

[8] Mark 10:23–25; Luke 1:33; John 3:5.

[9] See also Col 1:13; Heb 1:8.

[10] It is significant that Peter replaced "God" (*theos*) with "Lord" (*kyrios*), possibly to relate the quotation more clearly to Jesus. The next reference to "Lord," in 2:3, refers to Jesus.

refers to God) in 1 Peter 3:12 probably refers to Jesus.[11] Peter's encouragement to readers to sanctify "Christ as Lord" (1 Pet 3:15) a few verses later makes this association clear. The one who cares for and protects believers and who opposes their enemies, the one whom the OT text identifies as God, Peter also acknowledges to be Jesus who similarly cares for those who follow him and who suffer as a result.

The fact that Peter calls the Spirit who inspired the prophets not the Holy Spirit or the Spirit of God[12] but "the Spirit of Christ"[13] also elevates Jesus' status. Peter is affirming a number of truths in this statement, including the fact that Jesus existed prior to his incarnation and that he is in close association with the Spirit. Peter is not assuming that there is only one person who is called Christ or the Spirit. Rather, he is significantly elevating Jesus by speaking of him in such immediate proximity to the Spirit. The only parallel for this elsewhere is the Spirit being called the Spirit of God. It is significant for the believers who are suffering that Jesus' sufferings were the focus of the Spirit when inspiring the prophets (1 Pet 1:11). As the Spirit (of Christ) was aware of Jesus' sufferings, so also the Spirit is cognizant of the sufferings of Christ's followers. The Spirit prophesied, through the prophets, the glory that would envelope the suffering Jesus. The implicit hope is that such a reward awaits them as well.

Victorious over Death

Jesus is associated with power, majesty, honor, glory, and dominion.[14] He reigns over an eternal kingdom (2 Pet 1:11). The unique reference to his preaching "to the spirits in prison" (1 Pet 3:19–20), which is "the most remote and unlikely audience imaginable,"[15] further illustrates Jesus' supremacy. Even though Jesus died, death for him was a process to pass through, not a final state that enveloped him. Although he had died, Jesus was still alive, and he demonstrated this by speaking authoritatively to others who had also died.[16] Rather than death imprisoning

---

[11] So Bauckham, *Jude, 2 Peter,* 181.

[12] 1 Sam 10:6, 10; 19:23; 2 Chr 15:1.

[13] 1 Pet 1:11; also Rom 8:9.

[14] 1 Pet 1:7, 11; 4:11, 13; 5:10, 11; 2 Pet 1:16–17; 3:18.

[15] J. Ramsey Michaels, *1 Peter* (WBC; Waco: Word, 1988), 206.

[16] It is possible that those who died were: (1) fallen angels or demons who had been removed to this place prior to their eventual destruction (possibly those referred to in

him, he spoke to those who were in prison. Peter does not specify the content of his message. In the context of his death at the hands of those who opposed him, however, and with the reminder that the readers face a similar end from those who oppose them, it is likely that Peter reminds his readers of Jesus' victorious proclamation to encourage them to stand firm in the face of opposition.

Jesus' audience comprised the "spirits in prison, who in former times did not obey, when God waited patiently in the days of Noah" (1 Pet 3:19–2). It is likely, therefore, that he confirmed the truth of Noah's message and the integrity of the messenger. Jesus, far from being dead and defeated, preached a message of victory and vindicated truth and integrity.[17] Even though their disobedience occurred centuries earlier, Jesus had not overlooked or forgotten it. At the appropriate time, he revisited it. Jesus also stands as the advocate for all who suffer for doing right and for placing their faith in him.

His resurrection did not simply remove Jesus from sufferings. It enabled him to go to heaven to reside in the place of highest honor (1 Pet 3:21–22), at "the right hand" of God (Eph 1:20; Heb 1:3). There he is in the presence of "angels, authorities, and powers" who are all subject to him (1 Pet 3:22; also Heb 2:5–9). Because of his fundamental importance (1 Pet 2:6), he has the authority to judge (1 Pet 2:7–8) and "to keep the unrighteous under punishment until the day of judgment" (2 Pet 2:9).

The Majestic Son

Peter speaks of Jesus as the Son of "God the Father" (1 Pet 1:3; 2 Pet 1:17). Peter recalls the approval and affirmation that the Father

---

Gen 6:1–4); (2) OT believers who were being guarded until their resurrection; or (3) unbelieving people who had rejected the message of Noah. For support for option (3), see W. Grudem, *1 Peter: An Introduction and Commentary* (Tyndale New Testament Commentaries; Grand Rapids: Eerdmans, 1988), 157–61, 203–39. For option (1), see P. H. Davids (*The Letters of 2 Peter and Jude* [PNTC; Grand Rapids: Eerdmans, 2006], 139–40), who argues that the word "spirits" never refers to people but to demons and notes also that *1 En.* 21:6–10 refers to fallen angels who disobeyed in the days of Noah and who were imprisoned. For a useful summary, see Michaels, *1 Peter,* 206–9.

[17]The purpose of Jesus' preaching here is not to provide a chance for repentance but to announce that, even when it is unseen, truth is unconquerable. The term *euangelizomai*, which Peter uses in 1:12, 25; 4:6 to refer to evangelistic preaching, is not his choice here. Instead, he uses *keryssō*, "I declare."

offered to the Son at Jesus' transfiguration (2 Pet 1:17–18). He described Jesus as "precious" (1 Pet 2:6, 7) and having "majesty" (2 Pet 1:16).[18] The Father, who is "Majestic" (2 Pet 1:17), shares this portrait of majesty with the Son as they celebrate their exalted and dignified relationship.[19]

Jesus' high honor provides sufficient reason for the author's identification of himself as "an apostle of Jesus Christ" (1 Pet 1:1; "servant and apostle," 2 Pet 1:1). Followers of this exalted Savior are to love him (1 Pet 1:8), revere him (1 Pet 3:15), obey him (2 Pet 3:2), trust him to rescue them in their trials (2 Pet 3:9), and honor him with good behavior "in Christ" (1 Pet 3:16).

From Suffering to Glory

Costly Suffering

Peter graphically illustrates how much our salvation cost Jesus. He writes of the sprinkling of "his blood" (1 Pet 1:2)[20] and identifies Jesus as the "lamb without blemish or spot" (1 Pet 1:19).[21] Faith in Jesus results in salvation (1 Pet 1:5, 9) and Peter explicitly refers to Jesus as "Savior" (2 Pet 1:1).[22] The process of salvation involves Jesus bearing "our sins in his body on the cross" (1 Pet 2:24), which alludes to Isaiah 53:4, 12. This is reminiscent of Paul's reference to Jesus becoming sin (2 Cor 5:21).

Similarly, Peter declares that Jesus has died "for sins once for all" (1 Pet 3:18), even though he himself did not sin.[23] Indeed, 2 Peter 1:1

---

[18] This word describes God in Dan 7:27.

[19] Davids (*2 Peter and Jude,* 205) notes that Peter does not include the synoptic references to the cloud (or mountain) or the command to listen to Jesus. The focus is on the relationship between Jesus and the Father. There is no allusion to the inferior Moses, who also heard God speak on a mountain in a cloud (Exod 24:16). Jesus and the Father here are center stage.

[20] This is a reminder of the blood associated with a sacrificial offering. The blood acts as the seal of the covenant between God and his people (Exod 24:7–8; Heb 9:18–21).

[21] The reference is to the flawless Passover lamb (Exod 12:5; 29:1; Lev 4:19–20).

[22] Although this is an important term because it refers to Jesus saving people, it is also significant to readers who were used to the Caesar being identified as a savior. Jesus brings a superior salvation because he is a superior savior.

[23] 1 Pet 2:22, quoting Isa 53:9; see also 1 Pet 1:19, "without defect or blemish."

identifies Jesus as functioning in (ethical) righteousness.[24] His act of redemption (1 Pet 1:18) results in his being able to "bring you to God" (1 Pet 3:18). As a result of his death, believers are encouraged to "die to sin" so that they might "live for righteousness" because "by his wounds you have been healed" (1 Pet 2:24).[25] Something positive has resulted from physical pain and suffering, and this is a welcome message for readers. In response to Jesus' selfless act of grace and love, Peter exhorts believers to be "without spot or blemish" (2 Pet 3:14), as was Jesus (1 Pet 1:19).

God planned (and did not merely predict) the act of salvation before the creation of the world, because of his "great mercy." As a result, believers experience "a new birth," "into a living hope," "into an inheritance that is imperishable, undefiled, and unfading, kept in heaven for you" (1 Pet 1:3–4). To those who sacrifice all, including their lives, Peter promises substantially more than that which they will lose and he reassures them that God is guarding their reward for them. He is referring to the fact that God has granted believers "entry into the eternal kingdom of our Lord and Savior Jesus Christ" (2 Pet 1:11).

A Glorious Resurrection

1 Peter 1:3 refers to Jesus' resurrection, which authenticated his mission and guarantees the inheritance of believers, which is awaiting them in heaven.[26] Jesus' return is associated with hope, grace (1 Pet 1:13), glory, and honor (1 Pet 1:7). Peter exhorts believers to live in accordance with the hope that they have received through Christ, regardless of their circumstances. The message to readers is clear—they can place their confidence in Jesus (1 Pet 1:21), for he is their hope and the basis of their trust (1 Pet 1:13, 21). Just as Jesus died physically but remained spiritually alive, so also believers may die but will nevertheless retain spiritual life (1 Pet 3:18).[27]

---

[24] Elsewhere this term refers to righteousness as a lifestyle (2 Pet 1:13; 2:5, 7, 8, 21; 3:13).

[25] This healing relates to the forgiveness of sins, as the previous verse states, and not physical healing.

[26] See also 1 Pet 1:21; 3:18, 21.

[27] It is probable that *pneuma* (3:18) describes the new sphere of Jesus' life, dominated by the Spirit and therefore divine (so Michaels, *1 Peter*, 204–5). Jesus did not just die, leaving his body of flesh behind to take on a new mystical, spiritual bodily

Spiritual Temples and Spiritual Sacrifices

Peter also describes the present benefits of their salvation. As a result of Jesus' mission, believers are referred to as "living stones," reflecting Jesus who is also a "living stone" (1 Pet 2:4).[28] As a result of their relationship with Jesus, the cornerstone, believers are now part of the building that God is developing. God is building them "into a spiritual house." It is more appropriate to understand this house in terms of believers becoming an organism in which the Spirit dwells[29] rather than as a nonmaterial or mystical habitation. Furthermore, believers form "a holy priesthood,"[30] each member of which is able, because of Jesus, "to offer spiritual sacrifices acceptable to God" (1 Pet 2:5). Because of Jesus' sacrifice, believers offer their lives to God with the knowledge that he will be pleased with their contribution. Their gift is worthy not because of the intrinsic worth of their deeds or words, but because they present themselves, in Jesus, as fully fledged members of the family of God. Peter summarizes this section (1 Pet 2:1–9) by defining believers as "a chosen race, a royal priesthood, a holy nation, God's own people." While some of these terms also described the Jewish nation, now all believers, regardless of their race, are part of the people of God.[31] They are "in Christ" (1 Pet 5:14).

Through Jesus, believers receive significant resources—the gifts of "grace" and "peace" (2 Pet 1:2; 3:18). Jesus also enables them to know who they are and their true potential (2 Pet 1:2). Second Peter 1:3–11 provides a list of benefits that God grants to believers, including "everything needed for life and godliness," "precious and very great promises,"[32] and "entry into the eternal kingdom of our Lord and Savior Jesus Christ." The text does not clarify whether these attributes are from

form. Rather, he began to exist as he had done before his incarnation, in a way that was dominated and infused by the Spirit of God.

[28]The term "living stone" is a contradiction. Peter uses the term because of the "stone" in Isa 28:16, which he quotes a few verses later and relates to Jesus. In the OT, it refers to a stone God used as the basis for a new construction in Zion. To relate the stone to Jesus, Peter adds that it is "living."

[29]1 Cor 3:16; 6:19.

[30]The term *hierateuma* occurs only here and in 2:9 in the NT; the allusion is to Exod 19:6.

[31]1 Pet 2:10; alluding to Hos 1:6, 9–10.

[32]This is the only other reference to the word "promise" (*epangelia*) in the letter and is in the context of the return of Jesus.

God the Father or from Jesus, though the nearest antecedent is Jesus, in 1:2. Peter also refers to him by name ("Lord Jesus Christ") in verse 8. Verse 9 refers to his act of cleansing from sin and a reference to "our Lord and Savior Jesus Christ" ends the section in verse 11. It is appropriate, therefore, to see Jesus as the one who provides these gifts, which indicate his divine authority and beneficence.[33] Not only is he associated with "glory and goodness" (2 Pet 1:3), but he also grants to those he has cleansed the possibility of participating in "the divine nature" (2 Pet 1:4).[34] He is their example (1 Pet 2:21–24) and also the "shepherd" of straying sheep (1 Pet 2:25).

Conclusion

Writing to believers who were suffering as a result of opposition from those who rejected their message, Peter offers in these two letters guidance and support. Jesus is central to the hope that Peter offers his readers. In particular, Jesus' identity as Lord and victor helps believers put their present circumstances into perspective. Because Jesus himself suffered, he understands what they are experiencing. His resurrection encourages believers to focus on the promise that, whatever happens to them in this life, they will be with God in the next. Meanwhile, Jesus provides them with all the resources they need to persevere through their suffering. His gifts to them reflect the intimate relationship that they have with him.

---

[33] So D. Lucas and C. Green, *The Message of 2 Peter and Jude* (Downers Grove, Ill.: InterVarsity, 1995), 44–54.

[34] Although it is not clear what this phrase, "the divine nature," means, it must refer to believers benefiting from some aspect of God's character. Davids (*2 Peter and Jude,* 176), on the basis of the content of the previous verses, suggests that it relates to "the reception of an ethical nature like God's." Bauckham (*Jude, 2 Peter*, 180–91) prefers the notion of immortality. Although it is possible that the promise is actualized at salvation, the context may indicate the eschaton as the context for its fulfillment (so Bauckham, *Jude, 2 Peter,* 181–82). There is no reason, however, why this process should not take place from the point of salvation on, depending on what exactly it involves. Davids (*2 Peter and Jude,* 176), therefore, sees it beginning with salvation but not ending there. The fact that Peter does not clarify this may be significant in itself.

chapter 19

1–3 John

Jesus, Giver of Eternal Life

Although these letters do not identify their author,[1] they have long been associated with the Apostle John, the brother of James. We will refer to them simply as the letters of John. These letters address a number of issues including love (mentioned over 40 times), obedience to God, fellowship, and dealing with sin. John refers to "Jesus Christ" on a number of occasions.[2] His usage may indicate that this compound name for Jesus was a popular one by that time. It is also likely that he used the name to stress that Jesus is none other than the incarnate Messiah (i.e., Jesus, the Christ)—a fact that some of his readers were denying. John therefore stresses Jesus' incarnation (1 John 5:6; 2 John 1:7) as well as his messiahship (1 John 5:1). Indeed, John makes the acceptance of Jesus as the Son of God a condition of salvation and Christian orthodoxy (1 John 4:2; 5:5, 10). The antichrist is defined as the one who rejects this truth.[3]

John's brief second letter addresses an early error known as Docetism, which involved a denial of the reality of Jesus' physical nature. The third letter, addressed to a personal friend named Gaius, while it does not mention Jesus explicitly, calls upon his followers to show hospitality toward those who go out to spread the good news.

The Father and the Son

John emphasizes that Jesus is the Son of God[4] and he identifies his status as being unique.[5] To reject either the Father or the Son, John

---

[1] 2 and 3 John identify the author obliquely as "the Elder."

[2] 1 John 1:3; 2:1; 3:23; 4:2; 5:6, 20; 2 John 7.

[3] 1 John 2:22; 4:3; 2 John 1:7.

[4] 1 John 2:22, 23; 3:23; 4:15; 5:5, 10, 12–13; 2 John 1:3.

[5] 1 John 4:9; see also John 1:14, 18; 3:16, 18.

warns, is to lose one's relationship with the other (1 John 2:22; 2 John 1:9), for the Father is the constant supporter of the Son (1 John 5:9). John also identifies Jesus as the one who, in cooperation with the Father, grants grace, mercy, and peace to believers (2 John 1:3), while both the Father and the Son are identified as the ones with whom believers are able to have fellowship (1 John 1:3). At the same time, John affirms that Jesus is the one who destroys all that the devil has achieved (1 John 3:8).

Forgiveness and Life

John contradicts those who question if Jesus is the Savior. He asserts that not only is Jesus their Savior, but he is "the Savior of the world" (1 John 4:14).[6] As a result of the saving action of Jesus, fellowship with him and with the Father is now available (1 John 1:3, 7). John defines salvation as being not only about forgiveness but also about friendship with God, or abiding in the Son and the Father.[7] This metaphor demonstrates the intimacy of that relationship. It is a bond that the Spirit, who Jesus has given to believers, secures (1 John 3:24; 4:13). First John 4:15–16 reverses the metaphor and identifies God as the one who abides in those who confess that Jesus is the Son of God.

Finally, John reminds his readers that not only does Jesus know them intimately, but he also desires them to enjoy close relationship with him. Indeed, Jesus has devoted himself to facilitating this friendship (1 John 5:20; 2 John 1:9) and to responding to any prayer request that is aligned with his will (1 John 5:14–15), indicating that he listens and responds to all. Jesus achieved salvation as a result of loving people (1 John 4:9–10) and dying for them. Because he substituted his life for believers (1 John 3:16), the implication is that they should be prepared to lay down their lives for others.

Forgiveness of sins is, of course, fundamental to that relationship between Jesus and believers (1 John 1:7; 4:10) and is one of the benefits that believers enjoy (1 John 1:9; 2:1–2). Eternal life, the life that Jesus experiences to its fullest, is the promise to believers as a result of the salvation Jesus achieved.[8] This reference is not simply to everlasting life but also relates to the quality of life enjoyed by those whose destiny is

---

[6] This phrase appears only here and in John 4:42 in the NT.

[7] 1 John 2:24–25; 3:24; 4:15.

[8] 1 John 2:25; 5:11–13.

determined by the eternal characteristics that define God. In revealing their future to them, John records that they will see Jesus and be like him (1 John 3:2). He is probably referring to moral purity here, as the following verse intimates. As elsewhere, this promise has a practical consequence, for they are to prepare for eternal life by transforming their lives to be increasingly like his.

Conclusion

In letters written to believers who are facing a range of challenges caused by internal and external problems, John encourages his readers to focus on Jesus. His unique status, authority, love, and grace encourage believers' devotion. His incarnation in flesh and blood insures the authenticity of his suffering for sinners. Jesus not only provides believers with the opportunity to enjoy a relationship with God, but he also ensures that it lasts for eternity. As followers of Christ, believers are urged to demonstrate the authenticity of their faith by demonstrating practical love and caring for those in need.

chapter 20

Jude

Jesus, Just Judge and Merciful Master

This short letter identifies its author as Jude, the brother of James (1:1), the leader of the Jerusalem church, and one of the half brothers of Jesus Christ.[1]

Verse 3 indicates that Jude had originally intended to write a letter to believers about their faith but had changed his focus in the light of incorrect teachings that were affecting the church. It appears that those who were spreading error presented false views of Jesus and of grace while exhibiting arrogance and sexually inappropriate lifestyles. These false teachers also lacked experience of the Spirit.[2] The letter therefore offers a series of stern warnings, along with a passionate condemnation of false teachers,[3] and practical guidelines related to maintaining the true faith (vv. 20–23).

Jesus the Master and Lord

Jude identifies Jesus not only as Messiah but also as the Lord. He presents the authority of Jesus as being identical to that of God (v. 24). The crimes of those who were immoral and rejected Jesus were therefore particularly heinous because of his high status as "Master[4] and Lord" (v. 4). Because of his divine dignity, people are to believe Jesus as well as

---

[1] Mark 6:3 lists Jesus' brothers as James, Joses, Judas (the Greek form of Jude), and Simon.

[2] Vv. 4, 8, 10, 18, 19.

[3] Vv. 7, 10, 12–13, 16.

[4] The word here, Gk. *despotēs*, is unusual and rare in the NT. Elsewhere it refers to God (Luke 2:29; Rev 6:10), but generally it refers to the master of a slave (1 Tim 6:1; 1 Pet 2:18). Jesus is the believer's Master, both Sovereign and Lord.

the message brought by those he has sent. Jude reminds his readers of the prophecies of "the apostles of our Lord Jesus Christ" (v. 17). These predictions are trustworthy because those who represent the one who has supreme authority have delivered them. Jude is privileged to be a servant of such a remarkable leader (v. 1). He may be Jesus' brother, but he prefers to introduce himself as Jesus' servant.

Blameless before God

Because of the destabilizing situation that many in the church were experiencing, Jude reminds his readers that Jesus is in charge of their destiny (v. 1). They are being kept safe by him. This concept of being kept safe is central to the letter.[5] God's promise to protect his people (Isa 42:6; 49:8) now applies to the believers. Jesus is active in protecting them—not only for the future, but also for himself. Even though Jude's readers may be confused about certain aspects of the gospel because of the false teaching that has been circulating in the church, Jude asserts that Jesus is keeping them for himself. As Jesus keeps the faithless angels in captivity (v. 6), so also he keeps the faithful believers safe.

Jesus, as a result of his mercy, is committed to ensure that believers benefit from eternal life (v. 21). He will protect them from falling and ensure that they are presented "without blemish," blameless before God.[6] Jesus' mediatory role is particularly significant because of the division and uncertainty that Jude's original readers faced.

Conclusion

In a letter that focuses on the unsettling challenges caused by false teaching, Jude reminds his readers of the hope and certainty that Jesus' presence provides. While everything around them may seem unstable, Jesus, their preserver, is the basis for the eternal confidence of believers everywhere.

---

[5] Vv. 1, 6, 13, 21, 24.

[6] V. 24; see also Eph 1:14; Col 1:22.

chapter 21

Revelation

Jesus, Victorious Lamb of God

The book of Revelation (sometimes referred to as the Apocalypse) is a circular letter (intended for seven churches [1:11; Rev 1–3]) that exhorts readers to pursue spiritual transformation and encourages them to renew their faith in, and devotion to, Jesus. Although the authorship of the book has been much disputed, the author refers to himself simply as John in Revelation (1:4).[1] Following a series of letters to seven ancient churches, the book (ch. 4 onwards) explores the challenges facing believers who are experiencing opposition from within and outside the church. The vision of Jesus' ultimate victory over evil provides encouragement for persecuted believers.

In presenting the victorious Jesus, John reflects many themes from the OT and draws his imagery mainly from Daniel and Ezekiel. Much has been written about the interpretation of the book, its genre, and symbolism.[2] There has been much less written about the role and significance of the book's central character, Jesus. Many modern believers may even assume that the devil is more central to the message of Revelation, since so many popular books promulgate it as a prophecy of end-time events. The main message of the book of Revelation is that God, through Jesus Christ, will triumph over the devil and over evil. It is a book about assurance rather than angst, triumph rather than tribulation. Jesus, who easily vanquishes the devil, is the victor, who is in charge of the destiny of the church, the lives of believers, the present, the future, and even the devil (whose end is predetermined). In anticipation of his

---

[1] For a discussion of authorship, see G. K. Beale, *The Book of Revelation: A Commentary on the Greek Text* (NIGTC; Grand Rapids: Eerdmans, 1999), 34–36.

[2] See Beale, *Revelation*, 37–69.

certain victory, Revelation encourages readers to maintain their faith in, and witness to, Jesus.[3]

The First and the Last

A Trinitarian Portrait

The book of Revelation presents Jesus as fully divine and often portrays the partnership between God the Father and Christ (20:4, 6; 21:22). Several passages refer to him as "Lord,"[4] though 19:12 refers to his name being unknown.[5] Each reference to Jesus declares his authority. In a rare Trinitarian portrait, John combines the Father, Spirit, and Jesus in a greeting to believers that also refers to their provision of grace and peace (1:4–5). Jesus shares equality, therefore, with the Father and the Spirit. To him is offered "glory and dominion forever and ever" (1:6). All of these features help put the reference to Jesus being given the revelation into perspective. It is not that Jesus receives the revelation as an inferior benefiting from the gift of a superior—on the contrary, he is an equal member of the Godhead.

The portrait of Jesus in 1:12–20 (see also 19:12) is purposefully grand and reminiscent of the description of Jehovah in Daniel (7:6–10; 10:5–6) and Ezekiel (9:2; 43:2), some of which is later repeated in the introductions to the individual churches (2:1, 8, 12, 18). Of particular note is John's description of Jesus as the Son of Man (1:13; 14:14). His dress, appearance, and characteristics are like those of "the Ancient of Days" in Daniel.[6] It is not necessary to assume that Jesus actually looked like this. These metaphorical descriptions serve to identify him as being exalted as God.

His long robe and golden sash in the context of a temple scene in 1:13 probably imply his priestly role, though they could also indicate a regal role. The white hair, reminiscent of Daniel's vision of God (Dan 7:9), also conveys the ideas of wisdom, honor, and dignity.

---

[3] Revelation mentions Jesus' name 14 times (2 times 7), e.g., 2:10, 13, 19, 25; 3:8, 10–11; 12:17; 14:12; 19:10.

[4] 11:8; 17:14; 19:16; 22:20, 21.

[5] Earlier verses introduce the concept of the name (2:17; 3:5, 8, 12–13). Rev 19:12 declares that Jesus has the authority to decide when and to whom he will reveal his name.

[6] His eyes, voice, and face are similar to those of God in Dan 10:6.

The reference to feet of "burnished bronze" may indicate his moral purity. The two-edged sword[7] symbolizes precise perception and accurate judgment.

Titles that the Bible elsewhere ascribes to God now refer to Jesus, including "the first and the last" (1:17; 22:13), which is reminiscent of Isaiah 41:4; 44:6; 48:12, and the "Word of God" (19:13). Jesus is the one who had died but is now alive forevermore, which is a further reference to God (Dan 4:34; 6:27). He also has the highest authority to possess "the keys of Death and of Hades" (1:18), while the "I am" phrase, which God uses throughout the OT, now applies to Jesus.[8]

The introductions to the final three churches reveal new information about Jesus. He is associated with the Spirit (1:4; 5:6)[9] and the messengers of the churches (3:1). He is also the holy and true one, a phrase that regularly describes God in the OT (Isa 29:19, 23). He has the authoritative "key of David" (3:7), which is a clear reference to God's authority to decide who may be welcomed into his kingdom (Isa 22:22). Jesus is also the "Amen" and "the faithful and true witness"—phrases that, again, refer only to God in the OT (Isa 65:16).[10] Finally, the description of Jesus as "the origin of God's creation" (3:14) is possibly a reference to his resurrection rather than to his creative power.

King of Kings and Lord of Lords

In Revelation 22:16, John describes Jesus as "the bright morning star." Peter used this term (2 Pet 1:19) in a metaphorical reference to Jesus' certain and triumphal return. Revelation 5:5 describes Jesus as "the Lion of the tribe of Judah" who "has conquered" (Gen 49:9). Not only is he descended from the messianic line, "the Root of David" (5:5; 22:16), but he is also, like a lion, the epitome of authority and strength.

These pictures of Jesus would have been of particular encouragement to the book's original readers, who were living in an empire which presented a real threat to Christians because of their refusal to

---

[7] 1:16; 2:16; 19:15, 21, reminiscent of Isa 11:4; 49:2.

[8] 1:17, 18; 2:23; 22:16.

[9] The description of "seven spirits" may be intended to draw upon Jewish imagery associating the numeral 7 with perfection. If so, the image would refer to the unique, perfect Spirit working in partnership with Jesus.

[10] See Beale (*Revelation*, 297–301) for a full discussion.

participate in emperor worship. It was important for a church experiencing fear and uncertainty and facing the prospect of suffering, including martyrdom, to have an accurate picture of their supreme and sovereign Savior. Although it might have appeared that the emperor had the power of life and death, in reality he was a pawn in the hand of the one who was constantly present with the believers, caring for their eternal interests (1:20). The letters to the churches that follow demonstrate Jesus' intimate knowledge of their situations and his desire to guide and protect them. Although they were experiencing pressure caused by political powers, Jesus was present with them to provide for all of their needs.

John records the words of voices in heaven announcing that Jesus' kingdom, which he shares with God forever (11:15), will replace the kingdoms of this world. Jesus is described as "coming with the clouds" (1:7), or returning to earth. This picture derives from Dan 7:13, with reference to the coming of the Son of Man. Zechariah 12:10 prophesies the return of the one who was "pierced." While John's vision declares his present heavenly dwelling, it more specifically explores the impact that his return will have on those who killed him and, by extension, those who oppose his followers. His return will cause his desolate and doomed enemies much anguish and despair.[11] Although life is still in process, God has already determined the end, and Jesus will come to conclude it, powerfully and authoritatively.

Jesus is also the ruler, the judge (with "eyes . . . like a flame of fire," 1:14; 2:18), the conqueror of the kings on earth,[12] and the leader of heaven's armies (19:14). Although these facts define Jesus' sovereign authority over all other regal powers, natural and supernatural (12:10), John is also reminding his readers that even kings will be called to account for any measures they have initiated against believers. The authority of earthly kings is vastly inferior to Jesus' authority. Jesus is the Lord of believers. He is on their side and against their enemies. He is the "Lord of lords and King of kings" (17:14; 19:16) who wears "many diadems" (19:12),[13] the king of the cosmos.

[11] 1:7; 6:15–16; 14:10–11.

[12] 1:5; 14:14; 17:14; 19:11, 16. Although it will not be until 21:24 that John will explicitly reveal that the kings will submit to Jesus, it is announced at the start of the prophecy—their destiny is already determined.

[13] Jesus' many diadems are in contrast to the dragon, which has only 7 (12:3), and the beast, which has 10 (13:1).

A Secure Future

The opening of the scroll (5:1–13), which represents the future (4:1), is also of great interest to John's readers. The author's sadness (5:4) that no one is worthy to open the scroll is due to the fact that, without the future, past and present sufferings will receive no explanation or resolution. The scroll is thus important because of what it represents—the revelation of God's justice and the consummation of his eternal plans. Without the disclosure of the future represented by the opening of the scroll's seals, there would be no certainty of judgment on sin and all God's enemies, no eternal life for believers, and no fulfillment of all that God had planned for those he had saved. Such a prospect encapsulates the worst of all fears. Not only was the relatively small group of believers faced with a sea of antagonism against them, but they would remain uncertain about any prospect of relief without a revelation from God.

One of the elders then says, "Do not weep" (5:5), and a Lamb comes into focus. Tears are replaced with triumph, fears fade away, and hope comes home to stay because the Lamb is deemed worthy to open the seals (5:5, 7; 8:1). The fact that he is able to open the seals of the scroll confirms his supremacy. Graphically described, fearful events of judgment then occur (6:1–17). Jesus is this authoritative deity who presents this revelation and supervises the destinies of the churches (1:16).

Jesus is the Lamb with seven horns, which represent complete power, and seven eyes, which refer to the wisdom of the Spirit (5:6). He thus has supreme authority and comprehensive knowledge.

Worship the Lamb

It is little wonder that John devotes the rest of chapter 5 to the worship and exaltation of the Lamb. The Lamb has redeemed the people of God (5:9–10) and has given solid hope for the future. Those who serve God and are gathered around the throne, the twenty-four elders and the "four living creatures" (5:8–10, 14), therefore worship Jesus. These "living creatures" are reminiscent of the OT cherubim (Ezek 1:5–23). Thus Jesus receives honor from God's highest angels. They affirm him with a sevenfold acclamation: he is worthy to receive power, wealth, wisdom, might, honor, glory, and blessing from every living being forever (5:12–14).[14]

[14]The 24 elders and the 4 living creatures in 7:12 worship God with a similar sevenfold exaltation.

The Firstborn from the Dead

The Lamb Slain and Living

John describes Jesus as the one who was slain[15] and who functioned as a ransom (5:9). In the later chapters, he refers to Jesus' blood being shed.[16] He is the one who "loves us and freed us from our sins by his blood" (1:5). He knows the situations that believers face and has suffered in order to secure their salvation. Jesus achieved the greatest miracle—in the weakness of dying, he demonstrated supreme power. In the final act of his life, it appeared that he was bowing out as a failure. What actually happened, however, was that he simply moved from the penultimate scene to the climax of the drama as, with authority and ease, his victory humiliated all of the apparently superior forces opposing him. Not once was he the victim, even when circumstances seemed to indicate otherwise. There was no uncertainty or tension in heaven when Jesus was on the cross. On the contrary, God had already predetermined the end of the story.

John describes Jesus as the Lamb twenty-eight times[17] in the book of Revelation. This image, which reflects the Passover sacrifice of the OT,[18] is a striking reminder to readers of the redemption Jesus achieved. The language of conquest and victory (5:5), which perhaps alludes to similar themes in Jewish literature,[19] describes the redemption that the Lamb achieved. The Lamb who now stands alive and victorious, John says, has conquered his enemies by being slain (5:6, 12; 13:8). As the readers face death, John reminds them that Jesus also faced death and demonstrated the authenticity of his person and mission through death, for justice had determined that he would rise again, as would they. Like Jesus, too, believers will declare the validity of their faith most powerfully at the moment of death, when they appear to be weakest. The most compelling picture of the relationship between the Lamb and believers is that of the church as the bride of the Lamb

---

[15] 5:6, 9, 12; 13:8.

[16] 7:14; 12:11; 19:13.

[17] It is interesting that the number 28 can be configured as 4 (the symbol of the world, 7:1; 20:8) multiplied by 7 (the perfect number). Thus the Lamb achieves perfect salvation for the world.

[18] Isa 53:7–9; John 1:29, 36; 1 Cor 5:7.

[19] For a full discussion of this background, see David Aune, *Revelation 1–5* (WBC; Waco: Word, 1997), 367–73.

(21:9; 19:7–8) invited to "the marriage supper of the Lamb" (19:9).[20] John presents Jesus as the bridegroom, a metaphor that the OT applied to God.[21] As they worship God, so believers worship the Lamb of God—Jesus Christ (15:3).

The Firstborn Son

Revelation 1:5 refers to Jesus as the firstborn from the dead (see also Col 1:18). The term "firstborn" recalls the highly privileged status of the heir in a Jewish family in terms of inheritance and succession (Deut 21:15–17). Jesus has this privileged status. This is also, however, a reference to Jesus' resurrection from the dead and reminds believers of the salvation that Jesus achieved as well as of the prospect of their own resurrection after death. For those who are facing martyrdom, this message is powerfully therapeutic—another life and their Savior await them.

A Kingdom of Priests

Jesus' redemptive acts provided believers with life (13:8; 21:27) and formed them into a new kingdom of priests (1:6; 5:10; 20:6). Believers participate in the fulfillment of the ancient promise of Exodus 19:6 as they are able to serve God and receive royal dignity. As a result of the mission of the Lamb, believers will experience the fulfillment of their salvation in Jesus' presence (7:9–10). Jesus has promised to return (22:20) to be their shepherd and guide (7:17) —still more images that the OT uses to describe the ministry of God (Isa 49:10). Believers who have been sealed, meaning all who have followed Jesus, are redeemed (14:1–5) and reign with him (20:4, 6).

Jesus, Faithful and True

The letters to the seven churches in Revelation describe a number of the resources that Jesus provides for believers, each of which reflects some aspect of his character. Jesus is intimately present with believers

[20] See Beale (*Revelation,* 934–46) for a full discussion.

[21] Isa 54:5–8; 61:10; Hos 2:14–20.

(1:13), for he holds them and walks among them (2:1). As a priest's duty was to tend the candlesticks in the temple, so also Jesus cares for the church. Jesus is also aware of their strengths and weaknesses, of the sufferings they are experiencing and will yet experience (2:10, 13). He offers both challenges and words of encouragement (2:2–3:22). He has the authority to support them (3:3) but also to discipline them.[22]

These letters are of particular importance to believers who are uncertain about how long they have in this life, given the challenging times in which they live. Jesus provides them with eternal life (2:7), "the crown of life" (2:10), protection from "the second death" (2:11), membership in a new community and a new name (2:17; 22:4). Each of these metaphors indicates a future hope of eternal life. Each believer will have a new start, including a relationship with Jesus so intimate that he will choose their name. Jesus will fulfill the ancient prophecy of Isaiah 62:2, which says that God will give a new name to his people.

John also describes Jesus as "the faithful witness" (1:5; 3:14) and as "Faithful and True" (19:11). Although this is a reference to his trustworthy nature, it is more significant as a reminder that nothing happens to believers without his knowledge (1:9). As Jesus witnessed Stephen's martyrdom (Acts 7:55–56), so also he observes everything that happens to his followers. The implication is that he will also respond accordingly in judgment on the perpetrators who harm his people (2:22–23, 27; 3:9).

Jesus promises believers authority over the nations (2:26) and "the morning star" (2:28), which is a reference to their resurrection and the rule that they will be privileged to participate in (in fulfillment of Num 24:17). As symbols of everlasting life and Jesus' dedication and love they will receive white garments. He will always remember their names (3:5–6) and grants them admission into the presence of God (3:12) to sit with him on his throne (3:21; 7:17) that he shares with his Father.[23] These pictures, which the book of Revelation often portrays in symbolic terms, are there to encourage readers. Although they are isolated and marginalized by society, Jesus is aware of their situations and is able to support them, transform them, and promise them eternal security. Revelation expresses all of this in lavish terms that elevate believers to share positions of honor with Jesus.

---

[22] 2:5, 16; 3:3, 15–16.

[23] 5:6; 7:9–10; 19:4; 22:1, 3.

Conclusion

In this richly symbolic revelation of Jesus, John provides information that was of particular importance to his original readers in their very challenging circumstances. In so doing, John has written a detailed christology that demonstrates Jesus' deity. Jesus, the regal Savior with all the resources believers need, will care for them eternally even though they may suffer the consequences of persecution while on earth. Jesus, who is on their side and who has saved them and secured them for eternity, will decisively defeat and judge their earthly foes and will establish himself as the King of kings and Lord of lords for all eternity.

Postscript

Jesus is central to the NT, as all of the writers demonstrate. It is no surprise that the name of Jesus is prominent in the beginning and ending of most of the NT books.[1] He is the Savior of the world who has accomplished the salvation of believers through his death and resurrection, in association with the love of the Father and the facilitating work of the Spirit. The exaltation of Jesus is central to the message of the NT, which provides readers throughout with opportunities to be more and more impressed with Jesus.

Jesus is the mediator of salvation and the Savior and judge of all people. Although he is Messiah, the NT portrays him in exalted terms so that readers recognize that he is superior to the ancient expectations of Messiah. Although he is the Son of God, there is absolutely no indication of inferiority. On the contrary, Jesus shares a unique and equal relationship with the Father and the Spirit. As Son, he radiates divine characteristics, as do the Father and the Spirit.

Most remarkably, the NT consistently presents Jesus as fully God. The NT authors apply to Jesus many terms, titles, and OT texts that were previously associated exclusively with God. He is worshipped, receives prayer, and his equality with the Father and the Spirit, as members of the Godhead, is identified in various ways—the most common being the ascription of the title "Lord." He is the preexistent one, the creator, and the sustainer of all. He achieved the salvation that the OT had prophesied God would enact, when, though divine, he lived and died in human form. Along with the NT writers, readers are to marvel at his grandeur and divine worth. But more than this, the NT picture of Jesus

[1] Matthew, Mark, John, Romans, 1 and 2 Corinthians, Galatians, Ephesians, Philippians, 1 and 2 Thessalonians, 2 Timothy, Philemon, 1 and 2 Peter, Jude, Revelation. (Others either commence or end with Jesus in their introductory or concluding verses—Acts, Colossians, 1 Timothy, Titus, James, 1 John.)

as God in the flesh should motivate all readers in all times to be transformed into his likeness. Jesus our Savior is worthy of being followed and obeyed, worshipped and adored, and recognized as the supreme subject of one's eternal exploration. The wonder is that he welcomes all to begin enjoying that eternal journey of discovery now.

Bibliography

Aune, David. *Revelation 1–5*. Word Biblical Commentary. Waco: Word, 1997.

Barth, M., and H. Blanke. *The Letter to Philemon: A New Translation with Notes and Commentary*. Eerdmans Critical Commentary. Grand Rapids: Eerdmans, 2000.

Bauckham, R. J. *Jude, 2 Peter*. Word Biblical Commentary. Waco: Word, 1983.

Beale, G. K. *The Book of Revelation: A Commentary on the Greek Text*. New International Greek Testament Commentary. Grand Rapids: Eerdmans, 1999.

Bock, Darrell L. *Jesus according to Scripture: Restoring the Portrait from the Gospels*. Grand Rapids: Baker, 2002.

———. *Luke 1:1–9:50*. Baker Exegetical Commentary on the New Testament. Grand Rapids: Baker, 2003.

Bruce, F. F. *1 & 2 Thessalonians*. Word Biblical Commentary. Waco: Word, 1982.

Burridge, Richard A. *Four Gospels: One Jesus?* London: SPCK, 1994.

Cranfield, C. E. B. *The Epistle to the Romans: Romans 9–16: A Critical and Exegetical Commentary*. International Critical Commentary. Edinburgh: T. & T. Clark, 1979.

Cullmann, Oscar. *The Christology of the New Testament*. Louisville: Westminster John Knox, 1959, 1980.

Davids, P. H. *The Letters of 2 Peter and Jude*. Pillar New Testament Commentary. Grand Rapids: Eerdmans, 2006.

Dunn, James D. G. *Christianity in the Making, Volume 1: Jesus Remembered*. Grand Rapids: Eerdmans, 2003.

———. *Romans 9–16*. Word Biblical Commentary. Waco: Word, 1992.

Ellingworth, Paul. *The Epistle to the Hebrews*. New International Greek Testament Commentary. Grand Rapids: Eerdmans, 1993.

Fee, Gordon D. *Pauline Christology: An Exegetical-Theological Study*. Peabody, Mass.: Hendrickson, 2007.

Garland, David E. *1 Corinthians*. Baker Exegetical Commentary on the New Testament. Grand Rapids: Baker, 2003.

Green, Gene L. *The Letters to the Thessalonians*. Pillar New Testament Commentary. Grand Rapids: Eerdmans, 2002.

Grudem, Wayne. *1 Peter: An Introduction and Commentary*. Tyndale New Testament Commentaries. Grand Rapids: Eerdmans, 1988.

Guthrie, Donald. *The Pastoral Epistles*. London: Tyndale, 1957.

Harris, Murray J. *The Second Epistle to the Corinthians*. New International Greek Testament Commentary. Grand Rapids: Eerdmans, 2005.

Hawthorne, Gerald F. *Philippians*. Word Biblical Commentary. Waco: Word, 1991.

Hill, Charles E., and Frank A. James, eds. *The Glory of the Atonement*. Downers Grove, Ill.: InterVarsity, 2004.

Hoehner, Harold W. *Ephesians: An Exegetical Commentary*. Grand Rapids: Baker, 2003.

Hurtado, Larry. *Lord Jesus Christ: Devotion to Jesus in Earliest Christianity*. Grand Rapids: Eerdmans, 2003.

Knight, George W., III. *The Pastoral Epistles: A Commentary on the Greek Text*. New International Greek Testament Commentary. Grand Rapids: Eerdmans, 1992.

Lane, William L. *Hebrews 1–8*. Word Biblical Commentary. Dallas: Word, 1991.

Lincoln, Andrew T. *Ephesians*. Word Biblical Commentary. Waco: Word, 1990.

Lucas, D., and C. Green. *The Message of 2 Peter and Jude*. Downers Grove, Ill.: InterVarsity, 1995.

Marshall, I. Howard. *The Origins of New Testament Christology*. Downers Grove, Ill.: InterVarsity, 1977.

———. *The Pastoral Epistles*. Edinburgh: T. & T. Clark, 1999.

Michaels, J. Ramsey. *1 Peter*. Word Biblical Commentary. Waco: Word, 1988.

Moltmann, Jürgen. *The Source of Life*. Translated by M. Kohl. London: SCM, 1997.

Morris, Leon. *The Apostolic Preaching of the Cross*. Grand Rapids: Eerdmans, 1955.

———. *The First and Second Epistles to the Thessalonians*. Grand Rapids: Eerdmans, 1959.

Murray, John. *The Epistle to the Romans: Volume 2*. Grand Rapids: Eerdmans, 1965.

O'Brien, Peter T. *Colossians, Philemon*. Word Biblical Commentary. Waco: Word, 1982.

———. *The Epistle to the Philippians*. Word Biblical Commentary. Waco: Word, 1991.

Strauss, Mark L. *Four Portraits, One Jesus: An Introduction to Jesus and the Gospels*. Grand Rapids: Zondervan, 2007.

Towner, Philip H. *The Letters to Timothy and Titus*. New International Commentary on the New Testament. Grand Rapids: Eerdmans, 2006.

Wanamaker, Charles A. *The Epistles to the Thessalonians: A Commentary on the Greek Text*. New International Greek Testament Commentary. Grand Rapids: Eerdmans, 1990.

Warrington, Keith. *Discovering the Holy Spirit in the New Testament*. Peabody, Mass.: Hendrickson, 2005.

———. *Jesus the Healer: Paradigm or Unique Phenomenon*. Carlisle: Paternoster, 2000.

Wenham, David. *Paul: Follower of Jesus or Founder of Christianity?* Grand Rapids: Eerdmans, 1995.

Wright, N. T. "ἁρπαγμός and the Meaning of Philippians 2:5–11." *Journal of Theological Studies* 37 (1986): 321–52.

———. *The Climax of the Covenant: Christ and Law in Pauline Theology*. Minneapolis: Fortress, 1992.

———. *Jesus and the Victory of God*. London: SPCK, 1996.

Index of Subjects

Index of Ancient Sources

Mark

Luke

John

Acts

1 Corinthians

Philippians

Colossians

Other Ancient Writings

Homer

1 Maccabees

Psalms of Solomon

Virgil